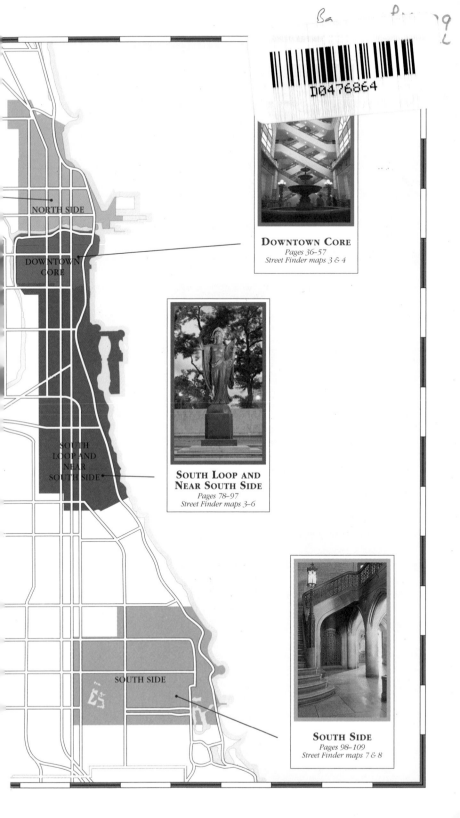

Ba          P          9
            L

**DOWNTOWN CORE**
*Pages 36–57*
*Street Finder maps 3 & 4*

**SOUTH LOOP AND
NEAR SOUTH SIDE**
*Pages 78–97*
*Street Finder maps 3–6*

**SOUTH SIDE**
*Pages 98–109*
*Street Finder maps 7 & 8*

NORTH SIDE

DOWNTOWN
CORE

SOUTH
LOOP AND
NEAR
SOUTH SIDE

SOUTH SIDE

# EYEWITNESS TRAVEL GUIDES

# CHICAGO

*Main contributors:*
LORRAINE JOHNSON AND JOHN RYAN

DK

DORLING KINDERSLEY
LONDON • NEW YORK • MUNICH
MELBOURNE • DELHI
www.dk.com

# A Dorling Kindersley Book

www.dk.com

Produced by International Book Productions,
Part of Denise Schon Books Inc.
Toronto, Canada

PROJECT EDITOR AND ART DIRECTOR Barbara Hopkinson
EDITOR Judy Phillips
DESIGNERS Dietmar Kokemohr, Stella Powelczyk
EDITORIAL AND MAP ASSISTANCE Terri Rothman
PICTURE RESEARCH Karen Taylor Permissions and Photo Research

MAIN CONTRIBUTORS
Lorraine Johnson, John Ryan

PHOTOGRAPHER
Andrew Leyerle

ILLUSTRATOR
William Band

Reproduced by Colourscan, Singapore
Printed and bound by L. Rex Printing Company Limited, China

First published in Great Britain in 2001
by Dorling Kindersley Limited
80 Strand, London WC2R 0RL

**Reprinted with revisions 2003**

Copyright 2001, 2003 © Dorling Kindersley Limited, London
A Penguin Company

A CIP CATALOGUE RECORD IS AVAILABLE FROM THE BRITISH LIBRARY.

ISBN 0 7513 4825 2

FLOORS ARE REFERRED TO THROUGHOUT IN ACCORDANCE WITH AMERICAN
USAGE; IE THE "FIRST FLOOR" IS ON GROUND LEVEL.

---

### The information in this
**Dorling Kindersley Travel Guide is checked annually**.
Every effort has been made to ensure that this book is as up-to-date
as possible at the time of going to press. Some details, however,
such as telephone numbers, opening hours, prices, gallery hanging
arrangements and travel information are liable to change. The
publishers cannot accept responsibility for any consequences arising
from the use of this book, nor for any material on third party
websites, and cannot guarantee that any website address in this
book will be a suitable source of travel information. We value the
views and suggestions of our readers very highly. Please write to:
Publisher, DK Eyewitness Travel Guides,
Dorling Kindersley, 80 Strand, London WC2R 0RL, Great Britain.

*Nuclear Energy* **by Henry Moore at
University of Chicago** *(see p100)*

---

# CONTENTS

## INTRODUCING
## CHICAGO

*Twisted Columns* **by Ricardo Bofill,
R.R. Donnelley Building** *(see p55)*

The ornate lobby of the Palmer House Hilton *(see p134)*

Raptor perched on a tree branch
in Washington Park *(see p104)*

Painted-glass window in St. James
Episcopal Cathedral *(see p67)*

Street-by-street map of South Loop *(see pp80–81)*

# HOW TO USE THIS GUIDE

THIS DORLING KINDERSLEY travel guide helps you get the most from your stay in Chicago. *Introducing Chicago* locates the city geographically, sets modern Chicago in its historical context, and describes events through the entire year. *Chicago at a Glance* highlights the city's top attractions. The main sightseeing section of the book is *Chicago Area by Area*. It describes the city sights, with photographs, maps, and drawings. It also offers suggestions for day trips outside the city center. *Beyond Chicago* delves into destinations in the region ideal either for day trips or longer sojourns, such as weekend getaways. Restaurant and hotel recommendations, as well as specially selected information about shops and entertainment, are found in *Travelers' Needs*. The *Survival Guide* gives practical information on everyday needs, from using Chicago's medical system and public transportation to the telephone system.

## FINDING YOUR WAY AROUND THE SIGHTSEEING SECTION

Each of the sightseeing areas in Chicago is color-coded for easy reference. Each chapter opens with a description of the area and a list of sights to be covered, located by numbers on an area map. This is followed by a Street-by-Street map, illustrating an interesting part of the area. Finding your way around the chapter is made simple by the numbering system used throughout. Sights outside Chicago have a regional map.

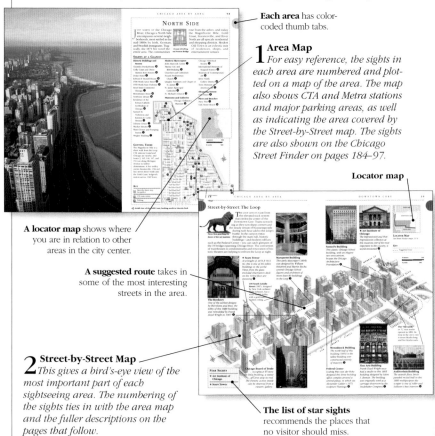

**Each area** has color-coded thumb tabs.

**1 Area Map**
*For easy reference, the sights in each area are numbered and plotted on a map of the area. The map also shows CTA and Metra stations and major parking areas, as well as indicating the area covered by the Street-by-Street map. The sights are also shown on the Chicago Street Finder on pages 184–97.*

**Locator map**

**A locator map** shows where you are in relation to other areas in the city center.

**A suggested route** takes in some of the most interesting streets in the area.

**2 Street-by-Street Map**
*This gives a bird's-eye view of the most important part of each sightseeing area. The numbering of the sights ties in with the area map and the fuller descriptions on the pages that follow.*

**The list of star sights** recommends the places that no visitor should miss.

## CHICAGO AREA MAP

The colored areas shown on this map *(see inside front cover)* are the four main sightseeing areas – each covered by a full chapter in *Chicago Area by Area (see pp34–109)*. The four areas are highlighted on other maps throughout the book. In *Chicago at a Glance (see pp18–29)*, for example, they help locate the top sights.

**Numbers** refer to each sight's position on the area map and its place in the chapter.

**Practical information** provides all you need to know to visit each sight, including a map reference to the *Chicago Street Finder (see pp184–97)*.

**3 Detailed information**
*All the important sights in Chicago are described individually. They are listed in order, following the numbering on the area map. Practical information such as address, telephone number, and opening hours is provided for each sight. The key to the symbols used is on the back flap.*

**The visitors' checklist** provides all the practical information needed to plan your visit.

**Façades** of important buildings are often shown to illustrate their architectural style, and to help you recognize them quickly.

**4 Chicago's major sights**
*These are given two or more full pages in the sightseeing area where they are found. Museums and galleries have color-coded floor plans to help you find important exhibits.*

**Stars** indicate the features no visitor should miss.

# INTRODUCING
# CHICAGO

# Putting Chicago on the Map

CHICAGO, A CITY of almost 3 million people, covers 228 sq miles (591 sq km) of the US's Midwest. Situated at the southwest edge of Lake Michigan, the world's fifth-largest freshwater body, Chicago claims 29 miles (47 km) of lakefront. Two airports handle international and internal flights. There are also interstate highways and rail links serving both the East and West Coasts and other parts of the country, and Canada.

### GREATER CHICAGO

Waukegan
Rockford
De Kalb
CHICAGO
Bolingbrook
Joliet
Ottawa
Hammond
*Lake Michigan*

0 kilometers 75
0 miles 50

MANITOBA

Hudson Bay

Churchill

Nelson

Seven

Winisk

ONTARIO

Attawapiskat

Albany

**A**

Winnipeg

Lake Nipigon

Winnipeg

MINNESOTA

Lake Superior

St Paul

WISCONSIN

Minneapolis

Minneapolis-St Paul

Mississippi

IOWA

Milwaukee

Lake Michigan

MICHIGAN

Lake Huron

Detroit

Lake Erie

Chicago

Chicago-O'Hare

ILLINOIS

INDIANA

Indianapolis

Lambert-St Louis

Kansas City

St Louis

Ohio

MISSOURI

KENTUCKY

WEST VIRGINIA

Cincinnati

Cincinnati-Northern KY

OHIO

Pittsburgh

Greater Pittsburgh

Montreal

Ottawa

MAINE

VT

NH

Logan

MA

Boston

RI

Lester B Pearson

Toronto

Hamilton

Lake Ontario

Buffalo

NEW YORK

CT

New York

JFK

PENNSYLVANIA

Philadelphia

NEW JERSEY

Philadelphia

DELAWARE

Baltimore

WASHINGTON, DC

MARYLAND

Dulles

VIRGINIA

NORTH CAROLINA

OKLAHOMA

Arkansas

ARKANSAS

Mississippi

TENNESSEE

Memphis

Tennessee

Atlanta

SOUTH CAROLINA

GEORGIA

ALABAMA

MISSISSIPPI

Alabama

Red

LOUISIANA

Dallas Fort Worth

Dallas

Houston

Houston

New Orleans

New Orleans

Jacksonville

FLORIDA

ATLANTIC OCEAN

The Bahamas

Miami

**KEY**

Greater Chicago

Airport

Interstate highway

Major road

Major railroad line

International border

State line

0 kilometers 500
0 miles 300

# THE HISTORY OF CHICAGO

**T**HE THIRD LARGEST CITY in the US is world famous for magnificent and innovative architecture, its colorful and turbulent political history and significance as a national transportation hub, the now-vanished stockyards, as well as its educational institutes and vibrant cultural venues.

The French missionary Jacques Marquette and French-Canadian explorer Louis Jolliet were the first Europeans to record a visit to this spot at the foot of Lake Michigan, in 1673. The peaceful, friendly local Potawatomi Indians called the low-lying swampy area "Checaugou," which likely means "wild onion" or "skunk cabbage." Jolliet and Marquette used this Indian name on the maps they drew, which were then used by later explorers.

**French-Canadian explorer Louis Jolliet**

More than 100 years passed before the first permanent settlement was established in 1779 by Jean Baptiste Point du Sable, an African-American trader from the Caribbean. Du Sable and his Indian wife built a house on the north bank near the mouth of the Chicago River.

A treaty negotiated with local Indian tribes in 1795 gave US citizens access to most of Ohio and a 6-sq-mile (15.5-sq-km) area of land where the Chicago River emptied into Lake Michigan – now the heart of Chicago's downtown.

In 1803, the US Army built Fort Dearborn along the river to protect settlers from the Indians, the British, and the French. Fort Dearborn was destroyed during the War of 1812 between the US and Britain; soldiers and their families were slaughtered by the Indians, allies of the British, as they fled the fort. Although the fort was rebuilt in 1816 and Illinois became a state in 1818, the area remained Indian territory until it was ceded in 1933 and the Natives relocated to reservations by the federal government. That same year, Chicago became a village.

### EARLY CHICAGO

With the land open for development, the rivers gained importance as shipping routes. In 1837, Chicago, its population now over 4,000, received city status. The expansion of the lake ports, completion of the Illinois and Michigan Canal connecting the Great Lakes with the Mississippi River, and arrival of the railroads spurred rapid growth. Public schools were established in 1840, and by 1847 the new city had two daily newspapers. From 1855 to 1858, Chicago literally pulled itself out of the mud, jacking up the downtown buildings and filling in the swamp muck with soil (see p57).

## TIMELINE

| 1673 Explorers Jacques Marquette and Louis Jolliet arrive at "Checaugou" | 1779 First settlement in Chicago established by trader Jean Baptiste Point du Sable | *Jean Baptiste Point du Sable* | 1803 Fort Dearborn built | 1848 Illinois & Michigan Canal completed (see pp118–19) |
|---|---|---|---|---|

| 1650 | 1700 | 1750 | 1800 | 1850 |
|---|---|---|---|---|

| 1682 Frenchman La Salle explores area and establishes forts | *A Potawatomi chief* | 1783 British cede land that is now Chicago to the newly established US government | 1825 Erie Canal opens  1837 Chicago incorporates as a city | 1858 Chicago becomes US's chief railroad hub  1847 *Chicago Tribune* newspaper founded |
|---|---|---|---|---|

◁ A contemporary lithograph depicting the Great Chicago Fire of 1871

Chicago's proximity to both the Mississippi River and the Great Lakes confirmed it as the nation's transportation hub. By 1860, 15 railroad companies had terminals here. Christmas Day 1865 saw the opening of the gigantic Union Stock Yards, the city's largest employer for decades. (It eventually closed in 1971.) Meatpacking laws, along with the Food and Drug Administration, were created after Upton Sinclair's stirring 1906 book, *The Jungle*, revealed the poor conditions of such stockyards. Although meat processing remained Chicago's major industry, positioning the city as the US's primary supplier, the grain-handling and manufacturing industries were also strong in 19th-century Chicago.

Detail of cow (1879) on the archway to Union Stock Yards

### THE GREAT FIRE

The Great Chicago Fire of 1871 burned for 36 hours, October 8 to 10, destroying most of the buildings in downtown Chicago, all of which were made of wood. At least 300 people died, and about 100,000 – one-third of the population – were left homeless. A cow, belonging to a certain Mrs. O'Leary, was blamed for kicking over a lantern and starting the fire. Although an inquiry confirmed that the blaze started in the O'Leary shed, the cause of the fire was not determined.

An 1874 bylaw prohibited the building of wooden structures downtown. Consequently, Chicago architect William Le Baron Jenney (*see pp24–5*) designed the Home Insurance Building (1884), a nine-story structure supported by a steel skeleton, regarded by many to be the first skyscraper. Jenney's design paved the way for the canyons of tall buildings found in city centers today.

### SOCIAL UNREST, SOCIAL REFORM

As Chicago's downtown rebuilt and the city continued to expand – to 500,000 inhabitants by 1880 – social divisions grew. In the 1873 Bread Riot, police trapped thousands of protesting hungry workers under a bridge, clubbing many to death. Four years later, during the 1877 national railroad strike, Chicago police fired on demonstrators, killing 30. On May 4, 1886, workers rallied at Haymarket Square to protest the police killing of two laborers demanding the shortening of the workday to eight hours. A bomb exploded in the midst of the police officers, starting a riot that

The aftermath of the Great Fire, as seen from Chicago Harbor

### TIMELINE

| 1860 Abraham Lincoln nominated for US president at Republican Convention | | 1871 Great Chicago Fire | | 1880 Chicago's population reaches 500,000 | |
|---|---|---|---|---|---|
| | *Lincoln Statue, in Lincoln Park* | | 1874 City council prohibits the building of wooden structures downtown | | 1886 Haymarket Riot |

| 1860 | | 1870 | | 1880 | |
|---|---|---|---|---|---|
| 1861 Civil War begins | 1865 Union Stock Yards, world's biggest stockyard, opens | 1873 Bread Riot | 1879 Art Institute of Chicago (*see pp46–9*) founded as the Chicago Academy of Fine Arts | | 1884 World's first skyscraper (*see pp24–5*) built |

**Protesters clash with police in the 1873 Bread Riot**

Christopher Columbus' journey to the Americas with the 1893 World's Columbian Exposition, held in Jackson Park *(see p105)*. Over 25 million visitors came to it, the largest fair yet to be held in the Americas. Despite a deep national economic depression, the city built a fabulous fairground, dubbed the "White City" because of its Neo-Classical white marble buildings. It was to have a huge impact on US architecture. Most of the buildings burned down or were vandalized after the fair.

eventually killed seven officers. The ensuing trial, in which eight men were charged with murder and four subsequently executed, is considered one of the worst miscarriages of justice in the US.

Into this social tumult stepped Jane Addams *(see p29)* and Ellen Gates Starr. In 1889, they founded Hull-House to help settle immigrants *(see p116)*. It would soon become a leader in US social welfare and reform.

### PROGRESS, AND THE **1893** WORLD'S COLUMBIAN EXPOSITION

Downtown, other initiatives were underway. The Art Institute of Chicago *(see pp46–9)* was founded in 1879, the Chicago Symphony Orchestra *(see p162)* in 1889, and the University of Chicago *(see pp100–101)* in 1891. The elevated tramway opened in 1892, its circle around the commercial core giving the downtown the nickname "The Loop." Chicago celebrated the 400th anniversary of

**Guidebook for the 1893 World's Columbian Fair**

### GROWTH AND GROWING PAINS

By 1890, Chicago's population climbed past one million. Awareness of public health issues led to concern that the city discharged, directly or indirectly, most of its waste into the Chicago River, and from there into Lake Michigan, the source of drinking water. In 1900, the Chicago Sanitary and Ship Canal opened, the direction of the Chicago River reversed so that the river flowed away from the lake rather than into it *(see p57)*.

A 1903 Chicago disaster affected both urban design and bylaws nationwide. More than 600 people died when a fire tragically destroyed the Iroquois Theater on December 30 *(see p51)*. Investigators blamed the fatalities on the doors. Many opened inward: impossible to open with a frantic crowd pressed against them. Most US cities now require that doors of public buildings open outward.

By 1914, waves of immigrants from Europe

| 1890 Chicago becomes second-largest US city, its population over 1 million | 1900 Chicago Sanitary and Ship Canal opens, reversing flow of Chicago River | 1907 University of Chicago's Albert Michelson is first US scientist to win a Nobel Prize in Physics, for measurement of the speed of light |
| --- | --- | --- |
| **1892** Elevated tramway ("The Loop") opens | | |
| **1890** | **1900** | **1910** |

| 1889 Hull-House *(see p116)* founded | 1893 Chicago hosts World's Columbian Exposition | *Opening of the new canal* | 1909 Plan of Chicago *(see p28)*, the first civic blueprint for a city, published |
| --- | --- | --- | --- |
| | 1891 University of Chicago *(see pp100–101)* founded | | |

**Speakeasy directions
written in chalk**

had arrived in Chicago. Industrialization now brought another wave: African Americans from the South, seeking work after being displaced from farm work by the cotton gin and other new machinery. Chicago's Black population skyrocketed, from about 14,000 in 1910 to almost 110,000 by the early 1920s. Previous arrivals did not always welcome the new migrants. A 1919 race riot that started at a segregated South Side beach raged for several days, leaving 38 dead and at least 500 injured.

Speakeasies, illicit social clubs offering liquor despite the prohibition of alcohol, flourished in the 1920s and made way for the bootlegging gangster. The most famous gangster – and the one most closely linked to Chicago in the public mind – was Al Capone, who arrived in 1920 from New York. Capone is legendary for his bloody gang war. In the notorious 1929 St. Valentine's Day Massacre, seven mobsters from a rival gang were killed execution-style by mobsters loyal to Capone.

Almost as famous were Elliot Ness and his team, who collected the evidence of income-tax evasion that put Capone in prison in 1931, where he died 16 years later.

## Chicago Milestones: 1920s–60s

The Chicago Municipal Airport (now Midway Airport) opened in 1927. From 1945 to 1958, it was the world's busiest airport, before being replaced by O'Hare, which was equipped to handle the new jetliners and is today one of the world's busiest airports.

The old airport brought visitors to the 1933–4 World's Fair. Showcasing innovative uses of electricity, the fair attracted 39 million people. Another kind of energy came to the fore when, in 1942, physicist Enrico Fermi from the University of Chicago conducted the world's first controlled atomic reaction (see p100).

After World War II, the city's economy boomed, its population peaking at 3.6 million. New arrivals included musicians from the Mississippi Delta and by 1950, they were recording a new form of blues.

**Physicist
Enrico Fermi**

The 1950s saw many milestones: Carl Sandburg won the Pulitzer Prize for Poetry in 1951; and Ray Kroc's first McDonald's opened in 1955 in Des Plaines, just outside Chicago.

**Chicago's O'Hare Airport, one of the world's busiest**

## Timeline

| 1920 | 1930 | 1940 | 1950 | 1960 |
|---|---|---|---|---|
| **1920** Mobster Al Capone arrives | **1928** Chicago River straightened to allow for expansion of downtown | **1942** First controlled atomic chain reaction, at University of Chicago | **1953** Hugh Hefner publishes first issue of *Playboy* magazine | 19 Luth brings mo |
| **1929** St. Valentine's Day Massacre | **1933** Chicago hosts Century of Progress World's Fair | **1943** Chicago's first subway opens | **1953** Richard J. Daley elected mayor | |
| | **1931** Elliot Ness succeeds in convicting Al Capone | | **1955** Richard J. Daley elected mayor | |
| | | | **1959** White Sox win American League baseball pennant | |

*Elliot Ness*

Richard J. Daley, mayor of Chicago for 21 years

## TURBULENT POLITICS

In 1955, Chicago elected Democrat Richard J. Daley as mayor, a position he held until his fatal heart attack in 1976. In 1966, Martin Luther King Jr. brought the civil rights movement to Chicago, challenging Daley's Whites-only political machine and the segregation of the Black population. Daley's administration survived the West Side riots, prompted by the assassination of King in Memphis, and the disastrous confrontations between police and demonstrators outside the Democratic National Convention, both in 1968. Daley was equally well known for his commitment to a clean city, in keeping with his motto "Keep Chicago beautiful."

Daley's successors include Jane Byrne, Chicago's first female mayor (1979–83), and Harold Washington, Chicago's first Black mayor (1983–7), called "the people's mayor" because he was considered to be in touch with the grassroots. Washington made significant structural changes in city operations before dying of a heart attack at his desk, shortly after his re-election as mayor in 1987.

In 1989, Chicagoans elected Richard M. Daley, son of former mayor Richard J. Daley, as mayor.

## CHICAGO TODAY

In 1990, Chicago's title of "Second City" became an honorific, as the population of Los Angeles surpassed that of Chicago and became the largest in the US after New York. But Chicagoans continue to glory in the city's triumphs. It remains the US's largest transportation center and the financial capital of the Midwest. Chicago Board of Trade, founded in 1848, continues to be the most important grain market in the nation. Sears Tower *(see p40)* recaptured the title of World's Tallest Building in two of four categories in 1997. The Chicago Bulls won six NBA championships. The 1999 Cows on Parade, a public-art project of 300 fiberglass cows decorated by Chicago artists, delighted locals and visitors alike.

Chicago has had its share of recent disasters. In 1992, the Chicago River poured into a hole pierced in an abandoned tunnel in the Loop. Water filled downtown basements, threatening to sink the city center below the level of the original swampland.

As a mature city, Chicago offers superb public art and architecture, and natural, cultural, and gastronomical delights. The city's dynamism is sure to linger in the memories of its visitors for decades to come.

One of the herd in the wildly popular Cows on Parade project

| 1971 Union Stock Yards close | 1979 Jane Byrne elected mayor of Chicago | 1983 Harold Washington elected mayor of Chicago | 1990 Chicago drops in ranking to third-largest US city | 2001 Millennium Park opens *(see p53)* |

| artin g Jr. ghts nt to :ago | 1970 | 1980 | 1990 | 2000 |

| Democratic National :ntion riots | 1973 Sears Tower *(see p40)* opens as tallest building in world | *Sears Tower* | 1986 Refurbished Chicago Theatre reopens *(see p54)* | 1992 Chicago River leaks into abandoned freight tunnel, threatening to collapse downtown |

# CHICAGO AT A GLANCE

M ORE THAN 100 places of interest are described in the *Area by Area* and *Beyond Chicago* sections of this book. They range from the Gothic-style Rockefeller Memorial Chapel *(see p102)* to the Post-Modern James R. Thompson Center *(see p56)*, from the offbeat neighborhood of Wicker Park *(see p114)* to tranquil Washington Park *(see p104)*. To help make the most of your stay, the following ten pages are a time-saving guide to the best Chicago has to offer. The guide highlights the city's best museums and architecture, as well as the people and cultures that have given Chicago its unique character over the years. Below are the top ten tourist attractions that no visitor to Chicago should miss.

## CHICAGO'S TOP TEN     TOURIST ATTRACTIONS

**Museum of Science and Industry**
See pp106–109

**John G. Shedd Aquarium**
See pp96–7

**Magnificent Mile**
See pp60–61

**Sears Tower**
See p40

**Navy Pier**
See p65

**Art Institute of Chicago**
See pp46–9

**Oak Park**
See pp114–15

**Lincoln Park Zoo**
See pp112–13

**Adler Planetarium and Astronomy Museum**
See pp92–3

**Field Museum**
See pp86–9

◁ **View of Chicago's River North district from Franklin Bridge**

# Chicago's Best: Museums

CHICAGO HAS some of the world's finest museums, and the buildings in which they are housed are often works of art themselves. The Art Institute of Chicago, world-renowned for its Impressionist and Post-Impressionist paintings, and Museum Campus – consisting of the Field Museum, Adler Planetarium, and Shedd Aquarium – are prominent on any visitor's itinerary. There are many smaller museums, too, celebrating Chicago's heritage and giving insight into the people and events that have left their mark on the city.

*North Side*

*Downtown Core*

**Chicago Historical Society**
*This museum traces Chicago's rich history, beginning with its first explorers and settlers, through the development of the city, to major events in modern-day Chicago (see p74).*

**International Museum of Surgical Science**
*The history of medicine and surgery, from blood-letting to X-rays, is brought to life at this fascinating museum (see p75).*

**Museum of Broadcast Communication**
*Visitors role-play as news anchorpeople at this unique museum showcasing radio and TV (see p53).*

**Spertus Museum**
*An outstanding collection of art and artifacts reflecting 5,000 years of Jewish culture and ritual is exhibited in this museum's thematic displays (see p84).*

| 0 kilometers | 2 |
| 0 miles | 1 |

### Museum of Contemporary Art
*Cutting-edge modern works by European and American artists such as sculptor Alexander Calder are featured in permanent and rotating exhibits (see p65).*

### Art Institute of Chicago
*One of the largest holdings of Impressionist and Post-Impressionist paintings outside France can be found here (see pp46–9).*

### Field Museum
*An encyclopedic collection of objects relating to the earth's natural and cultural history are explored in vivid displays at this museum (see pp86–9).*

### Adler Planetarium and Astronomy Museum
*One of the world's foremost planetariums, the Adler has a webcam atop its dome – offering a superb view of Chicago – and over 2,000 astronomical artifacts (see pp92–3).*

### Smart Museum
*The specialties within the wide-ranging collection of this compact museum are antiquities and Old Masters (see p103).*

South Loop and Near South Side

### Museum of Science and Industry
*Many of the technological inventions and scientific discoveries that have changed our world are on display at this very popular museum, a leader in interactive exhibits (see pp106–9).*

South Side

# Chicago's Best: Architecture

CHICAGO'S DOWNTOWN SKYLINE is characterized by high-rises, both modern and historic, while a range of residential architecture styles, such as Queen Anne and Prairie, are found in the city's neighborhoods. After the 1871 fire *(see p14)* and subsequent ban on wood as a building material, the use of terra-cotta and cast-iron – both fire resistant and durable – became prevalent. Terra-cotta was also an excellent material for decorative carving and so sheaths many of the city's steel-frame buildings. A detailed overview of Chicago's architecture is found on pages 24–5.

*North Side*

**Crilly Court**
*The Crilly Court row houses (see p71), with their turrets and bays, are one of the finest examples of Queen Anne style in the city.*

*Downtown Core*

**Newberry Library**
*Henry Ives Cobb, master of the Richardsonian Romanesque style, designed the library in 1890–93 (see p67). Its heavy stone walls and recessed, arched windows are typical of this style, popular in the second half of the 19th century.*

**333 Wacker Drive**
*A Post-Modern structure designed by the architect firm Kohn Pedersen Fox, this building (see pp56–7) was met with critical acclaim and local approval when constructed in 1983.*

0 kilometers                    2

0 miles                         1

**Harold Washington Library Center**
*This Post-Modern giant (see p82) alludes to Chicago's many historic buildings through its varied architectural features.*

## John Hancock Center
*The towering glass walls and horizontal beams of the John Hancock Center (see p64) are characteristic of the International Style.*

## Gage Group
*These three buildings reflect different approaches to the Chicago School: two, designed by Holabird and Roche, have minimal exterior decoration; the third, by Louis Sullivan, has a more ornate façade.*

## Water Tower
*The Gothic Revival-style castellated tower is one of the city's best-loved landmarks (see p63).*

## Field Museum
*Designed in white marble by Daniel H. Burnham, this monumental Neo-Classical building (1921) features a long colonnaded façade with Greek-style caryatids (see pp86–9).*

South Loop
and Near
South Side

## Christopher Bouton House
*This villa-like residence, with its tall windows and dominant cornice, was built in 1873 in the Italianate style popular in 19th-century Chicago.*

## Robie House
*Built 1906–1909, this house is considered by many to be Frank Lloyd Wright's Prairie School masterpiece (see pp102–103).*

South Side

# Exploring Chicago's Architecture

**Carving on the Rookery**

CHICAGO IS WORLD FAMOUS as a center of architectural innovation, a city where new building techniques have been developed and where architects have pushed the boundaries of creative expression. This reputation had its beginnings in the defining event of Chicago's history – the tragic fire of 1871. With a blank slate on which to build, architects rose to the challenge, transforming devastation into opportunity and reshaping the city. It was in Chicago that the world's first skyscraper was built, and here that Frank Lloyd Wright developed his distinctive Prairie School of architecture.

## GOTHIC REVIVAL

POPULAR IN the 1830s and 1840s, Gothic Revival was inspired by the medieval architecture of Europe, particularly of England. Steeply pitched roofs, pointed arches, turrets, and buttresses are typical features. One of Chicago's best examples of this style is the **Water Tower** (1869). Interest in Gothic continued through the 19th century and is reflected in many of the city's most impressive buildings, such as the **Fourth Presbyterian Church** (1914) and those of the **University of Chicago**.

## ITALIANATE STYLE

**The elegant Drake Hotel, built in the popular Italianate style**

POPULAR FROM the mid- to late 1800s, the Italianate design style is based on the historic architecture of Italy: the villas of northern Italy and the palaces of the Italian Renaissance. Characteristic features include asymmetrical balancing, low-pitched roofs, projecting eaves, and ornate door and window designs, the windows often grouped into arcades. Two notable examples are the **Samuel M. Nickerson House** (1883) and the **Drake Hotel** (1920).

## RICHARDSONIAN ROMANESQUE

RICHARDSONIAN Romanesque, or Romanesque Revival, was popularized in the US in the latter half of the 19th century by Bostonian Henry Hobson Richardson (1838–86). His architectural legacy is represented in Chicago by the severe yet subtly ornamented **Glessner House** (1887). Typical features of this style are heavy rough-cut stone, round arches, and deeply recessed windows. Richardson's influence can be seen in the work of Henry Ives Cobb, particularly Cobb's design of **Newberry Library** (1890–93) and the former home of the Chicago Historical Society *(see p74)* at Dearborn and Ontario streets.

## QUEEN ANNE

MAINLY USED in residential architecture, Queen Anne style was highly influential in Chicago from the mid- to late 1800s. The name does not reflect a historical period but was coined by English architect Richard Shaw. Queen Anne homes are built on a human scale. A mix of Classical, Tudor, and Colonial elements lead to a hybrid look. Victorian detailing, such as curlicue cutouts on the trim, is often prominent.

**Crilly Court** (1885) and the **Olsen-Hansen Row Houses** (1886) are fine examples of Queen Anne style. There are also many Queen Anne houses to be found in the **Pullman Historic District**.

**Crilly Court, the name of Crilly's son carved above the door**

## CHICAGO SCHOOL

NAMED AFTER the city in which it developed, the commercial style of the Chicago School led to both an engineering and aesthetic revolution in architecture. William Le Baron Jenney created the first skyscraper when he designed the nine-story Home Insurance Building (1884; demolished 1929), using skeletal steel

## BALLOON FRAME

Balloon-frame construction was first developed in Chicago by Augustine D. Taylor, in 1833 (though some credit George Washington Snow's 1932 Chicago warehouse as the first such construction). The name refers to the ease of construction: it was as simple as inflating a balloon, although critics said it referred to the ease with which the wind would blow away such structures. Raising a balloon-frame house required simply joining machine-cut lumber with machine-made nails, rather than interlocking time-consuming joints. Various interior and exterior surfaces could then be applied. Chicago's early balloon-frame houses fed the flames of the 1871 fire, but some built after the fire still exist in Old Town *(see pp70–71)*.

frames rather than the conventional height-limiting, masonry load-bearing walls.

Jenney trained many of Chicago's celebrated architects, including Louis Sullivan, William Holabird, Daniel Burnham, and Martin Roche, whose architect firm designed several Chicago School buildings, such as the **Rookery** (1885–8) and the **Reliance Building** (1890–95). The new window style of these buildings, made possible by Jenney's structural

**Reliance Building, Chicago School**

innovation, became known as Chicago windows. Each consists of a large central glass pane, flanked by two slender windows that open.

## NEO-CLASSICAL OR BEAUX-ARTS

NEO-CLASSICAL, or Beaux-Arts, style became popular in Chicago once it was chosen as the design style for the 1893 World's Fair. Based on classical Greek and Roman architecture, with its columns, pilasters, and pediments, these buildings are often monumental in scale. Many of Chicago's most notable cultural institutions, such as the **Chicago Cultural Center** (1893–7), are housed in Neo-Classical buildings.

## PRAIRIE SCHOOL

IN THE FIRST TWO decades of the 20th century, Frank Lloyd Wright developed a truly indigenous American architectural style. Reflecting the sweeping lines of the Midwestern landscape, Prairie style is characterized by low horizontal lines, projecting eaves, and rectangular windows. It is used mostly in residential architecture.

**Oak Park** is a treasure-trove of Wright-designed houses. Notable Wright buildings elsewhere in Chicago are **Robie House** (1906–1909) and **Charnley-Persky House** (1891–2).

Prairie School is considered a part of the Chicago School.

## INTERNATIONAL STYLE

THE INTERNATIONAL style developed primarily at Germany's Bauhaus School. Luminary Ludwig Mies van der Rohe immigrated to Chicago in 1938, after the Nazis closed the Bauhaus, and his ideas took root in the US. Simple, severe geometry and large expanses of glass are typical elements. One of the best places to see examples of Mies' "less is more" philosophy is at the **Illinois Institute of Technology** campus. Another landmark Mies' building is the austere but beautifully proportioned **IBM Building** (1971).

Chicago firm Skidmore, Owings and Merrill, architects of the **John Hancock Center** (1969) and **Sears Tower** (1974), is world famous for its International-style designs.

**The Post-Modern Harold Washington Library Center (see p82)**

## POST-MODERN

POST-MODERN architecture developed in the 1970s primarily in response to – and as a rejection of – the formal ideals of the International style. It is an eclectic style without strict rules or unified credo, although playful references to architectural styles of the past are typical features of Post-Modern structures.

The building at **333 West Wacker Drive** (1983), designed by the firm Kohn Pedersen Fox, and the **James R. Thompson Center** (1985), designed by architect Helmut Jahn, are notable examples of Post-Modern design.

**A balloon-frame house** is one of the most common building types in the US today.

**The balloon frame** consists of two-by-fours fastened with inexpensive, machine-made nails.

# Multicultural Chicago

**Chinatown street signs**

CHICAGO PRIDES ITSELF on being one of the most ethnically diverse cities in the US. In the 1840s, the Irish, fleeing their country's potato famine, arrived in droves in the young city of Chicago. Since then, successive waves of immigrants from countries around the world have shaped the city's many neighborhoods. These varied ethnic communities continue to celebrate their cultures at various festivals that are held throughout the year *(see pp30–33)*.

**Spanish sign welcoming visitors to Pilsen, once a Czech community**

## THE IRISH

**Irish police officers joining the St. Patrick's Day celebrations**

THE FIRST IRISH immigrants to Chicago worked as laborers, helping build the Illinois and Michigan Canal *(see p118)* in the mid-1800s. By 1870, the Irish represented over 13 percent of the city's population. Settled mostly in the South Side industrial town of Bridgeport, they soon became a powerful force in city politics. Over the years, there have been eight Irish mayors.

An Irish tradition not to be missed is a foaming glass of Guinness beer at one of the city's many Irish pubs.

## THE WESTERN EUROPEANS

GERMANS WERE some of the earliest immigrants to Chicago. Settling primarily in the North Side neighborhood of Old Town, by the 1870s they were Chicago's largest ethnic group. Today, the core of Germantown is Old Town's Lincoln Square, teeming with delicatessens and dance halls.

Swedes established, also in the mid-1800s, a small community just north of the Chicago River. They later moved to Clark Street and Foster Avenue, an area now known as Andersonville. The

community, with its many delicatessens and shops, retains its original character. Midsommarfest is celebrated here each June.

Prosperous Italians arrived in Chicago in the 1860s. By 1900, they were joined by poorer Italian farmers, many of whom settled between Van Buren and 12th Streets. Today, Taylor Street, between Madison and Halsted Streets, on Chicago's West Side, is the nucleus of Little Italy.

Greek immigration was spurred by the 1871 fire, when laborers came to help rebuild the city. By 1927, 10,000 shops, mainly selling fresh produce and flowers, were operated by Greeks. A short stretch of Greek restaurants is along South Halsted Street near Van Buren Street, on the West Side.

South Side neighborhoods such as Hyde Park and Kenwood *(see pp104–105)* were populated with wealthy German Jews. Over 125 Jewish congregations

**Jim's Original, a local favorite since 1939 for Maxwell Street-style Polish sausage**

worshiped in the city by the late 1920s, with the Jewish population and synagogues spread throughout the city, much like today.

## THE EASTERN EUROPEANS

THE POLITICAL UNREST in Czechoslovakia in 1848 led to the first wave of Czech immigrants to the US, many settling in the Midwest. By the 1870s, Chicago had a Little Prague along DeKoven Street on the West Side. Over the next few decades, a thriving Czech community developed nearby, along Blue Island Avenue from 16th Street to Cermak Road (then known as 22nd Street). Named Pilsen, after the west Czechoslovakian city Plzeň, the neighborhood today is predominantly Hispanic. Remnants of the Czech community, however, can be seen in buildings such as Thalia Hall *(see p116)*.

The Polish community, the largest outside Warsaw, is the largest White ethnic group in Chicago after the Hispanics. Poles began arriving in large numbers in the 1870s. By the turn of the century, the Polish Downtown had been established at Division Street and Milwaukee Avenue.

Ukrainians arrived in Chicago during the early 1900s, settling Ukrainian Village, an area bounded by Division Street and Chicago, Damen, and Western Avenues, northwest of the Loop. Two interesting museums in the community celebrate Ukrainian culture.

The Lithuanian community, centered at Western Avenue and Marquette Road, southwest of Hyde Park, also has a strong presence in Chicago, as does the smaller Latvian community, west of Lakeview.

Eastern European Jews settled the West Side's Maxwell Street at Halsted Street from the 1880s until the 1910s. Community life focused around the Maxwell Street Market (see p157), once the world's largest flea market.

## THE AFRICAN AMERICANS

**Jazz legend Nat "King" Cole, son of a Chicago Baptist minister**

DESPITE CHICAGO's first settler being mulatto (see p13), racist laws significantly affected African-American settlement in the early 1800s. By 1850, Chicago was a destination for fugitive slaves from the South. In the 1890s, a thin strip of the South Side, bounded by Van Buren and 31st Streets, State Street and Lake Michigan, became known as the Black Belt, with about half of the city's Black population living here.

The early 1900s saw another wave of settlement in the Black Belt: the "Great Migration" of Blacks from the South looking for factory work. Over the next decade, a lively jazz and blues scene developed in the area.

In the 1940s and 1950s, the Chicago Housing Authority replaced South Side tenements with public-housing projects, which soon became notorious for crime. But by the 1960s and 1970s, Chicago

also had several middle-class Black communities, such as Park Manor, as well as racially integrated areas, such as Hyde Park. The Black Metropolis Historic District (35th Street and Indiana Avenue) was created in 1984 to commemorate the vibrant Black Belt community of the early 1900s. Today, African Americans represent approximately 40 percent of Chicago's population.

## THE HISPANIC AMERICANS

THE FIRST FLOOD of Mexican immigrants was early in the 20th century, as laborers came to Chicago to help build the city's railroad. A second wave came after World War II, again as laborers. This time they were accompanied by Puerto Ricans. Cubans, fleeing from the 1959 revolution, joined Chicago's Hispanic community. Today, the Hispanic Americans – more than 20 percent of the city's population – continue to have an enormous impact on the cultural fabric of Chicago.

In the two southwest neighborhoods of Pilsen (see p116) and Little Village (south of Cermak Road between

**Menu and graffiti on the wall of Mi Barrio Taqueria, in Pilsen**

Western Avenue and Pulaski Road), the colorful streets are alive with Latin music, and inviting aromas waft from the numerous eateries.

## THE ASIANS

IN 1870 THERE WERE but two Chinese immigrants in Chicago. By the turn of the century, a Chinese community was growing in the South Side vice district of Custom

**Colorful Vietnamese and Chinese signs on bustling Argyle Street**

House Levee. That Chinatown dissolved in the early 1900s once the vice lords left. Chinese immigrants, faced with anti-Chinese sentiment reflected in excessive rent increases, found themselves forced to the fringes of the district. They settled at 22nd (now Cermak Road) and Wentworth Streets, an area that is now the heart of Chicago's Chinese community (see p94). There is also a new Chinatown on the North Side, marked by a pagoda at the Argyle CTA station entrance.

Chicago's Asian population swelled considerably in the 1980s with the arrival of Vietnamese, Cambodian, and Thai political refugees, as well as Filipino, Indian, Korean, and Japanese immigrants. Many settled in pockets on the North Side, where various Asian communities have developed, such as the Vietnamese neighborhood of Little Hanoi at Argyle Street and Broadway.

## THE MELTING POT

OTHER CULTURES are represented in Chicago but are not as distinctly defined. Chicago's American Indian population of approximately 17,000, concentrated in Uptown, north of Lakeview, is the highest of any US city after San Francisco and Los Angeles. Chicagoans of Middle Eastern origin are scattered throughout the city.

# Remarkable Residents

CHICAGO HAS ALWAYS BEEN a city at the forefront. It has nourished leaders in diverse fields, from music to industry, from architecture to sports. Some have been drawn to Chicago from other parts of the US and abroad; others were born and bred in Chicago and continue to call it home. All have left their mark on the city and, indeed, on the world. As the city where the skyscraper was developed, in the late 1800s, Chicago has long been a center for architectural innovation, with many of North America's influential architects based here for at least part of their careers. Having nurtured outstanding musicians since the 1910s, the city is also famous for its jazz and blues.

**Blues legend Muddy Waters playing his electric guitar**

**Frank Lloyd Wright, one of the world's most influential architects**

## ARCHITECTS

CHICAGO architects have literally shaped the city. Daniel Burnham (1846–1912) was one of Chicago's most successful architects. His partnership with John Wellborn Root (1850–91) led to buildings such as the Rookery (see p40), a stunning early skyscraper. His later partnership with Charles Atwood (1849–95) resulted in the groundbreaking Reliance Building (see p50).

Burnham was in charge of designing the 1893 World's Fair. However, it is for the 1909 Plan of Chicago he coauthored that he is best known. This document of civic planning became the vision for Chicago, proposing a series of riverfront public spaces and the widening of major roads to make the downtown easily accessible.

Louis Sullivan (1856–1924) has been called the first truly American architect. Celebrated for his organic style of

ornamentation, as seen on the windows of Carson Pirie Scott (see p50), Sullivan declared that form follows function. Indeed, the detailing allowed the architect artistic license while drawing in passers-by.

Sullivan nurtured a young draftsman with whom he worked, Frank Lloyd Wright (1867–1959). Over the next 70 years, Wright played a significant role in modern architecture, fathering the Prairie School (see p25) and designing such masterpieces as Robie House (see pp102–103).

Ludwig Mies van der Rohe (1886–1969) moved to Chicago in 1937. The impact of his International style (see p25) was profound.

## MUSICIANS

AN INNOVATOR of American music, Louis Armstrong (1901–1971) lived in Chicago from 1922 to 1929. Here he launched a revolution with his trumpet playing, popularizing the new art of jazz.

If Armstrong was the king of jazz, Benny Goodman (1909–1986) was the king of swing. His Russian parents settled in Chicago's West Side, where Goodman joined the Hull-House (see p116) youth band. Later, he led the US's first racially integrated band, inviting Black pianist Teddy Wilson to join his orchestra. Jelly Roll Morton (1890–1941), the great pianist from New Orleans, came to Chicago in 1922. Morton claimed to have invented jazz. Muddy Waters (1915–83) didn't claim to have

invented blues, but he did take credit for bringing the sound of the Mississippi Delta to Chicago, where his use of electric guitar was seminal.

Nat "King" Cole (1919–65) began his career playing the organ at his father's church. Cole, with his unique and velvety vocals, broke several color barriers in the 1950s. He was the first African American to have a radio show, and later, a weekly TV show.

## ACTORS AND COMEDIANS

PAUL SILLS and Bernie Sahlins opened Chicago's renowned improvisational comedy spot Second City in 1959. Many comics, including Gilda Radner (1946–89), Mike Nichols, Elaine May, Dan Aykroyd, and Joan Rivers, got their start here. Comic genius Jack Benny (1894–1974) and Saturday Night Live star John Belushi (1949–82) both lived in Chicago suburbs.

Several Chicago-based actors, including John Cusack and John Malkovich, have

**Chicago's Oprah Winfrey, a national TV personality**

gone on to international fame. One of the city's best-known TV personalities is talk-show host Oprah Winfrey *(see p161),* watched by nearly 15 million Americans each weekday morning. It was in Chicago that the TV talk show was born, in 1949, with NBC's *Garroway at Large.*

## ATHLETES

SPORTS TEAMS in Chicago are not known for their winning streaks, but they do boast a number of superstars. Chicago Bulls basketball player Michael Jordan is perhaps most famous, known as much for his product endorsements as for his basketball scoring.

Hockey legend Bobby Hull, as the star of the 1961 Chicago Black-hawks team, helped bring the Stanley Cup to the city – the team's only cup win in more than half a century.

Johnny Weissmuller (1904–1984) may be best known as the star of 18 Tarzan movies; however, the boy who swam at Oak Street Beach *(see p77)* became the man who held every world freestyle swimming record of the 1920s.

**Michael Jordan, the Chicago Bulls' No. 1 basketball player**

## WRITERS

CHICAGO'S MOST famous literary figure is Ernest Hemingway (1899–1960), who grew up in Oak Park *(see pp114–15).* He rejected the conservative mindset of

this Chicago suburb, saying it was full of "wide lawns and narrow minds."

Theodore Dreiser (1871–1945), considered the father of American literary natural-ism, wrote about Chicago, his home city, in his master-piece *Sister Carrie.*

African-American novelist Richard Wright (1908–1960) moved to Chicago at age 19, though he wrote his best-selling novel *Native Son,* about a man raised in a Chicago slum, in New York.

Illinois-native poet Carl Sandburg (1878–1967) moved to Chicago in 1912, where he worked as a lit-erary critic. His 1914 poem "Chicago" describes it as the "City of the Big Shoulders." Poet Gwendolyn Brooks (b.1917) has lived in Chicago her whole life, writing exclusively about it. She was, in 1950, the first African American to win a Pulitzer Prize, for *Annie Allen,* her collection exploring the Black experience in Chicago.

**Renowned poet Carl Sandburg**

## GANGSTERS AND CRIMINALS

THE CITY'S REPUTATION for lawlessness was secured in the 1920s with the rise of the US's infamous crime lord, Al Capone (1899–1947). Prohibition set the stage for mob warfare as gangsters monopolized the lucrative market of banned alcohol. More than 300 gang-related murders occurred in the 1920s, including the Capone-orchestrated St. Valentine's Day Massacre *(see p16).*

Bank robber John Dillinger's daring made him a folk hero of sorts. When he was killed by the FBI outside Lincoln Park's Biograph Theatre in 1934, onlookers dipped hand-kerchiefs in his blood for mor-bid mementos.

**A bank robber as folk hero, John Dillinger**

## ENTREPRENEURS AND INDUSTRIALISTS

**Charles Wacker, city planner**

YOUNG Chicago attracted many enter-prisers. Cyrus Hall McCormick (1809–1884) transformed wheat farming with his in-vention of the Virginia reap-er. In 1848, he concentrated his farm-implement empire in Chicago. He died the richest man in Illinois.

Real-estate developer Potter Palmer (1826–1902) built luxury hotels and is credited with creating the wealthy Gold Coast area *(see pp72–7).*

Marshall Field (1834–1906) built his fortune as a depart-ment store owner *(see pp50–51),* funding some of Chicago's most important institutes.

Brewer Charles H. Wacker (1856–1929), son of Frederick Wacker *(see p71),* helped shape the city as chair of the Chicago Plan Commission, overseers of the 1909 Plan of Chicago *(see p28).*

## SOCIAL REFORMERS

AT THE TURN of the 20th century, Chicago was home to three of the most influential women in the US.

Black civil-rights activist Ida B. Wells (1862–1931) success-fully sued a railroad company for racial discrimination. Her columns appeared in many of the nation's 200 Black papers during the 1890s *(see p95).*

Jane Addams (1860–1935) was involved with almost every US social movement of the early 20th century, winning a Nobel Peace Prize for her work. In 1889, she cofounded Hull-House *(see p116).* Suffragist Frances Willard (1839–98) helped found the World's WCTU, the first inter-national women's organization *(see Rest Cottage, p124).*

# CHICAGO THROUGH THE YEAR

CHICAGO'S NICKNAME "Windy City" originally referred to its blustery politicians who lobbied to host the 1893 World's Columbian Exposition. Visitors will be struck by the appropriateness of the label. Chicago is a windy city whatever the season – although it ranks only 14th for wind velocity in the country.

**Cyclist on Lincoln Park's lakefront path**

Springtime in Chicago begins in late March. The city bursts into bloom after a long winter, living up to its official motto, *Urbs in Horto*, or "City in a garden." In summer, Chicago's beaches offer cooling breezes and the sun-warmed waters of Lake Michigan. These same waters keep the city temperate during autumn. In winter, they lead to "lake effect" storms: plenty of snow and chilling breezes. Intrepid locals bundle up and take advantage of winter attractions such as the WinterBreak festival. City Visitor Centers and the mayor's office *(see p161)* provide event information.

**Irish reveler at Chicago's annual St. Patrick's Day Parade**

## SPRING

CHICAGOANS welcome the arrival of spring by jogging through Grant Park, enjoying Lincoln Park's magnificent flower displays, and cheering on the city's two baseball teams, the Chicago Cubs and the White Sox, whose seasons begin in April *(see pp162–3)*.

## MARCH

**Pulaski Day Reception** *(Mar 4)*, Polish Museum of America, 984 N Milwaukee Ave. Celebrations in honor of Polish freedom fighter and later US Civil War hero Casimir Pulaski.
**St. Patrick's Day Parade** *(Sat before Mar 17)*, the Loop. The Chicago River is dyed green in celebration.

**South Side Irish Parade** *(Sun before Mar 17)*, Western Ave from 103rd to 114th Sts. One of the largest Irish parades outside Dublin.
**Greek Independence Day Parade** *(last Sun)*, Halsted St from Randolph to Van Buren.

## APRIL

**Chicago Park District Spring Flower Show** *(early Apr–mid-May)*, Lincoln Park Conservatory. An exuberant display of colorful flowers.
**International Vintage Poster Fair** *(mid-Apr)*, Navy Pier. Everything from Hollywood movie posters to reproductions of works by master artists are for sale at this three-day event.

## MAY

**Bike Chicago** *(mid-May–mid-Jun)*, city wide. Month-long celebration of cycling, with architecture bike tours, group bike rides, and workshops.
**Great Chicago Places and Spaces** *(mid- or late May)*, 77 E Randolph St. Architecture in Chicago's downtown is celebrated through walking and lobby tours, special events, and exhibitions.
**Wright Plus** *(mid- or late May)*, Oak Park *(p114)*. Tour Frank Lloyd Wright-designed private residences and national historic landmarks in this annual housewalk.

## SUMMER

CHICAGOANS THRONG to art fairs, neighborhood festivals, and outdoor concerts during the summer. A long-standing Chicago tradition is the free evening concerts – from opera to blues, from country to pop – at Grant Park's *(see pp84–5)* Petrillo Music Shell. Chicagoans and visitors alike take advantage of this opportunity for a picnic dinner in the park.

## JUNE

**Chicago Gospel Festival** *(early Jun)*, Grant Park. A two-day free event featuring gospel composers, singers, and musicians.
**Chicago Blues Festival** *(early Jun)*, Grant Park. A three-day extravaganza of local blues musicians and southern artists.

**Navy Pier, Chicago's amusement park for the entire family *(see p65)***

**AVERAGE DAILY HOURS OF SUNSHINE**

Hours

Jan Feb Mar Apr May Jun Jul Aug Sep Oct Nov Dec

**Sunshine**
*More than 50 days a year on average have clear skies, whereas 240 are overcast. Night descends early during the winter months, but the days can be brilliantly clear. December is the cloudiest month of the year, with an average of just four cloud-free days.*

**Printer's Row Book Fair** *(early Jun)*, Dearborn Ave between Congress Pkwy and Polk St *(p82)*. Book dealers, and papermaking and bookbinding demonstrations.

**Old Town Art Fair** *(second weekend)*, 1800 W block of Lincoln Park W. Artists from around the world show and sell their work.

**Wells Street Art Festival** *(second weekend)*, Wells St between Division and North aves. Crafts and fine art on display and for sale.

**Ravinia Music Festival** *(mid-Jun–Labor Day)*, Ravinia Park. Dozens of performances in all musical styles *(p162)*.

**18th Street Cultural Festival** *(third weekend)*, 1617 W 18th St. Tastes, sights, and sounds of Hispanic culture.

**Gay and Lesbian Pride Parade** *(fourth Sun)*, Lincoln Park.

**JULY**

**Taste of Chicago** *(first week)*, Grant Park *(pp84–5)*. Concerts and cooking lessons accompany the cuisine of some of the city's finest restaurants.

**Kwanzaa Summer Festival** *(first Sat)*, 49 E 95th St. Musical entertainment, food, and activities for children of all ages.

**Chicago Country Music Festival** *(early Jul)*, Grant Park *(pp84–5)*.

**Rock Around the Block** *(mid-Jul)*, Lakeview *(p114)*. Annual weekend-long neighborhood festivities.

**Chicago Folks and Roots Festival** *(late Jul)*, Welles Park. An eclectic mix of musical styles from around the world.

**La Fiesta del Sol** *(Jul 29–31)*, Pilsen *(p116)*. Carnival rides, arts and crafts, local and visiting musicians, and Mexican cuisine are featured at this festival, one of Chicago's largest.

**Jazzfest** *(late Jul)*, South Shore Cultural Center, 7059 S Lake Shore Dr. Top jazz musicians perform.

**Venetian Night** *(late Jul)*, Monroe Harbor. Parade of boats and fireworks synchronized to music.

**Chinatown Summer Fair** *(late Jul or early Aug)*, Wentworth Ave between Cermak Rd and 24th St. Food, art, and dance.

**AUGUST**

**Pullman Jazz, Blues and Gospel Fest** *(early Aug)*, Gately Park *(p119)*.

**Bud Billiken Day Parade** *(second Sat)*, 39th and King Dr. One of the US's oldest African-American parades culminates with a picnic in Washington Park *(p104)*.

**Chicago Carifete** *(mid-Aug)*, Midway Plaisance *(p104)*. Music, dance, and food from the islands of the Caribbean.

**Air maneuvers over the North Side as part of the Air and Water Show**

**Rock the River** *(mid-Aug)*, Michigan Ave and Wacker Dr. River cruises, a fishing derby, and music in celebration of the Chicago River.

**Chicago Air and Water Show** *(late Aug)*, North Ave Beach. Planes and boats do stunts in the sky and water.

**Bucktown Arts Fest** *(late Aug)*, N Oakley Blvd *(p114)*. Local artists display their various works.

**Viva! Chicago Latin Music Festival** *(last weekend)*, Grant Park *(pp84–5)*.

**Visitors sampling delicacies of dozens of restaurants at Taste of Chicago**

## Average Monthly Rainfall

| MM | | Inches |
|---|---|---|
| 300 | | 12 |
| 240 | | 9 |
| 180 | | 6 |
| 120 | | 3 |
| 60 | | |
| 0 | | 0 |

Jan Feb Mar Apr May Jun Jul Aug Sep Oct Nov Dec

■ Rainfall
□ Snowfall

**Precipitation**
*Chicago's average
monthly precipitation is
much the same
throughout the year,
with a modest peak in
early summer. Summer
storms are brief but
dramatic, and provide
relief from humidity.
Winter brings blizzards.*

**Pumpkins at a local farmers'
market, a telltale sign of autumn**

## Autumn

Autumn is an invigorating
season in Chicago.
September's comfortable
weather provides an inviting
backdrop to the numerous
outdoor festivals held
throughout the city.

Autumn is also the season
when Chicagoans and visitors
alike test their mettle and
stamina during the
internationally celebrated
annual marathon.

Football season kicks off
the first week of September
with the Chicago Bears
playing at Soldier Field. The
city's many sports enthusiasts
also flock to the United
Center to see the Chicago
Bulls play basketball and the
Chicago Blackhawks play
hockey *(see p163)*.

In late autumn, the city gets
a head start on the Christmas
season, with many holiday
traditions beginning
immediately after Thanks-
giving, in November.

### September

**Chicago Jazz Festival** *(Labor
Day weekend)*, Grant Park
*(pp84–5)*. Swing to the lively
sounds of renowned jazz
musicians and singers.
**Around the Coyote** *(second
weekend)*, Wicker Park
*(p114)*. Arts festival and
gallery tours.
**Celtic Fest Chicago** *(mid-Sep)*,
Grant Park *(pp84–5)*. A celebration of Celtic music.
**Mexican Independence
Day Parade** *(mid-Sep)*, Little
Village. Floats, bands, and
dancers join to celebrate
Mexico's 1820 independence
from Spain.
**World Music Festival** *(mid-
to late Sep)*, various locations.
The eclectic sounds of world-
beat music.
**Art on Harrison** *(third weekend)*, Oak Park *(pp114–15)*.
Showcasing Oak Park's
artists, galleries, and studios,
with displays, demonstrations,
and food.

### October

**Haunted "L" Rides**
*(weekends)*, Chicago Cultural
Center *(p52)*. Free Loop train
tour with ghosts and goblins.
**Mayor Daley's Kids and
Kites Fest** *(early Oct)*, Lake
Shore Dr and Montrose Ave.
**Annual House Tour** *(second
weekend)*, Pullman *(p119)*.
A rare opportunity to see
inside this historic district's
19th-century houses.
**Chicago Marathon** *(second
Sun)*, downtown. One of the
world's largest marathons,
with thousands of partici-
pants, and spectators in the
hundreds of thousands
cheering runners along the

26.5-mile (43-km) course.
**Oktoberfest** *(mid-Oct)*,
Weed St from Dayton St to
Halsted Ave. Celebrates
German culture with food
and beer gardens.
**Pumpkin Plaza** *(mid- to late
Oct)*, Daley Plaza. An outdoor
haunted village kids will love.

### November

**Holiday Windows at
Marshall Field's** *(Nov–Dec)*.
Animated Christmas displays
in the windows of the State
Street store *(pp50–51)* are a
Chicago tradition.
**Christmas Around the
World and Holidays of
Light** *(mid-Nov–Jan)*,
Museum of Science and
Industry *(pp106–109)*.
Chicago's ethnic groups
decorate trees in an
"enchanted" forest and share
holiday traditions.
**Magnificent Mile Lights
Festival** *(third weekend)*,
Michigan Ave from the
Chicago River to Oak St.
Christmas lights are lit during
this annual procession.

**The Chicago Marathon, attracting
athletes from around the world**

AVERAGE MONTHLY TEMPERATURE

**Temperature**
*Spring in Chicago is generally mild. Most summer days are comfortably warm, but there may be some very hot and humid periods. Autumn is crisp, with unpredictable temperatures. Winter winds, rushing through the tunnels created by the city's tall buildings, are often bitingly cold.*

**Field's Jingle Elf Parade**
*(Thanksgiving Day),* State St between Congress Pkwy and Randolph St. Santa Claus and his elves delight children.
**Holiday Tree Lighting Ceremony** *(day after Thanksgiving Day),* Daley Plaza.
**Christkindlmarket** *(late Nov–Dec),*Daley Plaza. Holiday shopping in a German marketplace, complete with an 80-ft (24 m) tree.

## WINTER

THE CITY SPARKLES during winter with elaborate decorations, and buildings and trees festooned with seasonal green and red lights. The Merchandise Mart, on the north bank of the river, looks like a massive wrapped gift.

## DECEMBER

**Country Christmas**
*(throughout Dec),* Galena *(pp128–9).* Holiday traditions

and celebrations in the town's Victorian Historic District, including Santa visits, housewalks, and a Mistletoe Ball.
**Caroling to the Animals** *(first Sun),* Lincoln Park Zoo *(pp112–13).* Sing holiday favorites to the animals.
**Chicago Park District Christmas Flower Show** *(mid-Dec),* Lincoln Park Conservatory. Colorful holiday poinsettia displays.
**New Year's Eve** *(Dec 31),* Navy Pier *(p65).* An evening of celebration with laser-lights and fireworks.

## JANUARY

**New Year's Day** *(Jan 1),* Navy Pier *(p65).* Family activities and fireworks to start off the New Year.
**WinterBreak** *(Jan 1–Mar 31).* More than 100 city-wide indoor and outdoor events, including the Magnificent Mile Crystal Carnival, with its giant ice sculptures, as well as theme weekends.

**Illuminated Christmas tree in front of the Tribune Building**

## FEBRUARY

**Chinese New Year Parade** *(date varies),*Wentworth Ave from Cermak Rd to 24th St. Festivities include colorful floats, traditional music and dancing, and food.

### PUBLIC HOLIDAYS

**New Year's Day** (Jan 1)
**Martin Luther King Day** (3rd Mon in Jan)
**President's Day** (3rd Mon in Feb)
**Pulaski Day** (1st Mon in Mar)
**Memorial Day** (last Mon in May)
**Independence Day** (Jul 4)
**Labor Day** (1st Mon in Sep)
**Columbus Day** (2nd Mon in Oct)
**Veterans Day** (Nov 11)
**Thanksgiving Day** (4th Thu in Nov)
**Christmas Day** (Dec 25)

**Ice skaters enjoying a bright winter day outdoors**

# CHICAGO
# AREA BY AREA

# DOWNTOWN CORE

**B**ORDERED ON THE NORTH and on the west by the Chicago River, on the east by Lake Michigan, and on the south by the Congress Parkway, the Downtown Core is Chicago's historic and financial center. The downtown's nucleus is the Loop, named for the elevated train tracks encircling it. Even though the area was completely destroyed by the Great Fire of 1871, a mere two decades later it had been rebuilt with pioneering skyscrapers, including the Marquette Building. Along with this architectural legacy, the area is home to such famous museums as the Art Institute of Chicago. State Street is home to landmark department stores.

**Picasso sculpture at the Daley Center**

## SIGHTS AT A GLANCE

### Historic Buildings
Auditorium Building **6**
Carson Pirie Scott and Company **10**
Chicago Theatre **17**
Fine Arts Building **7**
Marquette Building **3**
Marshall Field and Company **12**
Monadnock Building **5**
Oriental Theater **13**
Reliance Building **11**
The Rookery **2**
Santa Fe Building **8**
35 East Wacker Drive **19**

### Modern Skyscrapers
Federal Center **4**
James R. Thompson Center **21**
R.R. Donnelley Building **20**
Sears Tower **1**
333 West Wacker Drive **22**

### Museums and Galleries
*Art Institute of Chicago pp46–9* **9**
Chicago Cultural Center **14**
Museum of Broadcast Communications **15**

### Bridges, Parks, and Streets
Michigan Avenue Bridge **18**
Millennium Park **16**
Wacker Drive **23**

## KEY

| | |
|---|---|
| ▨ | Street-by-Street map *See pp38–9* |
| **M** | CTA train station |
| ▤ | Metra train station |
| **P** | Parking |

## GETTING THERE

The Downtown Core is easily explored on foot. Frequent CTA elevated trains circle the Loop. CTA buses also provide frequent service. Downtown routes include 20, 22, 36, and 56. Twelve Metra lines service Chicago's suburbs. Trains depart from one of five stations surrounding the Loop (*see pp180–83*).

| 0 meters | 500 |
|---|---|
| 0 yards | 500 |

◁ **Atrium in Marshall Field's landmark department store**

# Street-by-Street: The Loop

THE LOOP GETS ITS NAME from the elevated track system that circles the center of the Downtown Core. Trains screeching as they turn sharp corners and the steady stream of businesspeople during rush hour add to the Loop's bustle. In the canyon vistas through the many tall, historic buildings – and modern edifices such as the Federal Center – you can catch glimpses of the 19 bridges spanning Chicago River. The conversion of warehouses to condominiums and renovation of historic theaters are helping to enliven the Loop at night.

*Stone lion guarding the doors of the Art Institute*

**The Rookery**
*One of the earliest designs by Burnham and Root, the lobby of this 1888 building was remodeled by Frank Lloyd Wright in 1907* ❷

**★ Sears Tower**
*At a height of 1,454 ft (443 m), this is one of the tallest buildings in the world. Views from the glass-enclosed observation deck on the 103rd floor are stunning* ❶

**190 South LaSalle Street** (1987), designed by New York architect Philip Johnson, has a white-marble lobby with a gold-leafed, vaulted ceiling.

**Marquette Building**
*This early skyscraper (1895) was designed by William Holabird and Martin Roche, central Chicago School figures and architects of more than 80 buildings in the Loop* ❸

STREET

CLARK

ADAMS

FRANKLIN

WACKER

STREET

DRIVE

---

**STAR SIGHTS**

★ Art Institute of Chicago

★ Sears Tower

---

**Chicago Board of Trade**
*occupies a 45-story Art Deco building, a statue of Ceres atop its roof. The frenetic action inside can be observed from a viewers' gallery.*

**Santa Fe Building**
*This classic Chicago School building, with an elegant two-story atrium, houses the Chicago Architecture Foundation* **8**

**★ Art Institute of Chicago**
*The Impressionist and Post-Impressionist collection at this museum, one of the most important in the country, is world famous* **9**

**LOCATOR MAP**
*See Street Finder maps 3 & 4*

**KEY**

– – – Suggested route

0 meters        100

0 yards         100

**Monadnock Building**
*The north half of this building (1891) is the tallest building ever constructed entirely of masonry* **5**

**Federal Center**
*Ludwig Mies van der Rohe designed this three-building office complex around a central plaza, which holds Alexander Calder's 1973 sculpture* Flamingo **4**

**Fine Arts Building**
*Frank Lloyd Wright once had a studio in this 1885 building designed by Solon S. Beman. The building was originally used as a carriage showroom by the Studebaker Company* **7**

**The "Elevated,"**
or "L," train tracks opened in 1892. Its loop in the city's core is seven blocks long and five blocks wide.

**Auditorium Building**
*The seventh-floor, birch paneled recital hall in this 1889 multipurpose sky-scraper is one of Adler and Sullivan's best interiors* **6**

# Sears Tower ❶

233 S Wacker Dr. **Map** 3 B2.
🅒 875-9696. 🅜 *Quincy.*
🅞 *May–Sep: 10am–10pm
daily; Oct–Apr: 10am–8pm
daily; last adm 30 min before
closing.* 🔣 🔣 🔣 🔣 🅿
🅦 *www.sears-tower.com*

**The 110-story
tower** soars to
1,454 ft (443 m) – or
1,729 ft (527 m) if
the higher of the
two antennas is
included.

**The tower top**
sways 6 inches (15
cm) in strong wind.

**The glass-
enclosed,** 103rd-
floor Skydeck, the
world's third-highest
observation deck,
provides views of
the far shores of
Lake Michigan and
four states on
clear days.

**The 16,000
bronze-tinted
windows** are
cleaned by six
automatic machines
eight times a year.

**Black aluminum**
clads the frame-
work, which is
made from 76,000
tons of steel.

**Alexander
Calder's mobile
sculpture** *Universe*
(1974) is on display
in the lobby.

IN JUNE 2000, Sears
Tower once again
became the world's
tallest building from
base to tip of antenna,
when a 22 ft (6.7 m)
extension was added to
one of the tower's two
broadcast antennas. It
had already regained
its title as the tallest
building in the world
in two of four
categories under
revised 1997
international
guidelines. Although
it no longer has the
tallest structural
height (Cesar Pelli's
Petronas Towers in
Kuala Lumpur has
that distinction,
which some say is
the most important),
it does have the
highest occupied
floor and also the
highest height to the
rooftop.

Sears Tower,
opened in
1974, was
designed by
Bruce Graham, a
partner at the Chicago
architectural firm of
Skidmore, Owings and
Merrill, with the assistance of
chief engineer Fazlur Khan.
Construction of the innovative
building took three years,
employing 1,600 people
during the peak period. More
than 110 concrete caissons
anchored in bedrock support
the tower's 222,500 tons.

Today, the tower contains
4.5 million sq ft (0.4 million
sq m) of office space, more
than 100 elevators. It also
contains approximately 43,000
ft (13,100 m) of telephone
cable, almost enough to
encircle the Earth twice.

The elevator to the Skydeck
travels at a stomach-churning
1,600 ft (490 m) per minute,

and a narrated history of the
tower provides a welcome
distraction for some.

During the summer, there
are often lengthy lineups for
the Skydeck, but diversions
include a short movie on
Chicago and an exhibition
on the city's ten
most significant
buildings.

**View of the Sears Tower and
Skydeck, looking northeast**

# The Rookery ❷

209 S LaSalle St. **Map** 3 C2. 🅒 553-
6150. 🅜 *Quincy; Jackson (blue line).*
🅞 *9am–8pm Mon–Fri; 9am–3pm
Sat.* 🅞 *major public hols.* 🔣

WHEN THE ROOKERY opened
in 1888, it was the tallest
building in the world. The 12-
story building, designed by
the influential firm Burnham
and Root in the Richardsonian
Romanesque style *(see p24)*,
has a dark red brick façade
with terra-cotta trim and a
rough granite base. The
building, now housing offices,
was constructed on a foundation of crisscrossing rails
– necessitated by the clay
soils unable to support the
weight of the massive
structure. While its thick
masonry walls are load
bearing, the iron framing
of the lower stories

**The Loop's glittering skyline as seen at sunset**

allows for the use of large windows – a welcome innovation when artificial lighting technology was in its infancy.

Framing the main entrance is a monumental arch with geometric carvings, including eponymous rooks. Inside is a two-tiered court, remodeled in 1907 by Frank Lloyd Wright, who covered the original iron columns and staircases with white marble, inlaid with gold leaf. The central staircase, framed with Wright's signature urns, leads to a mezzanine enclosed by a domed skylight. A magnificent, cantilevered cast-iron staircase leads from the second floor to the top. The building was made a National Historic Landmark in 1988.

Entrance to the Marquette Building

The Rookery's spectacular light court

# Marquette Building ❸

140 S Dearborn St. **Map** 3 C2.
📞 422-5500. Ⓜ Monroe (blue line).
🕐 24 hrs daily. ♿

CONSIDERED the premier remaining example of the Chicago School of architecture (see pp24–5), the Marquette Building was designed by Holabird and Roche in 1895.

Commissioned by the owners of the Rookery, the architects faced the demanding task of equaling the Burnham and Root original sophisticated design of that building.

The grid of this early commercial 16-story high-rise's steel-frame skeleton is easily seen in the terra-cotta and brick exterior.

The building's groundbreaking expansive horizontal windows became known as Chicago windows (see p25). They are one of the few remaining examples of this innovative window design.

Bronze bas-relief panels over the entrance doors, designed by Hermon Atkins MacNeil, illustrate Jesuit missionary Father Jacques Marquette's 1673–4 expedition to the area.

In the two-story lobby, mosaic panels of glass and mother-of-pearl designed by J.A. Holzer of Tiffany and Company depict scenes of the French exploration of Illinois. Sculpted heads inset above the elevators on the first and second floors pay tribute to the Native chiefs and early French explorers of the Chicago area (see p13).

The building underwent restoration in 1980.

# Federal Center ❹

219 S Dearborn St. **Map** 3 C2.
Ⓜ Jackson (blue line).
🕐 7am–6pm Mon–Fri. ⬤ major public hols. ♿

THE THREE-BUILDING Federal Center complex, designed by Ludwig Mies van der Rohe and completed in 1974, expresses the pared-down functionalism of Mies' International style (see p25). There is little ornamentation to distract from these austere curtain-wall structures made of glass and steel.

The 30-story Dirksen courtroom building stands on the east side of the complex; the 42-story Kluczynski office tower and one-story post office are to the west. The center is interesting for the expert arrangement of its buildings around the plaza and with each other.

The sterile plaza is graced with Alexander Calder's 53-ft (16-m) vermilion sculpture Flamingo (see p44), which seems almost to be dancing – its steel organic form a surprising complement to the rigid geometry of the buildings.

The Monadnock Building's
filigree wrought-iron staircase

# Monadnock Building ❺

53 W Jackson Blvd. **Map** 3 C2.
**M** *Jackson (blue line).* ⏰ *7am–6pm
Mon–Fri.* ⬤ *public hols.* ♿

CONSTRUCTED in two parts two years apart (and by two different architectural firms), the interestingly bisected Monadnock Building looks both to the past and to the future. The northern half of this office building, designed by Burnham and Root, was built first, in 1891. Sixteen stories tall and with masonry load-bearing walls (the building method at the time), it is the tallest masonry building ever constructed. The southern section, on the other hand, designed by Holabird and Roche, has a steel skeleton sheathed in terra-cotta, an innovation that in the 1890s allowed skyscrapers to soar.

The building is named after one of New Hampshire's White Mountains. "Monadnock" is also a geological term for a mountain surrounded by a glacial plain – an appropriate name for this most solid of buildings, as its walls are 6 ft (2 m) thick at the base. The interior was restored in the 1980s: the mosaic floor is a replica; the white-marble ceiling and

ornate staircase are original. At the north entrance to the building and at the south elevator banks, you can see, under glass, part of the original marble floor. A corridor bordered by shops and restaurants runs the full length of the building, much like an interior street.

# Auditorium Building ❻

430 S Michigan Ave. **Map** 4 D3. 🎫
341-3555. **M** *Library.* 🚌 *145, 147,
151.* ⏰ *7:30am–10:30pm Mon–
Thu; 7:30am–6pm Fri; 8am–5pm
Sat; 11am–4pm Sun (Sep–Apr only).*
⬤ *major public hols.* ♿ 🎟
**Building**: 341-3555; **Theater**: 922-
2110. See **Entertainment** p162.

DESIGNED BY Dankmar Adler and Louis Sullivan, their first major commission together, the Auditorium Building (1889), with its walls of smooth limestone typical of the Richardsonian Romanesque style *(see p24)* rising above the rough granite base, broke many records and achieved a number of firsts. Combining a 400-room hotel, a 17-story office tower, and a 4,300-seat theater, it was the tallest building in Chicago and the first building of its size to be electrically lighted and air-conditioned. Not surprisingly, it was also the most expensive, costing over $3 million to build. At 110,000 tons, it was the heaviest building in the world, and the most fireproof.

The building's crowning jewel is the lavish Auditorium Theatre, the

Roosevelt University admissions
office in the Auditorium Building

first home of the Chicago Symphony Orchestra. After many years of neglect (World War II servicemen used the stage as a bowling alley), it was restored in the 1960s and is now a venue for performing arts events. Four elliptical arches span the width of the theater, which is ornamented with stenciling, stained glass, and gold-leaf plaster reliefs. Its excellent acoustics enable guests in the last row to hear an unamplified whisper on stage, six stories below.

Stained-glass detailing in the
Auditorium Building

The grand lobby, with its onyx walls and ornate staircase, contains an exhibition on the building's history. The tenth-floor library, originally the hotel's dining room, has a dramatic barrel-vaulted ceiling and superb lake views.

The building also houses Roosevelt University.

Façade of the Auditorium Building, with cows from
Chicago's public-art project in the foreground

White-marble lobby of the Santa Fe Building

# Fine Arts Building ❼

410 S Michigan Ave. **Map** 4 D2.
📞 427-7602. Ⓜ Library. 🚌 3, 4,
60, 145, 147, 151. ⏱ 7am–10pm
Mon–Fri; 7am–9pm Sat; 10am–4pm
Sun. ⬤ major public hols. ♿

Although now closely associated with fine art and culture, the Fine Arts Building was originally commissioned by Studebaker Brothers Manufacturing to house a wagon carriage showroom. (The name "Studebaker" inscribed outside in stone is still visible above the first floor.)

Designed by Solon S. Beman and completed in 1885, the building, with its columns, rough stone, and arched entranceway and windows, is typical of the Romanesque style.

When the Studebaker Company moved to a new location, Beman was commissioned to renovate the building as a cultural center. The façade of the eighth floor was removed and replaced with a three-story addition. Inside, studios, shops, and offices were added, and the building quickly became a hub of artistic activity. The literary magazines *Dial*, *Poetry*, and *Little Review* were published here; the Little Theater staged dramas; and painters, sculptors, and architects (including Frank Lloyd Wright, *see p28*) had their studios on the tenth floor. In 1892, resident artists, including Frederic Clay Bartlett and Ralph Clarkson, formed a group called the Little Room and produced eight murals, which still can be seen on the walls of the tenth floor.

Today, the building, which has been given national historic landmark status, has a slightly frayed, run-down charm. Many arts-related enterprises remain in the building, including the Fine Arts Building Gallery in Suite 433, which showcases Chicago artists, with a new exhibition each month. There are also two movie theaters.

The sound of singers practicing scales can be heard echoing through the halls, and a ride in the old elevator (with an operator) is an experience not to be missed.

# Santa Fe Building ❽

224 S Michigan Ave. **Map** 4 D2.
📞 341-9461. Ⓜ Adams. ⏱ 24 hrs
daily. ⬤ major public hols.

The Santa Fe Building gleams – inside with white marble, and outside with white-glazed terra-cotta. Designed by D.H. Burnham and Co. in 1904 and originally known as the Railway Exchange Building, it is now called the Santa Fe because of the rooftop sign, erected in the early 1900s by the Santa Fe Railroad.

Porthole windows line the top floor; terra-cotta reliefs of ancient goddesses decorate the vestibule. The atrium's balustraded mezzanine, marble staircase, and elevators with

Decorative elevator door in the Santa Fe Building

grillwork are all notable. The building also houses the Chicago Architecture Center which is a "mini-museum" detailing the history of Chicago architecture and offering guided tours of the city.

The Artist's Snack Shop on the ground floor of the Fine Arts Building

# A Three-Hour Walk in the Downtown Core

DOZENS OF WORKS by world-renowned artists are on public display throughout Chicago's Downtown Core. This walk explores a selection from this huge outdoor art gallery and the buildings in the area, many of which are themselves works of art. The spectacular backdrop that the Loop's commanding architecture provides ensures excellent sights along the way.

### South Michigan Avenue to South Dearborn Street

Start at the Adams CTA Station ① and walk east on Adams Street, turning right onto South Michigan Avenue and past the stately Art Institute of Chicago *(see p46–9)*. Lorado Taft's (1860–1936) *Fountain of the Great Lakes* (1913) ②, with its five female figures, is at the

west along Van Buren Street, turning right at State. Continue north, bearing left at Jackson, to the Frank Metcalf Federal Building and the sculpture *Lines in Four Directions* (1985) ④ by American minimalist Sol Lewitt (b.1928).

Dearborn Street. Continue to walk north, passing the Marquette Building *(see p41)* on your left, to *The Four Seasons* (1974) ⑥ by Marc Chagall (1887–1985), at First National Plaza. This huge, four-sided mosaic consists of thousands of tiles in more than 250 colors that illustrate various

**View of buildings in the Loop looking east from Grant Park** ③

south end of the main building. One block farther south is the main entrance of Grant Park ③, from where there is a good view of the buildings along Michigan Avenue, including the Santa Fe Building *(see p43)*. Walk

*The Four Seasons* **by Marc Chagall** ⑥

### Dearborn Street to West Randolph Street

Cross Dearborn Street and enter the courtyard of the Federal Center *(see p41)* to see American sculptor Alexander Calder's (1898–1976) dramatic *Flamingo* (1974) ⑤. Retrace your steps to

Chicago scenes. Across the street is the groundbreaking Inland Steel Building ⑦. Steel pilings were driven 85 feet (26 m) down to the bedrock to support the building. Follow Dearborn Street to Washington, bearing left. On the left is Catalan artist Joan Miró's (1893–1983) *Chicago* (1981) ⑧, a surreal feminine figure made of plaster and bronze and studded with

*Miró's* **Chicago** ⑧

colorful ceramic tiles. County Building ⑨, with its 75-foot (23 m) Corinthian columns, can be seen at the corner of Washington and Clark. Continue along Washington Street, turning right onto LaSalle. Pass Chicago City Hall ⑩, the sister building of the County Building. On the northwest corner of Lasalle and Randolph is the Illinois State Office Building.

**Lantern on No. 35 East Wacker Drive ⑮**

On its exterior is *Freeform* (1993) ⑪, which Chicago sculptor Richard Hunt (b.1935) created to symbolize "a government supporting individual freedoms." Walk east on Randolph Street to the James R. Thompson Center *(see p56)* and French Art Brut artist Jean Dubuffet's (1901–1985) fiberglass sculpture *Monument with Standing Beast* (1984) ⑫. Its graffiti-like style is characteristic of the

**TIPS FOR WALKERS**

**Starting point:** *Adams CTA station, at the corner of Wabash Avenue and West Adams Street.*
**Time:** *Three hours.*
**Getting there:** *Take the brown, green, orange, or purple line CTA train to Adams Station.*
**Stopping-off point:** *Numerous cafés and restaurants can be found along the route, though many may be open only during weekday business hours. Sopraffina Marketcaffe, at 10 North Dearborn Street, serves Italian fare, from biscotti to pizza. West Egg Cafe, at 55 West Washington Street, offers breakfast and lunch at modest prices.*

## State Street to East Randolph Street

One block east, on State Street, is the elegant Chicago Theatre ⑭ *(see p54)*. Turn right at Wacker Drive. At No. 35 ⑮ *(see p55)* is the former Jewelers Building, designed in 1926. Follow Wacker Drive east, turning right at Michigan Avenue, then left at Randolph Street to Prudential Plaza ⑯, consisting of two buildings. No. 1, a towering limestone and aluminum structure built in 1952, was the first skyscraper to be built in the Loop since the 1930s. The design of No. 2, with its chevron top, suggests New York's Chrysler Building.

E WACKER DR
E LAKE ST
E RANDOLPH ST
COLUMBUS
E MONROE DR
DRIVE
E JACKSON DR
N MICHIGAN AVE
S MICHIGAN AVE

0 meters 250
0 yards 250

**KEY**

- - - Suggested route
Ⓜ CTA train station
🚇 Metra train station
Ⓟ Parking

artist's work. Just east, across the street in the Richard J. Daley Plaza, is the untitled sculpture by Pablo Picasso (1881–1973) ⑬. The piece created a stir when first erected, as Chicagoans debated its merits. Depending on where you stand, it is crowned with the head of a woman or of a hound dog.

**Façade of the Chicago Theater ⑭**

**The two buildings of Prudential Plaza, No. 1 on the far right ⑯**

# Art Institute of Chicago ❾

**Frieze on the west façade**

T HE EXTENSIVE COLLECTIONS at the Art Institute of Chicago represent nearly 5,000 years of human creativity through paintings, sculptures, textiles, photographs, cultural objects, and decorative artifacts from around the world.

The museum was founded by civic leaders and art collectors in 1879 as the Chicago Academy of Fine Arts, changing its name to the Art Institute of Chicago in 1882. Outgrowing two homes as wealthy patrons donated collections, it finally settled in a Neo-Classical structure built for the 1893 World's Fair. Today, the complex combines modern additions with the original structure designed by Shepley, Rutan and Coolidge.

**Visitors admiring works in the 19th-century European gallery**

**McKinlock Court**

**★ American Windows**
*Light from McKinlock Court streams through the azure stained glass designed by Marc Chagall, one of his last large-size works (1974–7), created in part as a tribute to the US bicentennial and to former Chicago mayor Richard J. Daley (see p17).*

## KEY TO FLOORPLAN

☐ Second floors

☐ First floors

☐ Lower levels

☐ Allerton Building

☐ Rice Building

☐ Rubloff Building

☐ School of the Art Institute

## STAR PAINTINGS

**★ *American Windows* by Marc Chagall**

**★ *Old Man with a Gold Chain* by Rembrandt van Rijn**

**★ *A Sunday on La Grande Jatte–1884* by Georges Seurat**

**Main Entrance**

## MUSEUM GUIDE

*The lower levels of the Rubloff and Rice buildings house European decorative arts from 1600 to 1900. The Allerton's is geared toward children, but photography and the Miniature Rooms are also here. First-floor galleries range from ancient Egyptian artifacts to Asian collections. Second floors are devoted mostly to European works from the 15th to 20th centuries.*

**The Bath** *(1891–2)*
*American artist Mary Cassatt employed a raised vantage point and cropped figures in her work – artistic devices uncommon at the time. This painting is influenced by the realistic style prominent in Japanese prints.*

**Time Transfixed** (1938), by René Magritte, is a juxtaposition of commonplace but unrelated items to create a surreal expression of reality.

**Mother and Child**, Pablo Picasso's 1921 painting, is exhibited along with a fragment that he removed from the final composition.

**★ A Sunday on La Grande Jatte–1884**
*Post-Impressionist Georges Seurat composed this image of promenading Parisians using tiny dots of color.*

**Self-Portrait by Vincent van Gogh**

*The Assumption of the Virgin*

**★ Old Man with a Gold Chain**
*Rembrandt van Rijn's interest in the wisdom of age can be seen in this character study (c.1631).*

**American Gothic**
*Grant Wood's 1930 portrait of an Iowa farmer and his spinster daughter, initially criticized as satire, has become an American classic.*

# Exploring the Art Institute of Chicago

THE MUSEUM'S HOLDINGS span the globe as well as centuries, from 3rd-millennium BC Egyptian and Chinese artifacts to 20th-century American art. Almost every major artistic movement of the 19th and 20th centuries is represented. The museum's Early Modernism collection is particularly strong; its Impressionist and Post-Impressionist collection – one of the most significant in the world – is outstanding. Important Renaissance and Baroque paintings complement these exhibits.

**Flower gardens in the grounds behind the Art Institute**

**Visitor to the European gallery appreciating works of old masters**

## ASIAN ART

SOME OF THE MUSEUM'S most exquisite pieces are in its distinguished Asian collection, which comprises 35,000 works of archeological and artistic significance.

The galleries of Chinese, Japanese, and Korean art include celebrated collections of ancient Chinese bronzes and jades, 19th-century Japanese woodblock prints, and early Korean ceramics.

The art from the Golden Age of the Tang dynasty (AD 618–907) is the prize of this exhibit, in particular, the magnificent brightly glazed earthenware funerary horses.

Indian, Himalayan, and Southeast Asian art dating from the 2nd to 19th centuries encompasses artifacts of the Hindu and Buddhist faiths. Among the gems here are the nearly life-sized 2nd- and 3rd-century bodhisattva sculptures from Gandhara (present-day Pakistan), and an elaborately carved 13th-century stone statute of Saraswati, the Hindu goddess of learning, from Southern India.

The Persian 16th-century illuminated manuscripts and miniature paintings are beautiful examples of that culture's precise and delicate art forms.

## ARMS AND ARMOR

REMARKABLE WORKS of late medieval and Renaissance metal-craft are showcased in the George F. Harding Collection. One of the finest such collections in North America, it consists of 3,000 pieces of arms and armor. These include finely etched helmets, chain mail, equestrian equipment, historic weaponry, and decorated breastplates.

One of the earliest pieces in the collection is a breastplate from northern Italy. Dating from 1380, its original fabric covering is still intact. Also striking is a 1575 northern Italian armor, used for foot combat. Made of etched and gilded steel and brass, the suit is decorated with large medallions depicting allegorical figures.

## DECORATIVE ARTS

FOR UNPARALLELED insight into the ever-changing taste of Western society, visit the decorative arts galleries. Their broad array embraces household items, including furniture and tableware, jewelry, and religious artifacts.

The impressive European collection contains 25,000 objects crafted from wood, metal, glass, ceramics, enamel, and ivory dating from 1100 to the present. It also includes sculpture from the medieval period to 1900.

The American collection includes an excellent selection of Arts and Crafts furniture, including a beautiful oak library table (1896) designed by Frank Lloyd Wright (see p28).

The fine European and American textile collection spans 15 centuries and

**The grand staircase and foyer of the Art Institute**

features vestments, tapestries, and embroideries. Highlights are a 19th-century William Morris-designed carpet and two rare fragments of Coptic cloth dating from between the 5th and 8th centuries.

Two of the quirkiest – and most renowned – collections are the Arthur Rubloff Paperweight Collection and the Thorne Miniature Rooms. The museum's holdings of more than 1,000 French, English, and American glass paperweights, popular in the mid-19th century, are one of the largest in the world.

The Thorne Miniature Rooms consist of 68 model rooms, painstakingly constructed to a scale of 1 inch (2.5 cm) to 1 foot (30 cm). The intricate European and American furnished interiors, ranging from the 16th to 20th centuries, are made with extraordinary technical precision.

**The Gourmet** (1901), painted by Pablo Picasso in his "Blue Period"

## 20TH-CENTURY ART

THE MUSEUM'S TROVE of more than 1,500 20th-century paintings and sculptures provides a comprehensive and provocative survey of the development of modern art. Representing every significant artistic movement in Europe and the US, the works are arranged in groupings that highlight stylistic affinities between varied artists.

The collection is divided into pre-1945 and post-1945 works. Particularly strong are the examples of Cubism, the precursor of all abstract art forms; German Expressionism, the embodiment of the search for a strong emotional language in art; and Surrealism, the liberation of the irrational.

Post-World War II art is represented with works by such influential artists as Willem de Kooning and Jackson Pollock.

## ARCHITECTURE

WHEN THE 1894 Chicago Stock Exchange (Adler and Sullivan) was demolished in 1972, its Trading Room was salvaged and reconstructed at the museum. Its ornate glory can still be seen in the room's stenciled ceiling and art-glass skylights. As memorable are the salvaged pieces from demolished Chicago buildings.

Special exhibits and a library with a comprehensive collection on Louis Sullivan complement the installations.

## IMPRESSIONIST AND POST-IMPRESSIONIST ART

GIFTS FROM WEALTHY patrons such as Bertha Palmer (see p77) and Frederic Clay Bartlett, who astutely began collecting works by Monet, Degas, and Seurat in the late 19th century, led to the Art Institute becoming the first in the US to include a gallery of Post-Impressionist art. Today, it is one of the foremost centers of Impressionist and Post-Impressionist paintings outside France.

United only by their fiercely held belief in artistic experimentation, the French Impressionists were a diverse group who

**The Basket of Apples** (c.1895) by Paul Cézanne

exhibited together in the late 1800s. Dedicated to a new form of art – one that eschewed the constraints of the prevailing formal style – these artists attempted to capture the textures and moods of fleeting moments, or impressions. Their final exhibition was in 1886.

The artists who followed in the Impressionists' footsteps – labeled Post-Impressionists by English art critic Roger Fry – created works of art exploring evocative color relationships and rules of composition.

Highlights of the museum's holdings include the highly estimable Helen Birch Bartlett Memorial Collection, featuring Paul Cézanne's *The Basket of Apples* (c.1895) and Henri de Toulouse-Lautrec's *At the Moulin Rouge* (1895).

No better illustration of Impressionist and Post-Impressionist principles can be found than Claude Monet's six versions of a wheat field, which combines the basic doctrine of Impressionism – capturing nature's temporality – with the Post-Impressionist concern for reconstructing nature according to art's formal, expressive potential.

**On the Seine at Bennecourt** (1868) by Claude Monet

## Carson Pirie Scott and Company ❿

1 S State St. **Map** 3 C2. ⟦ 641-
7000. Ⓜ Monroe; Washington (red
line). ☐ 9:45am–7pm Mon–Wed,
Fri; 9:45am–8pm Thu; 9:45am–6pm
Sat; 11am–6pm Sun. ◑ Easter,
Thanksgiving, Dec 25. ♿ 🍽 ▭
See **Shops and Markets** p155.

IT IS APPROPRIATE that such an
architectural gem as the
Carson Pirie Scott building,
housing one of Chicago's
oldest department stores, rests
at Chicago's ground-zero
address of State and Madison,
the starting point for the city's
street-numbering system.
The upper floors of the
building are of white terra-
cotta, but it is the ornamental
metalwork on the first two
floors that give this building,
designed by Louis Sullivan in
1899, its distinctive character.
A particularly noteworthy
feature of the store's exterior
is the corner entrance
pavilion, which extends 12
stories to the top of the
building and has ornamental
cast-iron motifs. Along with
intricately entwined botanical
and geometric forms,
Sullivan's initials, L.H.S., can
be seen above the corner
entrance. While this is the
showy heart of the building, it
is worth walking east along
Madison Street to view the
metalwork and Chicago
windows from a somewhat
less busy vantage point.

**The Reliance Building, precursor
to the modern skyscraper**

## Reliance Building ⓫

32 N State St. **Map** 3 C1. ⟦ 782-
1111. Ⓜ Washington (red line).
☐ 24 hrs daily. ♿ 🅿 See **Where
to Stay, Hotel Burnham** p134.

THE RELIANCE Building's
two-stage construction
(1890–95) was as unusual as
were the structural-support
techniques used. The leases
for the upper floors of the
original building on the site
did not expire until 1894, so

when work on the new
Reliance Building began in
1890, the upper floors of the
old building were supported
on jack screws and the lower
stories demolished. The
ground floors of the Reliance
Building were completed and
in 1894, when the leases
expired, the upper floors
were demolished and the
steel framing for 13 more
stories completed, in 15 days.
The new building, officially
opened in March 1895, was
considered revolutionary
because of its steel frame and
unusual two-story-column
design, allowing for the
masses of windows which
give the building its modern
look. The building's design
was undertaken by John Root
of Burnham and Root. Charles
Atwood completed it upon
Root's death in 1891.
The building was in serious
disrepair in the mid-1990s,
until the City of Chicago
purchased it and began an
exterior renovation, which
involved the replacement of
2,000 pieces of terra-cotta. In
1995, it was designated a
Chicago landmark. In 1998, a
hotel company bought the
building, undertaking a $27.5-
million refurbishment before
opening the Hotel Burnham
in 1999. Root's original bronze
and granite design of the first
floor has been re-created and
the 20-ft- (6-m-) high elevator
lobby reconstructed using
Italian marble, ornamental
metal elevator grills, and
elaborate mosaic floor tiles.

## Marshall Field and Company ⓬

111 N State St. **Map** 4 D1. ⟦ 781-
1000. Ⓜ Washington (red line).
☐ 9:45am–8pm Mon–Fri; 9am–9pm
Sat; 10am–8pm Sun. ◑ Easter,
Thanksgiving, Dec 25. ♿ 🛍 🍽 🅿
See **Shops and Markets** p155.

NO OTHER retail
establishment is, perhaps,
as important to Chicago's
cultural history as Marshall
Field's department store.
Originally a dry-goods shop
begun by wealthy businessman Marshall Field (see p77),
the store now occupies an

**Ornamental metalwork above the entrance to Carson Pirie Scott**

1925, when it was demolished. The Oriental, built on the site, opened in 1926. The 22-story building, with its 3,238-seat auditorium, was designed by renowned theater architects Cornelius W. and George L. Rapp.

The theater was used both as a movie palace and for live performances. Judy Garland, Jackie Gleason, and Bob Hope all performed here.

Inspired by the East Indian carnival-festival Durbar, the theater's interior is full of fantastic decorative elements, such as the elephant-head light fixtures in the foyer.

The Oriental is in what, for more than a century, was Chicago's bustling theater district: Randolph Street between Michigan Avenue and Wacker Drive. The Rice Theatre was the first to open in the area, in 1847 (since

Christmas window display at Marshall Field's

entire city block. Built in five stages as the company grew, the original building, a Renaissance Revival-style design by Charles B. Atwood of D.H. Burnham, still stands at Washington and Wabash.

Field is credited with transforming State Street into the retail heart of Chicago in the early 1900s and for coining the commercial credo "Give the lady what she wants." When the store opened in 1907, it was considered the largest in the world, with 1,339,000 sq ft (124,400 sq m) of retail space, including the basement (such use was until then unheard of

in US merchandising), 27,000 automatic fire sprinklers, 35,000 electric lights, 50 elevators, and 12 street-front entrances.

The store's most spectacular feature is its Tiffany mosaic dome, believed to be the largest piece of glass mosaic in the world. With more than 1.6 million pieces of iridescent glass covering 6,000 sq ft (557 sq m), it took 18 months and 50 artisans, supervised by designer Louis Comfort Tiffany, to complete.

Other interesting features of the store include the elegant Walnut Room restaurant and an exhibition tracing the store's history.

## Oriental Theater ⑬

24 W Randolph St. **Map** 3 C1.
【 782-2004. Ⓜ Washington (red line). ♿ ✉ 10:30am Sat; 11:30am Sun. See **Entertainment** pp162–3.

THE ORIENTAL Theater occupies the site of one of the worst theater fires in US history: just weeks after opening in 1903, fire broke out in the Iroquois Theater, claiming more than 600 lives (see p15). The theater was rebuilt and operated until

Signs such as this mark the Loop's theatrical district

burned down). By the 1880s, more than 25 entertainment palaces were offering vaudeville, musicals, opera, and drama. Although few of the original theaters remain, the district is being revitalized, spurred by the restoration of the Oriental, which reopened as the Ford Center for the Performing Arts Oriental Theater. Restoration of the theater was completed in 1998 after a 17-year closure; 62,500 sq ft (5,800 sq m) of gold leaf were used in the theater's renovation.

Tiffany glass dome in Marshall Field's southern atrium

Grand staircase leading to the third-floor Preston Bradley Hall

# Chicago Cultural Center ⓮

78 E Washington St. **Map** 4 D1. 🅲 744-6630. 🆔 744-2400, 877 244-2246. Ⓜ Randolph. ⏲ 10am–7pm Mon–Wed; 10am–9pm Thu; 10am–6pm Fri; 10am–5pm Sat; 11am–5pm Sun. ⚫ public hols. ♿ via Randolph St entrance. 🎦 2pm Tue–Sat. ☐ ☐ 🆔 *Weekly arts events*; call 346-3278. 🆆 www.ci.chi.il.us/tourism/culturalcenter

**B**UILT BETWEEN 1893 and 1897 as the city's main library, the building was dedicated in 1991 as the Chicago Cultural Center to showcase and celebrate the performing, visual, and literary arts.

Designed by the Boston firm Shepley, Rutan and Coolidge, this massive Neo-Classical *(see p25)* edifice features soaring arches of white marble and classical Greek columns. The 3-ft- (1-m-) thick masonry walls,

clad with Bedford limestone, rise 104 ft (32 m) above a granite base. The elegant building cost almost $2 million to construct.

There are two entrances to the building. The north entrance, at 77 East Randolph Street, with Doric columns and a massive portico, serves the four-story north wing; the deeply arched Romanesque portal with bronze-framed doors at the south entrance, at 78 East Washington Street, serves the five-story south wing. The Garland Court corridor connects the wings.

The interior of the building, which includes a grand Carrara marble staircase just inside the Washington Street entrance, is a monument to elegant ornamentation. Inset in the staircase are small medallions made from a rare Irish emerald marble. On the underside of the staircase, seen by looking up from each landing, are intricate mosaics.

Two spectacular glass domes complete the opulent detailing. At the south end of the building, on the third floor in Preston Bradley Hall, is a huge Tiffany dome. This 38-ft (11.5-m) jewel of sparkling colored glass, stone, and mother-of-pearl is valued at $35 million. It is the largest stained-glass Tiffany dome in the world. At the north end of the building, in the second-floor G.A.R. Rotunda, is a stained-glass dome in an intricate Renaissance pattern. It was created by the local firm Healy and Millet. Both domes were originally

Mosaic Tiffany dome in the G.A.R. Rotunda

skylights but have since been sheathed with copper and backlit to protect and preserve the glass.

On the fourth floor is the Sidney R. Yates Gallery, a replica of an assembly hall in Venice's 14th-century Doge's Palace. Arched, bronzed doorways are inlaid with antique marble, and the ceiling is coffered. The stairway leading to the fifth floor is modeled on the Bridge of Sighs in Venice.

Although the building itself rewards many hours of architectural exploration, allow enough time to view the center's many exhibits that reflect the city's rich cultural heritage and showcase local artists. The Museum of Broadcast Communications *(see p53)* is on the first floor. Along the western corridor on the same floor is the Landmark Chicago Gallery, displaying photographs of the city's architectural heritage.

The center also contains two concert halls, two theaters, a cabaret space, and a dance studio. More than 1,000 programs and exhibitions are presented annually; concerts, literary readings, and cultural events are held during the week.

One of several Visitor Information Centers operated by the Chicago Office of Tourism is on the first floor of the Chicago Cultural Center, near the Randolph Street entrance.

Façade of Chicago Cultural Center's Randolph Street entrance

# Museum of Broadcast Communications ⓰

78 E Washington St. **Map** 4 D1.
【 629-6000, 629-6016 (for tours) .
Ⓜ Washington (red line). ◯
10am–4:30pm Mon–Sat; noon–5pm
Sun. ● major public hols. ♿ ▣
▢ Ⓦ www.museum.tv

F OUNDED IN 1987 and
housed in the Chicago
Cultural Center (see
p52), the Museum of
Broadcast
Communications is
one of only three
broadcast
museums in the
US. Permanent
displays and special
exhibitions examine
popular culture
through the sights
and sounds of TV and radio.
A TV studio offers visitors the
opportunity to anchor the

**Antique mirror radio**

"news" and take home a
souvenir videotape. The
Sportscaster Café shows
replays of famous moments in
sports history, and, in the
Radio Hall of Fame, taped
voices from radio's golden
age, such as Jack Benny, Bing
Crosby, and Red Skelton, can
be heard throughout the
room. Two current weekly
radio programs (Chuck
Schaden's nostalgic "Those
Were the Days" and Bruce
DuMont's political talk
show "Beyond the
Beltway") are
broadcast from the
museum; visitors
can join the
studio audience.
Along with
displays of vintage
and contemporary
TV sets and radios,
the museum is also
home to "the camera that
changed America," the one
used to televise the 1960

**"His Master's Voice" dog
and early NBC microphone**

Kennedy/Nixon debate,
which marked a turning point
in the relationship between
TV and politics.
In the museum's research
center, you can, for a small
fee, hear from a collection of
over 50,000 hours of radio
programming, or view 15,000
TV broadcasts and 13,000 TV
commercials. A gift shop sells
postcards, books, and
broadcast memorabilia.

# Millennium Park ⓰

Bounded by Randolph & Monroe Sts,
Michigan Ave, & Columbus Dr. **Map**
4 D1. 【 742-7529. Ⓜ Madison;
Randolph. ▣ Ⓟ **Concerts**.

A PROJECT TO CELEBRATE the
21st century, Millennium
Park has provided year-round
recreational opportunities
since it opened in spring
2001. A northern expansion
of Grant Park (see pp84–5), it
covers more than 1 million sq
ft (93,000 sq m). This park-
within-a-park transforms an
unsightly rail yard into a
cultural destination.
The showpiece of the park
is the outdoor music pavilion,
designed by internationally
acclaimed architect Frank
Gehry in association with the
park's (and Sears Tower's)
designers, Skidmore, Owings
and Merrill. The pavilion
accommodates up to 14,000
people and is the new home
of the Grant Park Symphony
summer concerts (see p161).
The 1,500-seat music and
dance theater was built 40 ft
(12 m) below ground so as

not to interfere with views
through the park. Designed
by Hammond Beeby Rupert
Ainge, it features a glass
pavilion with an indoor
garden near its entrance.
The park's skating rink
converts to an activity plaza

in the summer, becoming a
venue for Chicago's summer
dance program (see p160).
The restoration of the site's
historic Peristyle – a semi-
circle of columns that were
torn down in the 1950s –
provides a classical detail.

## KEY TO MAIN SIGHTS

① Music and Dance Theater
Chicago Entrance
② Peristyle – North Lawn
③ Ice Rink
④ South Lawn and Fountain
⑤ Millennium Terrace
⑥ Monroe Garden
⑦ Great Lawn
⑧ Music Pavilion
⑨ Pedestrian Bridge

## Chicago Theatre

175 N State St. **Map** 4 D1. 443-1130. Washington (red line). 10am–6pm Mon–Fri.
See **Entertainment** pp162–3.

Slated for demolition in the 1980s but subsequently saved, this grand 3,800-seat theater has been restored to its former glory. The oldest surviving theater in Chicago, it was designed by Rapp and Rapp in 1921 and originally operated as a vaudeville movie palace. It now hosts musicals and other live performances.

Along with its Beaux-Arts white terra-cotta façade, the theater has the last-remaining cast-iron building front in Chicago. In 1902, architects Hill and Woltersdorf remodeled the west façade and added another floor. The elaborate decoration of the theater's marble-columned entranceway, triumphal arch (inspired by Paris' Arc de Triomphe),

**Chicago Theatre's marquee and sign**

and palatial lobby reflect the opulence of early theater design. The six-story-high "Chicago" sign above the marquee has become a glittering symbol of the city.

## Michigan Avenue Bridge

**Map** 2 D5. State.

Linking the loop with the Magnificent Mile, Michigan Avenue Bridge, the first double-deck trunnion bascule bridge ever built, was completed in 1920. Spanning the Chicago River, the bridge's two leaves, each weighing 3,340 tons, open by turning on enormous trunnion bearings on the banks. In 1991, it was designated a Chicago landmark.

The bas-relief sculptures, one on each of the four bridgehouses, commemorate important events in Chicago's history. A plaque on the southwest corner marks the

**Henry Hering's *Defence* depicting the 1812 massacre, on bridgehouse**

site of Fort Dearborn (1803–1812); brass markers embedded in the concrete outline the shape of the original fort.

At the bridge's north end, in the 401 North Michigan Avenue plaza, a plaque marks the homestead of Jean Baptiste Point du Sable, Chicago's first permanent non-American Indian resident.

Michigan Avenue Bridge is one of 20 downtown bridges spanning the Chicago River, in a city that has the greatest number of movable bridges of any city in the world.

**The opulent interior of the restored Chicago Theatre**

Visitors can also stroll along nearby Riverwalk, parallel to Wacker Drive from Wabash Avenue to Wells Street.

# 35 East Wacker Drive ⑲

**Map** 4 D1. 📞 726-4260. Ⓜ *Lake; State.* 🕐 *24 hrs daily.* ♿

Tнıs sandy-colored terracotta office building, which became a Chicago landmark in 1994, has been described as a "confection" –

**Frieze on 35 East Wacker Drive**

the dome at the top really does resemble a birthday cake! The building, designed by Thielbar and Fugard, opened in 1926. During Prohibition, the dome housed mobster Al Capone's notorious speakeasy, the Stratosphere Club.

The building once had private parking garages on each of the first 22 floors; jeweler tenants, concerned about security, drove into the elevator and were lifted up to their floors. A 1988 renovation restored the marble interior. Outside, a 6-ton clock with the gilded bronze figure of Father Time overhangs the Wacker Drive sidewalk.

**35 East Wacker Drive, seen from across the Chicago River**

**Corberó's *Three Lawyers and a Judge* in the R.R. Donnelley Building**

# R.R. Donnelley Building ⑳

77 W Wacker Dr. **Map** 3 C1. 📞 917-1177. Ⓜ *Clark.* 🕐 *24 hrs daily.* ♿

Tнe R.R. Donnelley Building (1992), a modern 50-story office tower overlooking the Chicago River, is one of the most recent skyscrapers to be built in the Downtown Core.

Designed by Chicago architect James DeStefano, with famed Catalan architect Ricardo Bofill as the design consultant, the building combines classical aesthetic with Chicago School *(see pp24–5)* functionality. The many classical references to ancient Greece and Rome include the four-pedimented roof, a contemporary take on a classically proportioned Greek temple. The building materials likewise conjure the classics: a grid of Portuguese white granite frames the exterior curtain wall of silver reflective glass.

The ground-floor marble lobby, with its 42-ft- (13-m-) high ceiling and huge, classical windows, is a monumental space housing two sculptural groupings: Ricardo Bofill's *Twisted Columns* (1992), a set of three Modernistic columns hand-carved from white Italian marble, and Catalan sculptor Xavier Corberó's *Three Lawyers and a Judge* (1992), rough-hewn basalt figures suggesting human forms.

At night, 540 high-intensity lamps dramatically illuminate the building in a lighting scheme designed by Pierre Arnaud, who also illuminated the Pyramids, the Parthenon, and the Louvre Museum.

**View of buildings along water-front Wacker Drive, at twilight**

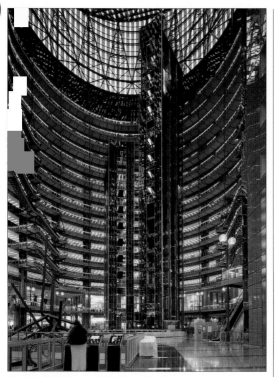

**The towering atrium in the James R. Thompson Center**

## James R. Thompson Center ㉑

100 W Randolph St. **Map** 3 C1.
Ⓜ *Clark/Lake.* ◯ *6:30am–6pm
(atrium 8am–6pm) Mon–Fri.* ♿ ▯
***Art exhibits.***

THE JAMES R. Thompson Center (1985) is a refreshing change from the rectangular skyscrapers that make up Chicago's Downtown Core. Architect Helmut Jahn designed the center as a symbol of open democratic government, one with no barriers between it and the people. The all-glass walls and roof in this multishaped structure provide a monumental, dazzling – and some say, chaotic – transparency.

Originally called the State of Illinois Building, and often still referred to as such, the building was later renamed after the former Illinois governor who commissioned it. The tricolor (patriotic but often criticized salmon, silver, and blue) center is home to almost 70 government offices and numerous restaurants and shops. Performances and fairs are often held in the atrium.

The interior rotunda, at 17 stories and 160 ft (49 m) in diameter, is one of the largest enclosed spaces in the world. A cylindrical skylight soaring 75 ft (23 m) above the roofline caps the rotunda. The building's steel frame weighs almost 10,500 tons.

Exposed escalator and elevator machinery echo the building's no-barriers theme.

Elevators run up glass shafts to a viewing platform on the 16th floor. Here, visitors brave enough to look down will have a stunning view of the marble rosette in the granite concourse floor marking the building's center.

Throughout the building are 14 specially commissioned artworks showcasing Illinois artists, and selections from the building's permanent art collection are also on view. Ask for a directory at the information desk.

On the second floor is the Illinois Art Gallery, with visiting exhibitions, and the Illinois Artisans Shop, selling artworks and crafts.

Not on view to the public are eight ice banks – each 40 ft (12 m) long, 12 ft (3.5 m) wide, and 14 ft (4 m) tall – in the sub-basement. In summer, up to 400 tons of ice are frozen each night in these giant cubes, then used to cool the building.

Outside the building, at the Randolph Street entrance, sits Jean Dubuffet's 29-ft (9-m) lighthearted fiberglass sculpture *Monument with Standing Beast* (1984) *(see p44).*

## 333 West Wacker Drive ㉒

**Map** 3 B1. ☎ *443-8254.*
Ⓜ *Washington (brown, orange, purple lines).* ◯ *7am–6:30pm Mon–Fri.* ♿ ▯

LOCATED AT A BEND in the Chicago River, this prominent Post-Modern, 36-story edifice echoes the curving form of its natural neighbor. Designed in 1983

**The massive James R. Thompson Center,** *Standing Beast* **in foreground**

by the architectural firm of Kohn Pedersen Fox, the office tower is sheathed with reflective, green-tinted glass that changes shade depending on the sun and water. Broad horizontal bands of brushed stainless steel run every 6 ft (2 m). Green marble and gray granite form the base of this elegant, wedge-shaped building, materials used again in the two-story lobby.

A cityscape reflected on 333 West Wacker Drive's convex surface

## Wacker Drive ❷

From N Wacker Dr to N Michigan Ave. **Map** 3 C1. **M** *Clark.*

WACKER DRIVE'S east-west segment offers one of the loveliest downtown walks of any US city. Running alongside the south bank of the main branch of the Chicago River and connecting to 17 of the city's bridges, this two-tiered street was the first of its kind in the world.

Named in honor of Charles Wacker, one of Chicago's civic planners *(see p71)*, the drive was built in 1926 to replace the run-down South Water Street Market.

The lower level is reserved for through traffic, but the upper level consists of a roadway, sidewalks, and a pleasant riverwalk, lined with public art.

Wacker Drive affords a splendid view across the river of impressive architecture, including the massive Merchandise Mart. Built by Marshall Field in 1931, it is, at

The fortresslike Merchandise Mart, best viewed from Wacker Drive

4.2 million sq ft (390,000 sq m), the world's largest commercial building.

State Street Bridge Gallery, in the bridge's mechanical room (open daily, no admission charge), offers visitors a rare opportunity to see the machinery at work behind this famous movable bridge. The gallery also displays local artwork.

At 75 East Wacker Drive is the city's thinnest skyscraper. This Gothic-style, 1928 building is clad in white terra-cotta.

The Chicago Architecture Foundation's river cruise tours, departing from Michigan Avenue Bridge at Wacker Drive, offer fantastic views of Chicago's towers.

## CHICAGO'S RIVER

No other natural feature played as important a role in the early development of Chicago as did the Chicago River. For Native Americans and settlers alike, the river served as a trade route connecting the Great Lakes and the heart of the continent. By the mid-1800s, as shipping became a major economic activity in the area, the Chicago River was the main thoroughfare of a growing metropolis.

One unsanitary result of such growth was that the Chicago River also served as the city's sewer, a dumping ground for waste. The swampy conditions, with the surface of the land near to the level of standing water, made it impossible to construct an underground sewer system.

In the mid-1800s, a Boston engineer, Ellis Chesbrough, was hired to fix the problem. Chesbrough developed the country's first

comprehensive sewer system – above ground. The streets, along with the buildings on them, were raised above the new system, sometimes by as much as 12 ft (3.5 m). The city's largest hotel at the time, the Tremont, was raised while still open for business, without breaking a pane of glass or cracking a plaster wall.

This new sewer system did not entirely eradicate the city's unsanitary conditions, however. In 1885, a devastating cholera and typhoid epidemic killed thousands of Chicagoans (12 percent of the population by some estimates) when sewage flowed into Lake Michigan, the city's source of drinking water.

In response to this tragedy, the city initiated the largest municipal project in the US at the time – the construction of the 28-mile- (45-km-) long Sanitary and Ship Canal. Built between Damen Avenue and the town of Lockport, the canal connected the Chicago

River to the Des Plaines and Illinois Rivers and involved the digging out of more rocks, soil, and clay than was excavated for the Panama Canal. This massive project reversed the flow of the main and south branches of the river, which now drain away from Lake Michigan and into the Sanitary and Ship Canal.

Drawbridge spanning the Chicago River opening for water traffic

# NORTH SIDE

JUST NORTH OF the Chicago River, Chicago's North Side encompasses several neighborhoods, most settled in the mid-1880s by Irish, German, and Swedish immigrants. Tragically, the 1871 fire razed the entire area. The communities

**Ornate detailing on Present Bridge**

rose from the ashes, and today the Magnificent Mile, Gold Coast, Streeterville, and River North are all upscale residential and shopping districts. Modest Old Town is an eclectic mix of residences, shops, and entertainment venues.

## SIGHTS AT A GLANCE

**Historic Buildings and Streets**
Charnley-Persky House **29**
Crilly Court and Olsen-Hansen Row Houses **22**
Drake Hotel **9**
Edward P. Russell House **28**
1500 North Astor Street **27**
1550 North State Parkway **24**
Hotel Inter-Continental Chicago **3**
Menomonee Street **20**
Newberry Library **18**
Residence of the Roman Catholic Archbishop of Chicago **25**
Samuel M. Nickerson and Ransom R. Cable Houses **15**
Tribune Tower **2**
Wacker Houses **21**
Water Tower and Pumping Station **5**
Wrigley Building **1**

**Modern Skyscrapers**
John Hancock Center **7**
Marina City and IBM Building **13**

**Churches and Cathedrals**
Fourth Presbyterian Church **6**
Quigley Seminary and Chapel of St. James **17**
St. James Episcopal Cathedral **16**
St. Michael's Church **19**

**Museums and Galleries**
Chicago Children's Museum **12**
Chicago Historical Society **23**
International Museum of Surgical Science **26**
Museum of Contemporary Art **10**
River North Gallery District **14**
Terra Museum of American Art **4**

**Shopping Streets**
Oak Street **8**

**Piers and Beaches**
Navy Pier **11**
Oak Street Beach **30**

## GETTING THERE

The Magnificent Mile is a short walk from the Loop. CTA stations Grand and Chicago are nearby, and buses 3, 145, 146, 147, and 151 run along Michigan Avenue to farther destinations. A free trolley circles Streeterville. CTA red line serves River North and the Gold Coast; Sedgwick station serves Old Town.

## KEY

Street-by-Street map
*See pp60–61*

**M** CTA train station

**P** Parking

# Street-by-Street: The Magnificent Mile

THE MAGNIFICENT MILE, a stretch of Michigan Avenue north of the Chicago River, is Chicago's most fashionable street. Although almost completely destroyed in the 1871 fire, by the early 1900s, Michigan Avenue had become a major traffic artery. The 1920 opening of Michigan Avenue Bridge led to a retail boom. In 1947, developer Arthur Rubloff, predicting that the street would be Chicago's premier shopping district, dubbed it the Magnificent Mile. His prediction came true and the name stuck. Exclusive shops line the wide boulevard, while modern retail complexes and mixed-use skyscrapers rub shoulders with historic buildings.

**Fourth Presbyterian Church**

*Fourteen carved stone angels, each holding a musical instrument, adorn the nave of this Gothic Revival-style church, the oldest structure on the Magnificent Mile after the Water Tower. A large fountain sparkles at the center of its inner courtyard* ⑥

**KEY**

– – – Suggested route

**STAR SIGHTS**

★ **Hotel Inter-Continental Chicago**

★ **John Hancock Center**

★ **Terra Museum of American Art**

★ **Water Tower and Pumping Station**

★ **John Hancock Center**
*This tower offers spectacular views from its open-air skywalk on the 94th floor. The ground-level plaza has a fountain, cafés, and, occasionally, live music* ⑦

★ **Water Tower and Pumping Station**
*These two historic castellated structures, the station housing a café and information-packed visitors' center, sit on an island in the street – a relaxing, shady retreat from busy Michigan Avenue* ⑤

**City Place**, a modern candy-colored granite building, houses shops at street level, a hotel on the middle floors, and offices on the upper floors.

**Chicago Place** *contains specialty shops and an airy food court with an excellent view of Michigan Avenue. Historical murals decorate the building's lobby.*

### ★ Terra Museum of American Art

*One of the major cultural attractions on the Magnificent Mile, this museum's highlight is its collection of American Impressionist paintings* **4**

**LOCATOR MAP**
*See Street Finder map 2*

**Water Tower Place**
contains eight floors of upscale boutiques and numerous restaurants, as well as two major department stores.

**Tribune Tower**
*Rock fragments from famous sites around the world, including St. Peter's Basilica in Rome, are embedded in the exterior of this Gothic-style tower* **2**

### ★ Hotel Inter-Continental Chicago

*An eclectic mix of detailing – from Mesopotamian-inspired carvings to knights in armor – vie for attention in this 1926 hotel* **3**

**Wrigley Building**
*This structure, one of Chicago's most beloved, boasts a giant four-sided clock and a quiet courtyard, which is open to the public. The building is particularly dazzling at night, when it is illuminated* **1**

NORTH MICHIGAN AVENUE

```
0 meters        200
0 yards         200
```

**View of the two-part Wrigley Building, to the left of Tribune Tower**

## Wrigley Building ❶

400–410 N Michigan Ave. **Map** 2 D5. 923-8080. Grand (red line). 3, 11, 145, 146, 147, 151. **North lobby** 24 hrs daily; **South lobby** 7am–6pm Mon–Fri. **South building** public hols.

THE WRIGLEY BUILDING rests on a historical site: it was to here that Jesuit missionary Jacques Marquette and explorer Louis Joliet made their first portage west of the Great Lakes in the 1670s, and here that La Salle planted the flag of France *(see p13).*

Chewing-gum manufacturer William Wrigley, Jr. commissioned the architectural firm Graham, Anderson, Probst and White to design the building. The 30-story south tower was built in 1920, the 21-story north tower in 1924. They are connected by three arcades. The circular temple and cupola rising above a massive four-faced clock were inspired by Seville's Giralda Tower.

Six shades of white enamel, from gray to cream, were baked onto the terra-cotta cladding. Illuminated at night, the building shimmers.

## Tribune Tower ❷

435 N Michigan Ave. **Map** 2 D5. 222-3232. Grand (red line). 24 hrs daily.

THE 36-STORY limestone Tribune Tower is the winning design of a 1922 international competition sponsored by the Tribune Company to celebrate the 75th anniversary of the *Chicago Tribune.* Architects were challenged to create the most beautiful office building in the world. From 263 submissions, that of New York firm Howells and Hood was chosen. Their Gothic design, reflected in the flying buttresses of the crowning tower, echoes France's Rouen Cathedral.

The building's ornate three-story arched entrance is carved with figures from Aesop's fables. Gargoyles, such as the monkey symbolizing human folly (below the south-side fourth-floor windows), embellish the façade. More than 100 rock fragments from famous sites, including Beijing's Forbidden City and London's Westminster Abbey, are embedded in the exterior walls, as is a 3.3-billion-year-old piece of moon rock, collected by the Apollo 15 mission. A guide to the rocks is available in the lobby.

## Hotel Inter-Continental Chicago ❸

505 N Michigan Ave. **Map** 2 D5. 944-4100. Grand (red line). 24 hrs daily. P See **Where to Stay** p138.

ORIGINALLY the Shriners' Medinah Athletic Club, this magnificent building was renovated at a cost of $130 million, reopening in 1990 as the Hotel Inter-Continental Chicago. Designed in 1929 by Walter W. Ahlschlager, it is topped with a large onion-shaped gilt dome.

Many of the building's exterior and interior details reflect the Shriners' interest in all things Egyptian, medieval, and Renaissance. Ask the concierge for the free self-guided tour audiotape, which will explain the building's historic features.

Carved on the 2nd-floor staircase to the Hall of Lions, two lions guard the intricate terra-cotta fountain. Inside the King Arthur Foyer and Court on the 3rd floor, colorful paintings on the ceiling beams depict King Arthur's life. On the 5th floor, classical Renaissance paintings adorn the walls of the Renaissance Room Foyer. The Spanish Tea Court features a fountain lined with Spanish Majolica tiles.

A gem is the 11th-floor swimming pool, named after the swimmer and actor Johnny Weissmuller. A recent renovation created a common entrance for the north and south towers.

**The Johnny Weissmuller Pool at Hotel Inter-Continental Chicago**

**Terra Museum's marble exterior**

# Terra Museum of American Art ❹

664 N Michigan Ave. **Map** 2 D4.
🆔 664-3939. Ⓜ️ *Chicago (red line);
Grand (red line).* 🚌 *3, 11, 125, 145,
146, 147, 151.* ⏰ *10am–8pm Tue;
10am–6pm Wed–Sat; noon–5pm
Sun.* ⬤ *major hols.* 🎫 *(free Tue,
Thu & 1st Sun every month).* ♿ 🛍
*noon weekdays (except Mon); 2pm
weekends.* 📋 *Lectures.*

AMIDST THE Magnificent
Mile's retail bustle is the
Terra Museum of American
Art. Daniel J. Terra, a former
US ambassador-at-large for
cultural affairs, founded the
museum in 1980 in Evanston
to display his extensive personal art collection.
    The museum, now in its
new five-story location,
houses more than 700
American works, including
paintings, prints, and sculptures from the 18th, 19th, and
20th centuries. Particularly
noteworthy are the American
Impressionist paintings by
artists such as Theodore
Robinson (1862–1948).
    Other important artists rep-
resented include Mary Cassatt,
Georgia O'Keeffe, Milton
Avery, John Singer Sargent,
and James A.M. Whistler. An
early American masterpiece
in the collection is Samuel
F.B. Morse's *Gallery of the
Louvre* (1831–3).

# Water Tower and Pumping Station ❺

806 N Michigan Ave. **Map** 2 D4. Ⓜ️
*Chicago (red line); Grand (red line).*
**Tower** 🆔 744-0808. ⏰ *10am–
6:30pm Mon–Sat; 10am–5pm Sun.*
⬤ *public hols.* **Station** 🆔 744-
2400. ⏰ *7:30am–7pm daily.* ⬤
*Thanksgiving, Dec 25.* ♿ *station
only.* 🖥 🏧 🛈

BUILT JUST BEFORE the fire of
1871, the Water Tower
(1869) and the Pumping
Station (1866), housing
Chicago's waterworks,
were two of the few
buildings in the city to
survive the conflagration.
    Designed by William W.
Boyington, these struc-
tures look like Gothic
castles. The 154-ft (47-m)
tower consists of lime-
stone blocks rising in five
sections from a square
base. The tower origi-
nally housed a stand-
pipe that stabilized
pressure of the
water flowing in
the mains. It is
now home to a
City Gallery,
which specializes
in photography.
Lookingglass
Theatre is also
based here.
    In addition to
housing a
Visitor Infor-
mation Center (163 E.
Pearson St.), the Pumping
Station still fulfills its original
purpose, pumping up to 250
million gallons (946 million
liters) of water per day.

**The Water Tower survived
Chicago's Great Fire of 1871**

# Fourth Presbyterian Church ❻

866 N Michigan Ave. **Map** 2 D4.
🆔 787-4570. Ⓜ️ *Chicago (red line).*
🚌 *10, 145, 146, 147, 151.* ⏰ *9am–
5pm Mon–Fri; 8:30am–9pm Sun.*
✝ *8:30am, 11am, 6:30pm Sun.*
♿ *via 126 E Chestnut St.* **Concerts**
*12:10pm Fri.*

THE 1871 FIRE destroyed
the original Fourth
Presbyterian Church the
night it was dedicated.
The new building (1914)
was the first major structure built on Michigan
Avenue after the fire.
    Designed by Ralph
Adams Cram, architect of
New York's Cathedral of
St. John the Divine, the
church is Gothic Revival
in style *(see p24).* Its
exposed buttresses,
stone spire, and
recessed main window
all reflect the influences
of medieval Euro-
pean churches.
    The illuminated
timber ceiling
rises ten stories;
the stained-glass
windows are
magnificent.
    A covered
walkway leads
to a tranquil
courtyard, sur-
rounded by
parish buildings, which was
designed by Howard Van
Doren Shaw.
    The church's organ – a
Chicago treasure – can be
heard at weekly concerts.

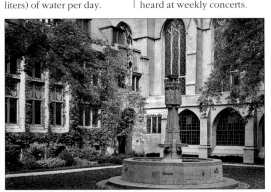

**The peaceful courtyard of the Fourth Presbyterian Church**

## John Hancock Center **❼**

875 N Michigan Ave. **Map** 2 D4. **Observatory** 📞 751-3681. Ⓜ *Chicago (red line).* ⭘ *9am–11pm daily.* 🖼 *to observatory (children under 4 free).* ♿ 🍴 🍸 🅿

A**FFECTIONATELY** called "Big John" by Chicagoans, John Hancock Center stands out as a bold feature of the Chicago skyline. The 100-story building has 18-story-long steel braces crisscrossing the tapering obelisk tower like stacked Xs.

The center's major attraction is the Hancock Observatory on the 94th floor. Here, 1,000 ft (305 m) above the Magnificent Mile, you can actually go outside, onto Chicago's only open-air (screened) skywalk. Designed by architect Bruce Graham of Skidmore, Owings and Merrill and engineer Fazlur R. Khan, the Hancock Center opened in 1969, and has offices, condominiums, and shops in 2.8 million sq ft (0.26 million sq m) of space.

**Open-air deck topping the Hancock Center**

The elevator ride to the top is touted as the fastest in North America. At 20 miles (32 km) per hour, you reach the observatory in just 40 seconds. On a clear day, you can see for up to 80 miles (130 km). The view is especially dazzling when late-afternoon sun falls upon the downtown buildings. A wall-to-wall exhibition in the observatory traces Chicago's history.

The Chicago Architecture Foundation shop and tour center is in the concourse. The lower courtyard has cafés, with patios in summer.

**Entrance to the 1920s Drake Hotel**

## Oak Street **❽**

Between Rush St & N Michigan Ave. **Map** 2 D3. Ⓜ *Chicago (red line).* See **Shops and Markets** pp156–9.

T**REE-LINED** Oak Street at the north end of the Magnificent Mile is home to many upscale boutiques: Giorgio Armani, Hermès, Sonia Rykiel, and Gianni Versace. The Daisy Shop specializes in vintage couture resale clothing. Wolford Boutique sells European hosiery and swimwear.

Along with its chic fashion boutiques, Oak Street has numerous art galleries, such as Billy Hork Galleries, which sells limited-edition prints and vintage posters, and Colletti Antique Poster Gallery, specializing in original works from 1880 to 1940. The Watermark offers stationery and unique gift-wrapping: it seals gifts in a can.

The 20-story apartment building (1929) at No. 40 was designed by Ben Marshall, architect of the Drake Hotel.

## Drake Hotel **❾**

140 E Walton Pl. **Map** 2 D3. 📞 787-2200. Ⓜ *Chicago (red line).* ♿ 🍴 🏨 🍸 See **Where to Stay** p137.

T**HE ESSENCE** of luxury in the heart of the Magnificent Mile, the 537-room Drake Hotel opened in 1920. Designed by Marshall and Fox in the Italian Renaissance style *(see p24)*, this 13-story hotel is clad in limestone.

The lobby, paneled in marble and oak, is graced with grand chandeliers, elegant red carpets, and a magnificent fountain.

The elegant Palm Court, in the lobby, offers traditional afternoon tea and is also a fashionable place for cocktails, with live jazz Fridays and Saturdays. The Cape Cod Room has an extensive seafood menu.

Chicago jive-legend Buddy Charles plays regularly at the hotel's splendid piano bar, the Coq d'Or. When Prohibition ended in 1933, this bar served the second drink in Chicago.

**Upscale boutiques lining Oak Street**

**The Museum of Contemporary Art's grand entrance**

# Museum of Contemporary Art ⑩

220 E Chicago Ave. *Map* 2 D4. 📞 280-2660. Ⓜ *Chicago (red line).* 🚌 10, 66. 🕐 *10am–8pm Tue; 10am–5pm Wed–Sun.* ● *Jan 1, Thanksgiving, Dec 25.* 🎫 *(free Tue).* ♿ 🛍 🎧 ☐ 🍴 ℗ ⓦ *www.mcachicago.org*

Founded in 1967, the Museum of Contemporary Art's mission is to preserve, interpret, and present contemporary art. Designed by Berlin architect Josef Paul Kleihues, the sleek building has four floors of naturally lit exhibition space. On display are selections from the museum's extensive collection of works by internationally acclaimed artists, including Andy Warhol, René Magritte, Cindy Sherman, and Alexander Calder. Don't miss Richard Long's *Chicago Mud Circle* (1996), an exuberant application of mud on the gallery wall. There are also temporary exhibitions.

Once a month, the museum hosts an evening of live music.

# Navy Pier ⑪

600 E Grand Ave. *Map* 2 F5. 📞 800-595-7437. 🚌 29, 56, 65, 66, 120, 121, 124. 🕐 *10am; closing times vary by day and season.* ● *Thanksgiving, Dec 25.* ♿ 🍴 ☐ 🍷 ℗ 🚻 *Lake cruises.*

Navy Pier is a bustling recreational and cultural center. Designed by Charles S. Frost, the 3,000-ft- (915-m-)

**Tranquil fountains and palms at Navy Pier's Crystal Gardens**

long and 400-ft- (120-m-) wide pier was the largest in the world when built in 1916. Over 20,000 timber piles were used in its construction.

Originally a municipal wharf, the pier was used for naval training during World War II. After a four-year renovation, Navy Pier opened in its present incarnation in 1995.

Navy Pier Park has a 150-ft- (45-m-) Ferris wheel; old-fashioned carousel; outdoor amphitheater; ice skating; miniature golf; and IMAX 3D theater. The Smith Museum displays stained glass.

Free trolleys run between Navy Pier and State Street.

# Chicago Children's Museum ⑫

700 E Grand Ave. *Map* 2 F5. 📞 527-1000. 🚌 29, 56, 65, 66. 🕐 *10am–5pm Tue–Sun; Memorial Day–Labor Day.* ● *Thanksgiving, Dec 25.* 🎫 *(free 5–8pm Thu).* ♿ 🍴 ℗ *Special activities daily.* ⓦ *www.chichildrensmuseum.org*

Chicago Children's Museum, focusing on activating the intellectual and creative potential of children age 1 to 12, is an activity center for the whole family. All exhibits are hands-on. Kids can build a fort in the Under Construction exhibit, be part of a TV crew in the Info-Tech Arcade, or make a flying machine in the Inventing Lab. In the WaterWays, they can channel water with dams and locks.

The Dinosaur Expedition gallery has a reproduction of a huge *Suchomimus* skeleton. Kids can dig for bones in an excavation pit. Along with these educational exhibits, children can simply climb, slide, and jump around.

**Chicago Children's Museum, at the main entrance to Navy Pier**

# Marina City and IBM Building ⑬

**Marina City:** 300 N State St.
**Map** 1 C5. 🚇 222-1111. Ⓜ State.
🅾 24 hrs daily. ♿ 🍴 🅿
**IBM Building:** 330 N Wabash Ave.
**Map** 2 D5. Ⓜ State. 🅾 24 hrs daily.
♿

THE TWO TOWERS of Marina
City pay symbolic tribute
to the Midwest's farming
economy – they look like
giant corncobs. Designed by
Bertrand Goldberg Associates
and opened in 1967, these
twin circular towers function
like a city within a city, with
apartments, offices, shops,
parking, a theater, marina,
and even a bowling alley and
skating rink.

To the east of Marina City,
and in stark contrast to its
organic form, rises the IBM
Building, a sleek modern
monument. Designed by Mies
van der Rohe *(see p28)* with
C.F. Murphy Associates and
opened in 1971, the 52-story
office tower has an exposed
steel frame and dark bronze-
tinted glass walls.

A small bust of Mies van
der Rohe, who died before
construction of the building
was complete, is located in
the lobby. In winter, the
exterior plaza can be quite
bleak and frigid. Strung ropes
prevent people from being
blown into the Chicago River.

**Marina City's twin towers, flanked
on the right by the IBM Building**

**Shops and galleries lining the streets of the River North Gallery District**

# River North Gallery District ⑭

Between N Wells & N Orleans Sts,
from W Huron St to W Chicago Ave.
**Map** 1 B4. Ⓜ Chicago (brown,
purple lines). 🚇 649-0064.
See **Shops and Markets** pp156–9.

RIVER NORTH is home to
some of Chicago's finest
antique and home-furnishing
shops. There are also more
than 50 art galleries here –
the largest concentration
outside New York City.

West Superior Street is the
center of the district. Galleries
here and on adjoining streets
offer a wide range of artwork
by both international and local
artisans. Unusual pieces by
American folk artists, African-
American art, glass sculpture,
photography, and superb Arts
and Crafts objects are just
some of the treasures to be
found. Most galleries are
closed Sundays and Mondays.

# Samuel M. Nickerson and Ransom R. Cable Houses ⑮

40 & 25 E Erie St. **Map** 2 D4. Ⓜ
Chicago (red line); Grand (red line).
**Nickerson House** 🚇 640-1300.
🅾 9am–5pm Mon–Sat.
**Cable House** ⬤ to public.

SAMUEL M. NICKERSON House
offers a glimpse into the
wealthy world of late-1800s
Chicago high society. Commissioned by Nickerson, a

distillery owner and banker,
this Italian Renaissance
palazzo was designed in 1883
by Chicago church-architects
Burling and Whitehouse. The
mansion's owners, R.H. Love
Galleries, restored the interior
in the late 1980s.

It has 23 rooms on its three
floors, each room seemingly
more opulent than the next.
More than 20 varieties of
marble, along with onyx and
alabaster, were used to build
the main hall and great
staircase. Even the ceiling is
marble. The largest room is
the first-floor Picture Gallery,
illuminated by a domed,
Tiffany leaded-glass skylight.

Across the street, the
Ransom R. Cable House now
quarters a securities and
capital management corpora-
tion. Designed by Cobb and
Frost, the 1886 Richardsonian
Romanesque *(see p24)* man-
sion was built for the presi-
dent of the Chicago, Rock
Island and Pacific Railway
Company. It features rough-
hewn rusticated masonry.
Both houses are designated as
Chicago landmarks.

**Charming coach house belonging
to the Ransom R. Cable House**

# St. James Episcopal Cathedral ⑯

65 E Huron St. **Map** 2 D4. 787-7360. Chicago (red line). for mass only. **Cathedral** 9am, 11am Sun; **Chapel** 12:10pm Mon–Fri; 5:30pm Wed; 9am Sat; 8am Sun. Concerts.

T HE PARISHIONERS of St. James have worshiped at this site since 1857. After their original building was destroyed in the Great Fire of 1871 (only the 1867 bell tower survived), architects Clarke and Faulkner were hired to design a new building. The St. James Episcopal Cathedral, a Gothic Revival *(see p24)* structure of Joliet limestone, was completed in 1875.

Inside is a fine example of Victorian stencil work (1888), designed by Edward J. Neville Stent, a student of British designer William Morris. The stencils were restored in 1985 by the Chicago architects Holabird and Root.

The Chapel of St. Andrew is at the north end of the cathedral. Designed by Bertram G. Goodhue in 1913, it is said to be based on a private oratory in an ancient Scottish abbey. The painted-glass windows portray the figures of St. Paul, Mary Magdalene, and St. Francis.

**The majestic altar and windows in the Chapel of St. James**

**Statue of Archbishop Quigley outside Quigley Seminary**

# Quigley Seminary and Chapel of St. James ⑰

831 N Rush St. **Map** 2 D4. 787-8625. Chicago (red line). **Seminary** 787-9343. to public. **Chapel** mandatory: noon, 2pm Tue, Thu–Sat. **Concerts**.

T HE QUIGLEY Seminary, a high-school-level seminary for the archdiocese of Chicago, was designed by Zachary T. Davis (architect of Wrigley Field) and Gustave E. Steinback. Completed in 1919, this Gothic monument has carved buttresses and spires.

Ten statues in the niches along the north wall represent saints, such as St. Cecilia, patron of music, and St. Elizabeth, patron of pregnant women. Adorning the spire of the library tower is a statue of St. George, his iron spear serving as the building's lightning rod. A statue of Archbishop James E. Quigley (1854–1915), known for his commitment to building Catholic schools in Chicago in the early 20th century, perches at the northwest corner of the grounds.

The school's Chapel of St. James was inspired by Paris' Gothic Sainte-Chapelle. The spectacular Rose Window, 28 ft (9 m) in diameter, depicts the life of the Virgin Mary. Smaller windows relate stories from the Bible. The pictorial scheme represents 245 events of scriptural and church history. More than 700,000 pieces of glass are set in limestone frames.

The magnificent 50-ft- (15-m-) tall limestone altar, adorned with sculptures, was hand-carved in France.

# Newberry Library ⑱

60 W Walton St. **Map** 1 C3. 943-9090. Chicago (red line). Hrs for lobby, book rooms, and exhibits vary; call ahead. public hols. 3pm Thu; 10:30am Sat. **Exhibits, lectures, concerts**.

A T THE NORTH end of Washington Square Park, the city's oldest park, is the impressive Newberry Library. Founded in 1887 by Walter Newberry, a merchant and banker, this independent research library for the humanities – one of the best in the US – opened to the public in 1893. Henry Ives Cobb, master architect of the Richardsonian Romanesque style, was the designer.

Strengths of the collection include cartography, Native American history, and Renaissance studies. Rarities include a 1481 edition of Dante's *Divine Comedy* and first editions of Milton's *Paradise Regained* and the King James Version of the Bible.

Through the triple-arched entranceway, the lobby features a grand marble staircase, terrazzo flooring, galleries, and a bookstore.

**Jeweled cover of the first edition of Milton's *Paradise Regained***

## St. Michael's Church ❶⑨

1633 N Cleveland Ave. **Map** 1 B1.
📞 642-2498. Ⓜ *Sedgwick.*
🕐 *8am–7pm daily.* ✝ *8am, 5:30pm Mon, Wed, Thu, Fri; 8am, 6pm Tue, Sat; 8am, 11am, 7pm Sun.* ♿ *weekends or by arrangement.* 🅿

THE ORIGINAL St. Michael's Church was a small brick building built in 1852. As St. Michael's small congregation expanded, it outgrew the building. The cornerstone for a new church was laid in 1866. Just three years later, the building's construction was complete.

Just two years later, the Great Fire of 1871 destroyed the roof and floors of the church. However, the thick, brick walls survived and remain to this day, incorporated into the 1872 Romanesque-style structure designed by architect August Wallbaum.

**Angel in St. Michael's**

The steeple, added to the bell tower in 1888, rises 290 ft (88.5 m) above the ground. The bell tower is adorned with a large four-faced clock with wooden hands. Each of the five bells in the tower weighs between 2,500 and 6,000 lbs (1,135 and 2,720 kg). By tradition, if you can hear the bells of St. Michael's, you are in Old Town.

Restoration of the church began in the 1990s. The first phase involved removing two tons of pigeon excrement from inside the bell tower.

The colorful, high-domed interior has stained glass, murals, and sculptures depicting the life of Christ. The carved high altar and its four subsidiary altars illustrate St. Michael, flanked by the arch-angels Gabriel and Raphael, triumphant over Lucifer.

A small monument on the grounds is dedicated to Catholic war veterans.

**The high-domed interior and main altar of St. Michael's Church**

**335 Menomonee Street, a wooden cottage typical of Old Town**

## Menomonee Street ❷⓪

From N Sedgwick St to Lincoln Park W. **Map** 1 B1. Ⓜ *Sedgwick.*

MENOMONEE STREET lies in the heart of Old Town Triangle Historic District (bounded by Cleveland Street and North and Lincoln Avenues), a delightful area of vintage cottages and Queen Anne-style *(see p24)* row houses settled in the mid-1800s by working-class German immigrants.

In the 1940s, community concern over the area's falling fortunes led to one of the city's earliest neighborhood revitalization efforts. Today, the Old Town Triangle's narrow tree-lined streets are home to picturesque houses and numerous interesting shops and restaurants.

Walk along Menomonee Street to view the residences that typify mid- to late-19th-century Old Town. Most of the original houses in the area were small cottages built using the method of balloon framing, so-called because such structures were report-edly as easy to construct as blowing up a balloon *(see p25).* The lightweight wood-en frames provided ample kindling when the 1871 fire swept through the area.

The whitish gray clapboard house at No. 350 is a rare surviving example of the fire-relief shanties the Chicago Relief and Aid Society built for people made homeless by the fire. These two-room structures, costing the City about $100 each, were transported on wagons to charred lots, providing fire victims with instant lodging.

The shanties were later replaced with permanent wooden cottages, constructed before an 1874 city ordinance prohibited the building of wooden structures. The high basements and raised front staircases typical of these cottages were designed to accommodate the above-ground sewage system *(see p57)*. The cottages at Nos. 325–45, although built after 1871, are typical of those in the neighborhood before the ravages of the Great Fire.

## Wacker Houses ㉑

1836 & 1838 N Lincoln Park W. **Map** 1 B1. **M** *Sedgwick.* ● *to public.*

**B**OTH THE Charles H. Wacker House and the Frederick Wacker House, designed in the early 1870s by an unknown architect, are highly ornate examples of the Chicago cottage style.

Commissioned by Frederick Wacker, a Swiss-born brewer, No. 1836 was built as a coach house but served as the Wacker's temporary home until No. 1838, a wood-frame structure built just before the ban on wood as a building material, was completed.

Charles Wacker, Frederick's son and the city planner after whom Wacker Drive is named *(see p57),* remodeled the

**Frederick Wacker House, with its alpine-style overhanging porch**

**The elaborate Queen Anne-style Olsen-Hansen Row Houses**

coach house after moving it to its present location beside the main family home.

No. 1838's elaborately carved trim is an excellent example of the handcrafted details on many houses in the Old Town neighborhood.

## Crilly Court and Olsen-Hansen Row Houses ㉒

**Crilly Court**: north of W Eugenie St between N Wells St & N Park Ave; **Olsen-Hansen Row Houses**: 164–172 W Eugenie St. **Map** 1 C1. **M** *Sedgwick.* ● *to public.*

**R**EPRESENTING TWO different approaches to Queen Anne-style row-house design are Crilly Court and the Olsen-Hansen Row Houses.

Crilly Court was created in 1885 by real-estate developer Daniel F. Crilly, when he bought a city block and cut a north-south street through it, which he named after himself. Over the next ten years, Crilly built a residential and retail development, creating what is now one of the quaintest streets in Chicago.

Two columns frame the entrance to the court. On the court's west side are two-story stone row houses. On the east side is a four-story apartment building, the names of Crilly's four children carved above the doors.

The renovation of the development in the 1940s, led by Crilly's son Edgar, included

closing off alleys behind the residences to create private courtyards and replacing wooden balconies with wrought-iron ones, giving the complex a New Orleans-like atmosphere. This redevelopment of Crilly Court initiated the renewal of the Lincoln Park neighborhood.

The Olsen-Hansen Row Houses, on West Eugenie Street, are more elaborate expressions of the Queen Anne style *(see p24).* The row houses were designed by Norwegian-born architect Harald M. Hansen in 1886 for Adolph Olsen. Only 5 of the original 12 remain.

Turrets, various window styles, Victorian porches, irregular rooflines, and a mixture of building materials – ranging from red brick to rough stone – give each of the row houses a distinctive identity. Hansen himself lived here, at No. 164.

**Daniel F. Crilly, developer of Chicago's handsome Crilly Court**

# Astor Street

FOR MORE THAN 100 YEARS, Astor Street, named for fur tycoon and real-estate magnate John Jacob Astor, has been the heart of fashionable Gold Coast. Wealthy Chicagoans flocked to the area in the 1880s and built over the next 60 years the striking houses in myriad architectural styles that line the street, though interspersed today with more modern buildings. Just six blocks long, the charming Astor Street district, designated a Chicago landmark in 1975, is ideal for leisurely strolling.

### STAR SIGHTS

- ★ **Charnley-Persky House**

- ★ **Edward P. Russell House**

- ★ **Residence of the Roman Catholic Archbishop of Chicago**

## JOHN JACOB ASTOR

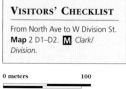

German-born John Jacob Astor (1763–1848) made his fortune in the fur trade. In 1808 he chartered the Chicago-based American Fur Company, creating a monopoly in the Great Lakes area. Astor's successful fur business helped fund later, highly profitable, real-estate ventures. When he died, he was the richest man in the US.

0 meters          100

0 yards          100

**Astor Street East Side** ‹ ‹ ‹ ‹ ‹ ‹ ‹ ‹ ‹ ‹ ‹ ‹ ‹ ‹ ‹ ‹ ‹ ‹ ‹ ‹ ‹ ‹

### VISITORS' CHECKLIST

From North Ave to W Division St.
**Map** 2 D1–D2. **M** *Clark/Division.*

0 meters          100

0 yards          100

**May House** (No. 1443) is a granite Romanesque Revival-style mansion designed in 1891 by celebrated residential architect J.L. Silsbee, one of Frank Lloyd Wright's *(see p28)* first employers. The mansion's grand arched entranceway with ornate carving is one of its most striking features.

### William D. Kerfoot

*This real-estate businessman lived at No. 1425. The first Chicagoan to reopen for business in the Loop after the fire of 1871, he posted outside his hastily erected shanty a sign the day after the fire: "All gone but wife, children, and energy."*

### 1400 Block North Astor Street

*The buildings lining this handsome block of the Gold Coast reflect an eclectic mix of architectural styles, ranging from a Tudor Revival country-style house at No. 1451 to a Gothic-style chateau at No. 1449.*

**John L. Fortune House (No. 1451)**

**Astor Street West Side**    ‹ ‹ ‹ ‹ ‹ ‹ ‹ ‹ ‹ ‹ ‹ ‹ ‹ ‹ ‹ ‹ ‹ ‹ ‹ ‹ ‹ ‹ ‹ ‹ ‹ ‹ ‹ ‹ ‹

**KEY**

◄ ◄ ◄ ◄  East side walking south

► ► ► ►  West side walking north

### ★ Edward P. Russell House

*Carvings in a floral motif decorate the Art Deco façade and window metalwork of this 1929 Holabird and Root-designed townhouse (No. 1444)* **28**

### ★ Residence of the Roman Catholic Archbishop of Chicago

*Built in 1880 of red brick, this massive Queen Anne-style mansion is the oldest home in the area. Decorative exterior features include floral carvings and limestone trim* **25**

**Patterson-McCormick Mansion (No. 1500;** *see p76)*

### ★ Charnley-Persky House

*This superb house (No. 1365) is, appropriately, now the national headquarters of the Society of Architectural Historians. The building reflects the architectural styles of its two collaborators, Louis Sullivan and Frank Lloyd Wright, and is a masterpiece of Prairie School design (see p25)* **29**

### Astor Court

*This Georgian-style mansion (No. 1355) was designed in 1914 by Howard Van Doren Shaw for William C. Goodman, who also commissioned Shaw to design the Goodman Theatre. An iron gate with decorative brass doorknobs opens to a courtyard. The building now contains luxury apartments.*

**Edwin J. Gardiner House (No. 1345)**

# Chicago Historical Society ㉓

1601 N Clark St. **Map** 1 C1. **☎** 642-4600. **Ⓜ** Clark/Division then bus 22, 36. **🚌** 11, 151, 156. **⏰** 9:30am–4:30pm Mon–Sat; 11am–5pm Sun. **⬤** Jan 1, Thanksgiving, Dec 25. **🎫** (free Mon) **⚬** **♿** **📷** (call for times). **🍴** **🚻** **Ⓟ** **Concerts, lectures**. **ⓦ** www.chicagohs.org

Founded in 1856, the Chicago Historical Society (CHS) is the city's oldest cultural institution. A major museum and research center, it boasts more than 20 million objects, images, and documents relating to the history of Chicago and Illinois. Permanent exhibits, supplemented with temporary exhibits, trace the early recorded history of the Chicago area, beginning with the expeditions of 17th-century French explorers such as Father Jacques Marquette.

The first-floor Fort Dearborn and Frontier Chicago gallery includes early portage maps and a wall built of logs salvaged from the second Fort Dearborn (see p13). The Illinois Pioneer Life gallery tells the settlers' story. Visitors are introduced to daily life on the Illinois frontier through the re-creation of a pioneer home and barn. The Please Touch section, where visitors are encouraged to handle old farming tools, exemplifies the hands-on friendliness of the CHS.

Among the highlights of the collection are the Chicago history dioramas on the second floor. Behind glass in a darkened room, eight

The original, Neo-Georgian entrance to the Historical Society

miniature scenes show Chicago's rapid growth in the 18th and 19th centuries. The dioramas begin with a depiction of the signing of the 1795 Treaty of Greenville, in which American Indians ceded 25,000 sq miles (64,750 sq km) of land, including 6 sq miles (15 sq km) at the mouth of the Chicago River. The dioramas illustrate great events, such as the Great Fire of 1871 and the 1893 World's Columbian Exposition, and historic scenes, such as the Chicago River during the Civil War, and bustling LaSalle Street in the mid-1860s.

American-history buffs shouldn't miss the American Wing on the second floor, which features 1 of only 23 surviving copies of the Declaration of Independence (the version printed in Philadelphia on July 4, 1776). As well, there's a rare copy of the American Constitution first printed in a Philadelphia newspaper, alongside the Bill of Rights drafted in 1789. Abraham Lincoln's deathbed is also on display.

Along with the fascinating exhibits, the building itself is noteworthy, as it presents two dramatic faces to the world – one modern, one historic. Both are imposing but welcoming. The original Neo-Georgian structure, designed by architects Graham, Anderson, Probst and White in 1932, is best appreciated from Lincoln Park. The 1988 addition faces North Clark Street with a three-story, glass-and-steel atrium entrance. The most dramatic feature is the curving glass section at the south end, containing a restaurant.

Contemporary sculptor Sheila Klein's *Commemorative Ground Ring,* a giant ring with symbolic references to landmarks of Chicago's architectural heritage, such as a Prairie-style roof and the façade of the Wrigley Building, stands at Clark Street and North Avenue.

1550 North State Parkway, once the epitome of Gold Coast luxury

# 1550 North State Parkway ㉔

**Map** 1 C1. **Ⓜ** Clark/Division then bus 22, 36. **⬤** to public.

When it opened in 1912, this apartment building overlooking Lincoln Park epitomized the luxury of the Gold Coast. Designed by Marshall and Fox (architects of the Drake Hotel, see p64), the 12-story Beaux-Arts (see p25) structure is faced with white terra-cotta.

Depiction of the 1871 Great Fire from the society's excellent collection

Originally, each of the floors comprised a separate apartment with 15 rooms (5 for servants) and 9,000 sq ft (835 sq m) of living space – more than four times the size of the average modest home. The luxurious apartments have since been subdivided.

The black grillwork of the iron balconies, bowed windows, and the large urns on top of the balustrade are all interesting features.

**The imposing home of Chicago's Roman Catholic archbishop**

# Residence of the Roman Catholic Archbishop of Chicago ㉕

1555 N State Pkwy. **Map** 2 D1.
**M** *Clark/Division.* ● *to public.*

**B**UILT IN 1880 on the site of an early Catholic ceme-tery, the building is home to the archbishop of Chicago's Roman Catholic diocese. Archbishop Patrick A. Feehan was the first resident of this, the area's oldest home.

The two-and-a-half-story Queen Anne-style *(see p24)* mansion was designed by Alfred F. Pashley. Although not highly ornamented, its decorative features include Italianate windows and 19 chimneys rising from a peaked and gabled roofline, a landmark of the area.

The property surrounding the archbishop's residence was subdivided in the late 1800s by the Chicago Archdiocese and sold to Chicago's wealthy, who built their houses on the lots.

Today, the archbishop's residence has attractive landscaped grounds, complete with papal flag.

# International Museum of Surgical Science ㉖

1524 N Lake Shore Dr. **Map** 1 D1.
**C** 642-6502. **M** *Clark/Division* then bus 22, 36. ○ *10am–4pm Tue–Sat.* ● *Sun, Mon, public hols.* 🎟 *by donation.* 📷 🔓 **P**

**T**HE INTERNATIONAL Museum of Surgical Science, with its cranial saws and bone crushers, is an unusual museum and well worth a visit. Where else in the world can one marvel at the var-iety, size, and intriguing shapes of gallstones and bladder stones?

Opened to the public in 1953, the museum is handsomely lodged in a historic (1917) four-story mansion designed by Howard Van Doren Shaw.

Fascinating exhibits from around the world trace the history of surgery and related sciences. Some of the earliest artifacts are 4,000-year-old Peruvian trepanning tools used to release evil spirits from the skull. Amaz-ingly, some of the trepanned skulls on display show bony tissue growth,

*Hope and Help,* **by Edouard Chaissing, at museum entrance**

proof that patients survived the procedure.

Less grisly exhibits include a re-creation of a turn-of-the-20th-century apothecary, complete with medicine bottles, labels claiming to cure every ill. The Hall of Immortals showcases 12 larger-than-life sculptures of important figures in medical history, such as the earliest-known physician, Imhotep (c.2700 BC), and Marie Curie.

One of the most unusual exhibits is the 1935 Perfusion Pump created by Charles A. Lindbergh and Alexis Carrel, a device that enabled biologists to keep a human organ functioning once removed from the body.

The scale model of a 1594 anatomical theater at the University of Padua, the extensive collection of early X-rays, a working iron lung, and a Chippendale conva-lescent wheelchair are also worth seeing.

The museum's library holds more than 5,000 books, including rare and antique volumes – some from as early as the 15th century. A fourth-floor art gallery displays medically related, contemporary artworks – just one more of the many surprises in this inimitable place.

**Turn-of-the-20th-century apothecary shop, Museum of Surgical Science**

**Façade of 1500 North Astor Street, with its classical detailing**

## 1500 North Astor Street ㉗

**Map** 2 D1. Ⓜ *Clark/Division then bus 22, 36.* ⬤ *to public.*

THIS OPULENT four-story Italian Renaissance palazzo was built in 1893 for *Chicago Tribune* publisher Joseph Medill as a wedding gift for his daughter. Designed by McKim, Mead and White, it is built of orange Roman brick, with terra-cotta trim. The most impressive feature of this house, the largest on Astor Street, is the two-story front porch with Doric and Ionic columns.

Cyrus Hall McCormick II, son of the inventor of the Virginia reaper *(see p29),* bought the mansion in the 1920s. He then commissioned an addition to be built at the north end, doubling the building's size. It now contains luxury condominiums.

**Art Deco window on the exterior of Edward P. Russell House**

## Edward P. Russell House ㉘

1444 N Astor St. **Map** 2 D2. Ⓜ *Clark/Division.* ⬤ *to public.*

A UNIQUE, four-story townhouse, the Edward P. Russell House was designed in 1929 by the architect firm of Holabird and Root. Designed in the Art Deco style popular in the 1920s and 1930s, the house is, perhaps, the finest example of this architectural style in Chicago.

Graceful carvings in a floral motif decorate the building's smooth, white stone façade. These carvings are repeated in the metalwork on the windows. Although the shapes of the windows vary, they all unite to create a harmonious balance.

The stone on the townhouse's façade, which was quarried in Lens, France, is trimmed with polished granite. A subtle three-story bay of black metal embodies the grace and elegance of this truly refined, much-admired, building.

## Charnley-Persky House ㉙

1365 N Astor St. **Map** 2 D2. 〖 573-1365. 𝕔 915-0105. Ⓜ *Clark/Division.* ⬤ *mandatory.* ⬤ *public hols.* 🖼 ⊡

FRANK LLOYD WRIGHT called Charnley-Persky House (1891–2) "the first modern house in America." Two of America's most influential architects collaborated on the design: Wright *(see p28),* then a draftsman in the early stages of his career, and Louis Sullivan *(see p28),* known for his architectural detailing. They were commissioned by lumberman James Charnley and his wife Helen.

Charnley-Persky House is a pivotal work in the history of modern architecture. Its design embraces abstract forms, every interior view providing a perfectly balanced composition. The house's relatively simple façade of brick and limestone contrasts with the elaborate fronts of the exclusive Astor Street neighborhood.

An atrium reaching from the oak-paneled entry to a skylight two floors above is the interior's focal point. Dramatic arches frame the rooms on the first floor.

Along with the house's bold geometrical forms and organic abstractions are surprising details, such as windows in the closets. One of the most striking aspects of the house is the elegantly tapering wooden screen, on the second floor.

**The elegant second-floor stairway screen at Charnley-Persky House**

Oak Street Beach at dusk, looking southeast across Lake Michigan

Restored in 1988 by the architect firm of Skidmore, Owings and Merrill, the house now headquarters the Society of Architectural Historians. It was renamed in honor of Seymour Persky, who bought it for the society.

## Oak Street Beach ③⓪

Between E Division & E Oak Sts, at N Lake Shore Dr. **Map** 2 D3.
▐ *742-7529 (Chicago Park District)*
▐ *Chicago (red line) then bus 36; Clark/Division.* ▬ *145, 146, 147, 155.*

JUST STEPS from Chicago's Magnificent Mile is the fashionable Oak Street Beach, just one of the city's several beaches that together form a sandy chain along Chicago's lengthy lakefront.

As well as providing a great view of Lake Michigan, the Gold Coast, and towering North Side buildings such as the John Hancock Center and the Drake Hotel, Oak Street Beach presents a good opportunity to shed shopping bags and loafers and don swimsuit and sandals. Throngs of joggers, bicyclists, dog walkers, and in-line skaters make the broad expanse of Oak Street Beach a lively place to enjoy the sun and watch the waves. At the southern end of the beach is a promenade – a pleasant, if somewhat crowded, spot for strolling during the summer.

The din of cars heading along Lake Shore Drive is a constant reminder that the beach is in the city, but the sounds of squawking gulls provide noisy competition.

To reach the beach, use the pedestrian tunnels at Oak or Division Streets. There are washrooms at the beach, but the nearest changing rooms are at North Avenue Beach.

View of the Gold Coast skyline from Oak Street Beach

## OLD MONEY

Chicago has a beautiful sound because Chicago means money – so the late actress Ruth Gordon reputedly said. By the turn of the century, 200 millionaires flourished in the city. One of the most prominent was dry-goods merchant and real-estate mogul Potter Palmer who, with his socialite wife Bertha Honoré, had an enormous impact on the city's social, cultural, and economic life.

Chicago's wealthy began to flock from the Prairie Avenue District to the Gold Coast after Palmer built, in 1882, an opulent home (since demolished) at present-day 1350 North Lake Shore Drive. Palmer quadrupled his investment when he subdivided and sold Gold Coast land he had astutely purchased before moving to the area.

Potter Palmer

Perhaps no feature of the Palmer mansion epitomized the family's wealth as much as did the doors: there were no outside handles, since the doors were always opened from inside – by the Palmer's servants.

Department-store owner Marshall Field *(see pp50–51)*, was less ostentatious in his display of wealth. Although he rode in a carriage to work, he always stopped short of his store to walk the last few blocks so people would not see his mode of transport. Likewise, he asked the architect of his $2-million, 25-room mansion not to include any frills. The influential Field provided major funding to the Field Museum *(see pp86–9)* and the 1893 World's Fair.

Marshall Field

## GETTING THERE
The South Loop is a short walk from the Downtown Core and is easily accessible from the Harrison and Roosevelt CTA stations, and via the State Street and Dearborn Street buses. The Near South Side, 3 miles (5 km) south of the city center, is best reached by car, taxi, or Michigan Avenue bus 3.

◁ **T. Thomas Memorial, Grant Park**

# SOUTH LOOP
# AND NEAR SOUTH SIDE

TWO OF CHICAGO'S neighborhoods have always been areas of diversity, with dereliction and gentrification coexisting side by side. South Loop developed as an industrial area in the late 1800s. But after World War II, manufacturers left and the area declined. Not until the 1970s did it again show signs of prosperity. The Near South Side also had cycles of boom and bust. After the 1871 fire, the city's elite created a wealthy enclave here that lasted until the early 1900s. Decay followed, as brothels and gambling houses formed the Levee vice district. In the 1940s, the Illinois Institute of Technology (IIT) transformed the area yet again.

The contrasts remain striking. The oldest residence in the city, the Henry B. Clarke House, is minutes from the sleek IIT campus; the city's teeming Chinatown borders the historic Black Metropolis.

## KEY

Street-by-Street map
See pp80–81

M CTA train station

Metra train station

P Parking

0 meters 500

0 yards 500

# Street-by-Street: South Loop

JUST SOUTH OF DOWNTOWN, the South Loop has changed dramatically in recent decades, from a run-down industrial area to a residential and retail neighborhood. With the 1970s conversion of the district's derelict warehouses to fashionable lofts, businesses sprang up as Chicagoans took advantage of the area's proximity to downtown. Today, the South Loop's diversity is evident in its industrial heritage, the green expanse of Grant Park, and the lively retail scene next door to several outstanding museums.

**Sculpted owl on the roof of Harold Washington Library**

**★ Harold Washington Library Center**
*Dominating the South Loop is the world's largest public library building, artwork displayed throughout* ❶

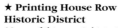

**★ Printing House Row Historic District**
*Many of this area's historic warehouses, built for the printing trade, have been converted into fashionable apartments, with numerous shops and cafés at street level* ❷

**The Transportation Building** was one of the earliest buildings in Printers' Row to be converted to residential use and helped start the area's revival.

**Details on the** *Lakeside Press Building, at 731 S Plymouth Street, are typical of the rich decoration of buildings in this area.*

## STAR SIGHTS

- **★ Harold Washington Library Center**
- **★ Printing House Row Historic District**
- **★ Spertus Museum**

**The Second Franklin Building** *has handsome tilework illustrating the history of printing over its entranceway.*

**Museum of Contemporary Photography**
*Focusing on American photography produced since 1959, the museum presents selections from its extensive collection and excellent temporary exhibitions* **7**

★ **Spertus Museum**
*This world-renowned collection of Judaic art highlights decorative objects and religious artifacts that span centuries of Jewish history* **6**

**LOCATOR MAP**
*See Street Finder maps 3 & 4*

**KEY**

- - - Suggested route

**South Michigan Avenue**
*Featuring a spectacular row of historic buildings, this is one of Chicago's grandest streets, an excellent place to window shop and from which to admire the varied architectural styles for which the city is famous* **4**

**Hilton Chicago**
*Decorated in the French Renaissance style, this 25-story building is one of Chicago's most opulent hotels and was the largest in the world when it opened in 1927* **5**

**Buddy Guy's Legends**
*presents both big-name and local blues acts. Proprietor and blues legend Buddy Guy can often be found among the club's patrons.*

**Dearborn Station Galleria**
*Chicago's oldest surviving passenger train station building, an 1885 Richardsonian Romanesque design, has been converted into a shopping mall. Its square clock tower is a local landmark* **3**

| 0 meters | 100 |
|---|---|
| 0 yards | 100 |

**Harold Washington Library Center's ninth-floor Winter Garden**

# Chicago Public Library, Harold Washington Library Center ❶

400 S State St. **Map** 3 C2. 747-4300. Ⓜ Library. 🚌 2, 6, 29, 36, 62, 145, 146, 147, 151. 🕐 9am–7pm Mon–Thu; 9am–5pm Fri–Sat; 1pm–5pm Sun. ● major hols. ♿ call 747-4252. 📷 noon, 2pm daily. ▢ ⬤ Exhibits, lectures, films. Ⓦ www.chipublib.org

THIS, THE LARGEST public library building in the world, was designed by Thomas Beeby – winner of a competition voted on by Chicagoans – and opened in 1991. It is named in honor of Chicago's first Black mayor.

Inspired by Greek and Roman structures – with five-story arched windows, vaulted ceilings, and decorative columns – the design also pays tribute to many of Chicago's historic buildings: the rusticated granite base recalls the Rookery *(see p40)*, for example. Perched on each roof corner is a gigantic sculpted barn owl representing wisdom; over the main

entrance, a great horned owl with a 20-ft (6-m) wingspan grips a book in its talons. The library holds close to 7 million books and periodicals on its 70 miles (110 km) of shelving. Artwork is displayed throughout the building, including work by Cheyenne artist Heap of Birds. On the ninth floor is the Beyond Words Café.

**Rowe Building on Dearborn Street, in the Printing House Row District**

# Printing House Row Historic District ❷

S Federal, S Dearborn, & S Plymouth Sts; between W Harrison & W Polk Sts. **Map** 3 C3. Ⓜ *Harrison.*

BY THE MID-1890s, Chicago was the printing capital of the US. The majority of this industry centered in a two-block area now known as Printing House Row Historic District. Nearby Dearborn Street railroad station *(see p83)* facilitated rapid industrial development in the neighborhood. However, by the 1970s, when the station closed, most of the printing companies had already moved out of the area.

Many of the massive, solid buildings erected to hold heavy printing machinery remain today. Their conversion into stylish condominiums and office lofts has led to the revitalization of the

**Carved detail on façade of the historic Lakeside Press Building**

neighborhood and an influx of commercial activity.

The landmark Pontiac Building (542 South Dearborn Street; 1891) is the oldest surviving Holabird and Roche *(see p25)* building in Chicago. Several other noteworthy buildings line South Dearborn Street. The 1883 Donohue Building (Nos. 701–721) has an impressive arched entranceway, Romanesque Revival styling *(see p24)*, and a birdcage elevator in the lobby. The Rowe Building (No. 714, c.1882) houses the excellent Sandmeyer's Bookstore, specializing in local authors and travel literature. The Second Franklin Building (No. 720) is significant for the ornamental tilework gracing its façade. Above the entrance is a delightful terra-cotta mural of a medieval print shop.

## Dearborn Station Galleria ❸

47 W Polk St. **Map** 3 C3.
▐ 554-4408. Ⓜ *Harrison.*
🕑 *7am–9pm Mon–Fri; 8am–5pm
Sat.* ⚫ *major hols.* 🔳 🖥 🍸

**D**EARBORN STATION, built in
1885, is the oldest surviving passenger railroad station
building in Chicago, and is a
monument to the historic
importance of the nation's
coast-to-coast rail system. By
the turn of the century, more
than 100 trains (from 25 different railroad companies)
and 17,000 passengers
passed through the station
each day.

Designed by Cyrus L.W.
Eidlitz, the station features
masonry walls and terra-cotta
arches in the Richardsonian
Romanesque style *(see p24)*.
A 1922 fire destroyed the
roof, attic, and upper story.
The clock tower was rebuilt
and stands today as the striking terminus of Dearborn
Street, visible from the northern Loop.

The station closed to rail
traffic in 1971, its trains and
platforms removed. In 1976,
amid much controversy, the
building's train shed was
demolished. The building
was converted in 1985 into a
shopping mall and office
complex, and many of its
original features have since
been restored.

**Dearborn Station Galleria's
high-ceilinged atrium**

**View along South Michigan Avenue looking north**

## South Michigan Avenue ❹

S Michigan Ave from E Madison St
to E Balbo Ave. **Map** 4 C2–C3.
Ⓜ *Madison.*

**S**OUTH MICHIGAN AVENUE is
the place to revel in the
monumental solidity of late
19th- and early 20th-century
architecture. This historic
street has been described
variously as a "cliff" and a
"wall." Be warned: you may
strain your neck gazing up to
the tops of these massive
structures. The longest span
of pre-1920 buildings in
Chicago, South Michigan
Avenue contains numerous
architectural styles, from the
Gothic-inspired *(see p24)*
Chicago Athletic Association
Building (No. 12) to the
Chicago School *(see pp24–5)*
Gage Building (No. 18), one
of three buildings making up
the Gage Group. The Gage
Building was designed by
Holabird and Roche; Louis
Sullivan designed the terra-
cotta façade.

At Nos. 24 and 30 are striking examples of Chicago
windows *(see p25)*, which
allowed in plenty of light
for the milliners once working here.

The School of the Art
Institute of Chicago residence (No. 112) contains a
frieze of the Greek god
Zeus overseeing athletic
games, a decorative detail
that reflects the original
1908 purpose of the building
as the home of the Illinois
Athletic Club.

## Hilton Chicago ❺

720 S Michigan Ave. **Map** 4 D3.
▐ 922-4400. Ⓜ *Harrison.* 🕑 *24
hrs daily.* 🛗 🔳 🍸 🅿 *See **Where
to Stay** p139.*

**W**HEN IT OPENED in 1927,
this 25-story hotel had
3,000 rooms, a rooftop
18-hole miniature golf
course, its own hospital, and
a 1,200-seat theater. After the
owner went bankrupt in the
mid-1930s, the World War II
Army Air Corps purchased
the Holabird and Roche-
designed redbrick building,
converting the grand ballroom to a mess hall.

In 1945, Conrad Hilton
acquired the building,
reopening the hotel in 1951.
Further renovations in the
1970s and 1980s secured the
hotel's reputation for
opulence. Its lofty centerpiece is the ballroom, a space
decorated in the French
Renaissance style, featuring
mirrored doors and walls,
arched windows, and huge
crystal chandeliers. The hall-
way is equally ornate, with
fluted columns, a marble
stairway, and a cloud mural
painted on the ceiling.

**Marble fountain, lobby of
the Hilton Chicago**

## Spertus Museum ❻

618 S Michigan Ave. **Map** 4 D3.
**C** 322-1747. **M** Harrison. **O** 10am–
5pm Sun–Wed; 10am–7pm Thu;
10am–3pm Fri. **●** Sat, major public
and Jewish hols. **⚱** (free Fri). **&** **☑**
**☐** Concerts, lectures, films.

T HE SPERTUS MUSEUM, in the
Spertus Institute of Jewish
Studies, has one of the largest
permanent collections of
Judaic art in the US. Five
thousand years of religious

**Children excavating in a re-created
dig at the Spertus Museum**

and cultural history are
represented in the collection's
10,000 artifacts, arranged by
themes relating to holy days
and rituals. Ceremonial
objects, paintings, sculptures,
jewelry, and coins fill this
somewhat labyrinthine space,
covering two floors.

Highlights include ornate
torah arks and scrolls from
around the world. The 5-ft-
(1.5-m-) tall Aron Ha-Kodesh
torah ark (1913–23) from
Jerusalem is embellished with
etched and bas-relief brass
depicting biblical events
accompanied by Hebrew
quotations. Decorative
candelabras and Hanukkah
lamps include 18th-century
eastern European examples
and modern Israeli designs.

A computer in the deeply
moving Zell Holocaust
Memorial room lists the
names of people lost by
Chicago families in the
Holocaust; it takes a full day
to read the list. Shoes and a
spoon from Auschwitz and a
prisoner's outfit are likewise
haunting reminders of this
horrific period of history.
Temporary exhibitions are

**Interior of the Museum of Contemporary Photography**

held in the museum's second-
floor gallery.

Kids can excavate artifacts
in a 32-ft- (10-m-) long re-
created dig site in the
ARTiFACT Center – a hands-
on archeological adventure.

Asher Library, on the fifth
floor, is the largest public
Jewish library in the central
US, with over 100,000 books.

## Museum of Contemporary Photography ❼

600 S Michigan Ave. **Map** 4 D3.
**C** 663-5554. **M** Harrison. **▥** 1, 2,
3, 3L, 4, 6, 10, 14, 29, 127, 130,
146. **O** 10am–5pm Mon–Wed, Fri;
10am–8pm Thu; noon–5pm Sat. **●**
major hols, Dec 25 –Jan 1. **◎** **&**
1st, 2nd floors only. **Lectures, films**.

F OUNDED BY Columbia
College Chicago in 1984 to
collect, exhibit, and promote
contemporary photography,
the Museum of Contemporary
Photography is the only
museum in the Midwest
devoted exclusively to the
medium of photography.

Wide-ranging provocative
and innovative exhibitions,
housed in the college's
historic 1907 building,
change regularly as do
selections from the collection
of more than 5,000
American photographs pro-
duced since 1959.

Temporary exhibitions
explore photography's many
roles: as artistic expression,
as documentary chronicler,
as commercial industry, and
as a powerful scientific and
technological tool. The Midwest Photographers Project,
work by regional photographers, rotates annually.

## Grant Park ❽

From Randolph St to Roosevelt Rd,
between Michigan Ave & Lake
Michigan. **Map** 4 E2–E4.
**M** Randolph; Madison; Adams.
**◈** See **Through the Year** pp30–33.

G RANT PARK is the splendid
centerpiece of the 23-
mile- (37-km-) long band of
green stretching along the
Lake Michigan shoreline from
the city's south end to its

**The main entrance to Grant Park, Ivan Mestrovic's** Bowman **to the right**

**View of Grant Park, looking north**

northern suburbs. Although bisected by busy streets, the park offers a tranquil retreat from noisy downtown, serving as Chicago's "front yard" – playground, promenade, garden, and sculpture park all in one, and hosting summer concerts and festivals.

The park is built on landfill and debris dumped after the 1871 Fire. Originally called Lake Park, it was renamed in 1901 for the 18th US president, Ulysses S. Grant, who lived in Galena (see p128). In

**Reading Cones** by Richard Serra in Grant Park

1893, the World's Columbian Exposition was held in the south end of the park.

Although the park was intended as public ground, free of buildings, various structures were erected. Not until 1890, when businessman Aaron Montgomery Ward initiated a series of lawsuits which dragged on for more than 20 years, was the preservation of Grant Park for public recreation secured.

Daniel H. Burnham and Edward H. Bennett's 1909 Plan of Chicago (see p28) envisioned the park as the "intellectual center of

Chicago." The renowned landscape-architecture firm Olmsted Brothers designed the park in a French Renaissance style reminiscent of the gardens at Versailles. The symmetrical layout includes large rectangular "rooms," grand promenades, formal tree plantings, sculptures, and the central Buckingham Fountain.

A noteworthy footnote is that the park was the site of the 1968 Democratic Convention riots, when anti-Vietnam War protesters clashed with police.

# Buckingham Fountain ❾

In Grant Park, east of Columbus Dr, at the foot of Congress Pkwy. **Map** 4 E3. **C** 742-7529. **M** Harrison.

THROUGHOUT the summer, one of the showiest and most impressive sights in Chicago is the water shooting from the 133 jets of Grant

Park's Buckingham Fountain, culminating dramatically in a spray 150 ft (45 m) high. The fountain's one-and-a-half million gallons (5.7 million liters) of water recirculate through a computer-operated pumping system at a rate of 14,000 gallons (53,000 liters) per minute.

Hundreds of spotlights hidden within the fountain are used to create a dazzling show of colored lights. The 20-minute shows, set to music, are held from dusk to 11pm every hour on the hour, from April to October.

Financed by Kate Sturges Buckingham (1858–1937) in honor of her brother, Clarence (1854–1913), a trustee and benefactor of the Art Institute of Chicago, the fountain was designed by Marcel Francois Loyau (sculptor), Jacques Lambert (engineer), and Edward H. Bennett (architect).

The design, based on the Latona Basin in the gardens of Versailles but twice the size of that fountain, incorporates a ground-level pool 280 ft (85 m) wide, with three concentric basins rising above. In 1927, it was dedicated as the world's largest decorative fountain.

Constructed of pink marble, the Beaux-Arts fountain symbolizes Lake Michigan. The four pairs of 20-ft- (6-m-) tall seahorses diagonally across the fountain from each other represent the four US states bordering the lake: Illinois, Wisconsin, Indiana, and Michigan.

**Buckingham Fountain, sculpted seahorses in the foreground**

# Field Museum ⑩

**Xochipilli, Aztec god of flowers**

T HE FIELD MUSEUM is one of the world's great natural history museums, with a collection of over 20 million specimens (just under 5 percent are displayed). Following the success of the 1893 World's Columbian Exposition, a group of prominent Chicagoans decided to create a museum with objects from the fair. With funding from Marshall Field *(see p77)*, they opened, in 1894, the Columbian Museum of Chicago in Jackson Park's Palace of the Fine Arts, one of the fair's finest buildings. This lodging soon proved too small for the museum. In 1921, its current home – a white-marble Neo-Classical structure designed by Daniel H. Burnham – was built, and the Field Museum, with its celebrated collection of anthropological, botanical, zoological, and geological artifacts, opened to the public.

**★ Underground Adventure**
*Walk through worm tunnels, meet giant bugs, and feel reduced to insect size in this "subterranean" exhibit.*

**Egyptian Mummy Mask**
*This decorative linen-and-plaster burial mask encased a mummified child.*

## KEY TO FLOORPLAN

- ☐ Animals, plants, and ecosystems
- ☐ Rocks and fossils
- ☐ Ancient Egypt
- ☐ Americas
- ☐ Pacific cultures
- ☐ Special exhibits
- ☐ Nonexhibition space

**Ground Level**

## MUSEUM GUIDE

*The museum has three levels: ground, main, and upper. Most of the exhibition galleries are on the main and upper levels. Each level has east and west wings; those of the main and upper are bisected by a large central hall. The upper level features exhibitions on nature (plants and earth sciences), dinosaurs, and Pacific cultures. Exhibits on the main level focus on animals, birds, and American Indians. The highlight of the ground level is the Underground Adventure exhibition.*

**Lions of Tsavo**
*The two lions that, in 1898, terrorized a Kenyan outpost, killing 140 workers before being shot, are on display in the Mammals of Africa gallery.*

### Life over Time
*Evolution – from single-cell DNA life through the age of dinosaurs to the development of humans – is explored in this fascinating exhibit.*

**Upper Level**

### ★ Mammoth-Bone Hut
*This hut is modeled on a 15,000-year-old shelter found in Ukraine, made of 300 bones from 13 mammoths. The bones of an 18-year-old Cro-Magnon woman are exhibited nearby.*

**Main Level**

### ★ Pawnee Earth Lodge
*The only precise re-creation of a fully furnished Pawnee earth lodge, this interactive exhibit showcases the traditions of these 19th-century Great Plains Indians.*

**Field Museum Store**

**Egyptian Mastaba** is a reconstruction incorporating two rooms from a 4,400-year-old tomb. Visitors can roam through it, as the deceased's spirit was meant to.

**Main Entrance**

### African Elephants
*These bull elephants are 1905 specimens from Kenya. One bull is poised to plunge its only tusk into the other as it rears.*

### STAR EXHIBITS

★ **Mammoth-Bone Hut**

★ **Pawnee Earth Lodge**

★ **Underground Adventure**

# Exploring the Field Museum

**W**ITH ITS ENCYCLOPEDIC COLLECTION of cultural objects and biological specimens from around the globe, the Field Museum warrants many trips. More than 40 permanent exhibitions are supplemented with fascinating temporary shows. Particular strengths of the museum are dinosaur fossils – highlighted by the recently opened exhibit on Sue, the most complete *Tyrannosaurus rex* skeleton ever found – American Indian artifacts, botanical specimens, and displays relating to mammals and birds. Major crowd pleasers, especially for children, are Underground Adventure, which explores the rich diversity of life in the soil, and Inside Ancient Egypt, focusing on that civilization's funerary practices.

**Tlatilco female figurine**

**The monumental Neo-Classical entrance to the Field Museum**

## ANIMALS, PLANTS, AND ECOSYSTEMS

**O**NE OF the museum's missions is to encourage prudent stewardship of our environment. This theme is highlighted in the animal, plant, and ecosystem exhibits, which emphasize the interconnectedness of all life on Earth. The Messages from the Wilderness gallery is a good place to start your exploration. Eighteen wilderness park settings, from the Arctic to Argentina, incorporate representative mammals and their habitats.

Also here is the Local Woodlands Four Seasons Diorama, completed in 1902 by taxidermist Carl Akeley, who transformed the way museums displayed animals.

**A golden eagle clutching its prey, by taxidermist Carl Akeley**

For Akeley, habitat accuracy and the authenticity of background details were equally important. Thus, each of the 17,000 wax leaves in the diorama is cast separately from a real one.

The main-level galleries in the west wing provide an overview of animal biology, behavior, and habitats, with samples from the museum's 17 million zoological specimens. Outstanding exhibits are Mammals of Asia and Mammals of Africa. Suspended from the ceiling in the World of Mammals gallery is the massive skeleton of a right whale. The museum's collection of birds is also particularly strong, with its informative Bird Habitats, World of Birds, and North American Birds galleries.

A popular attraction is Bushman, a lowland gorilla brought from West Africa to Lincoln Park Zoo in the 1920s. So beloved by Chicagoans that the mayor gave him a voter's registration card, Bushman died in 1951. He was then moved to the museum where, preserved, he continues to delight visitors.

The museum's 2.6 million botanical specimens encompass all major plant groups and every continent. Particularly rich in flowering plants and ferns of the Americas, this is the world's largest museum exhibit dedicated exclusively to plants. Be sure to stop at the

tropical aerial garden. Its reproductions made from wax, glass, and wire look remarkably lifelike.

## ROCKS AND FOSSILS

**T**WO OF THE TWELVE Martian meteorites on display in museums around the world are here at the Field Museum. You can touch non-Martian meteorite pieces on the upper floor, in the Earth Sciences galleries. Other fascinating

**A collection of marine skeletons, exoskeletons, and fossils**

and beautiful rocks in the 500-specimen display are a topaz the size of a pear, in the sparkling Grainger Hall of Gems, and a 312-lb (142-kg) block of lapis lazuli, one of the largest ever found and its origin still a puzzle.

The centerpiece of the museum's renowned collection of dinosaur fossils is 67-million-year-old Sue, the largest, most complete *Tyrannosaurus rex* skeleton ever found. It was discovered near the Black Hills of South Dakota in 1990 by fossil-hunter Sue Hendrickson. The

**A gargantuan *Apatosaurus* skeleton in Genius Dinosaur Hall**

restored skeleton, the skull alone weighing 750 lb (340 kg), was unveiled in 2000. Interactive exhibits tell the story of its discovery and preparation for exhibit. Scientists still do not know whether creatures preying on Sue's remains left the teeth marks on her skull or if these marks are the signs of a deadly battle with another *Tyrannosaurus rex,* the fiercest dinosaur known.

The Genius Dinosaur Hall showcases fossils of seven dinosaurs and the evocative Charles Knight murals. Commissioned by the Field Museum in 1927, these 28 striking paintings of dinosaurs, Ice Age mammals, and early humans were for years the standard depictions of prehistoric life.

## ANCIENT EGYPT

THE MUSEUM'S Ancient Egyptian holdings consist of more than 1,400 rare artifacts, including statues, hieroglyphics, and mummies. The predynastic burial exhibit

**Isty's Book of the Dead, an ancient papyrus scroll**

reveals Egypt's intriguing burial practices before the development of intricate pharaonic tombs. Here, the remains of a 5,500-year-old woman are displayed, along with items such as pottery jars thought to be needed in the afterlife. A partial reconstruction of a *mastaba*, a multiroom "mansion of eternity," features a false door at which the earthbound and the wandering spirits meet.

Other extraordinary artifacts include the fully preserved inner coffin of Chenet-a-a, a woman who lived between 945 BC and 712 BC. It is not known what is inside the coffin since it has never been opened or X-rayed.

**A Pacific Coast Indian carved figure, once a house entranceway**

## AMERICAS

THE MUSEUM'S HOLDINGS of artifacts from North American Indian tribes reflect one of the Field's main missions: to encourage improved understanding among cultures. Ceremonial objects and splendid totem poles – two Haida examples rise to the ceiling of Stanley Field Hall – are just some of the treasures in this exhibit.

The Pawnee Earth Lodge, a life-size reproduction, was built in conjunction with the Pawnee, a group of American Indians based in Oklahoma.

The 19th-century cedar Kwakiutl transformation masks are colorful and vivid. Such masks are often used

**Ceremonial dance mask worn by Alaskan Eskimo shamans**

during the ceremonies of this Pacific Northwest tribe. Panels on the mask are opened and closed by the dancer wearing it to show various faces.

## PACIFIC CULTURES

THE HIGHLIGHT of the Pacific cultures exhibits, with a section on headhunting and a re-creation of a Tahitian market, is the sacred Maori meetinghouse, Ruatepupuke II. Built in 1881 in New Zealand, it was acquired by the museum in 1905. The 55-ft- (17-m-) long, beautifully carved house symbolizes the body of the Maori ancestor Ruatepupuke, credited with sharing the art of wood-carving with the world. The house's ridgepole represents his spine, the rafters his ribs, and the expansive roof-boards his arms, open in greeting. It is the only Maori meetinghouse in the western hemisphere and remains governed by Maori customs.

**Spirit mask from Papua New Guinea**

## John G. Shedd Aquarium ⓫

*See pp96–7.*

## Adler Planetarium and Astronomy Museum ⓬

*See pp92–3.*

## Prairie Avenue Historic District ⓭

Prairie Ave, from 18th to Cullerton Sts.
**Map** 6 D1. Ⓜ *Cermak-Chinatown
then bus 21.* ☑ *May–Oct: 1pm,
2pm 2nd & 4th Sun; call 326-1480.*

W HEN THE CITY of Chicago
was incorporated in
1837, the area now known as
the Prairie Avenue Historic
District was not much more
than a strip of sandy prairie
bordering Lake Michigan. Its
fortunes changed dramatically
when the 1871 fire destroyed
the city center. Chicago's
wealthy, including George
Pullman *(see p119)* and
Marshall Field *(see p77)*,
moved to the Near South
Side, building their grand
mansions along Prairie
Avenue. It remained a mecca
for the city's socialites until
the late 1800s and
early 1900s, when
the rapidly

The imposing Richardsonian Romanesque façade of Glessner House

growing Gold Coast area
superseded Prairie Avenue as
the address of choice. Many
mansions fell to the wrecker's
ball (plaques along Prairie
Avenue mark the sites of demolished houses), but those
that remain offer a glimpse
into 19th-century splendor.
    Along with Glessner House
and Clarke House, highlights
of the district include the
Kimball House (No. 1801).
This mansion, designed by
Solon Spencer Beman in
1890, is one of the best
remaining examples in the US
of the Chateauesque style.
    Elbridge G. Keith House
(No. 1900) is the oldest extant
mansion on Prairie Avenue.
Built in 1870, it was designed
by John W. Roberts in the
Italianate style *(see p24)*. Now
home to the Woman Made
Gallery, which exhibits
contemporary art, it is one
of the few mansions
whose interior is open to
the public.
    At 1936 South
Michigan Avenue is the
magnificent neo-Gothic
Second Presbyterian
Church, designed by
James Renwick in 1874.
Inside are 22 stained-
glass windows by Louis
C. Tiffany and 2 win-
dows painted by British
Pre-Raphaelite artist
Edward Burne-Jones.
    The district is reput-
edly close to the site
of a grim event: the
1812 massacre of
settlers fleeing Fort
Dearborn *(see p13)*.

**Elbridge G. Keith House
on Prairie Avenue**

## Glessner House ⓮

1800 S Prairie Ave. **Map** 6 D1.
☎ *326-1480.* Ⓜ *Cermak-
Chinatown.* ☑ *mandatory: 1pm,
2pm, 3pm Wed–Sun (except public
hols).* 🎟 *(free Wed).* 🎤 **Lectures**.

T HE ONLY EXTANT residential
design in Chicago by
Boston architect Henry
Hobson Richardson, whose
signature style became known
as Richardsonian Romanesque
*(see p24)*, Glessner House
helped change the face of
residential architecture.
    Commissioned by farm-
machinery manufacturer John
J. Glessner and his wife,
Frances, in 1885 and
completed in 1887, the two-
story house represented a
radical departure from
traditional design and created
a furor in the exclusive Prairie
Avenue neighborhood.
George Pullman is said to
have proclaimed: "I do not
know what I have ever done
to have that thing staring me
in the face every time I go
out of my door."
    A fortress-like building of
rough-hewn pinkish gray
granite with three modified
turrets, the house dominates
its corner site. The main
rooms and many of the large
windows face a southern
courtyard. The striking
simplicity of the design is
perhaps best reflected in the
main entrance arch, which
frames a heavy oak door
ornamented with grillwork.
    The beautifully restored
interior boasts a world-class

collection of decorative accessories. Most were purchased or commissioned by the Glessners, who were keenly interested in the British Arts and Crafts movement of the late 19th and early 20th centuries. Adherents of the philosophy that everyday objects should be artistically crafted, they filled the house with tiles, draperies, and wallpaper designed by William Morris. Handcrafted pieces, from furniture to ceramics, by American designer Isaac E. Scott grace the rooms.

*Untitled* (1995) by Stephen Ham, at the Vietnam Veterans Art Museum

# National Vietnam Veterans Art Museum ⓯

1801 S Indiana Ave. **Map** 6 D1.
🆑 *326-0270.* Ⓜ Cermak-
Chinatown then bus 21. 🚌 *1, 3, 4.*
◻ *11am–6pm Tue–Fri; 10am–5pm
Sat; noon–5pm Sun.* ⬤ *major hols.*
🖼 📷 ♿ 🛍 *(for groups).* 🍴 🏪

THE NATIONAL Vietnam Veterans Art Museum is the only museum in the world with a permanent collection that focuses on the subject of war from a personal point of view. Bringing together more than 700 works of art in diverse media created by 140 artists who participated in one of America's most divisive wars, this collection presents a humanist statement on behalf of veterans of all wars.

This adamantly apolitical museum began when two Chicago veterans, Ned

Broderick and Joe Fornelli, began collecting artworks created by fellow veterans. The City of Chicago donated an abandoned warehouse and the museum opened in its new home in 1996.

The artworks explore powerful themes with unflinching honesty. The belongings of prisoner-of-war Major General John L. Borling, who lived in captivity in North Vietnam for seven years, is documented in the display *My Cup Runneth Over.* There is also a comprehensive collection of North Vietnamese and Viet Cong medals, uniforms, and weapons.

# Henry B. Clarke House ⓰

1827 S Indiana Ave. **Map** 6 D1.
🆑 *326-1480.* Ⓜ Cermak-
Chinatown then bus 21. 🎫 *mandatory: noon, 1pm, 2pm Wed–Sun (departs from Glessner House).*
⬤ *public hols.* 🖼 *(free Wed).* ♿

BUILT IN 1836, Clarke House is Chicago's oldest surviving building, a Greek Revival-style house constructed for merchant Henry B. Clarke and his wife Caroline. The house originally stood on what is now South Michigan Avenue but was then an old Indian path. When the house sold in 1872, the new owners moved it 28 blocks south, to 4526 South Wabash Avenue. In 1977, the City purchased the house and then, in a feat of engineering, hoisted the 120-ton structure over the 44th Street "L" tracks, moving

**The dining room in the Henry B. Clarke House**

it to its present location one block southeast of the original Clarke property.

Four Roman Doric columns mark the east entrance to the house. Solidly constructed of timber frame, with a white clapboard exterior, the two-story house was damaged in a 1977 fire. It now has been painstakingly restored, even adhering to the original color scheme, which researchers determined by delving under 27 layers of paint.

Now a museum showcasing an interior reflecting the period 1836–60, Clarke House offers a fascinating glimpse into early Chicago domestic life. It is so historically accurate that the first-floor lighting simulates gas lighting, and the upper floor has no artificial lights. A gallery in the basement documents the history of the house.

Behind the house is Clinton Women's Park, an outdoor cultural center named in honor of former first lady Hillary Rodham Clinton.

**The classical façade of the Henry B. Clarke House**

# Adler Planetarium and Astronomy Museum ⑫

THE ADLER PLANETARIUM and Astronomy Museum has one of the finest astronomical collections in the world, with artifacts dating as far back as 12th-century Persia. It also has the world's first virtual-reality theater. Spectacular light shows complement displays on navigation, the solar system, and space exploration. State-of-the-art technology enables visitors to explore exhibits hands-on.

**Diptych sundial, c.1665–1700**

When the Adler opened in 1930, it was the first modern planetarium in the western hemisphere. Businessman Max Adler funded the 12-sided, granite-and-marble Art Deco structure, designed by Ernest Grunsfeld. This original building, with its copper dome and a bronze depiction of a sign of the zodiac on each of the 12 corners, is now a historical landmark.

**★ StarRider Theater**
*The world's first digital theater offers an unrivaled virtual-reality environment in which visitors can participate in a journey beyond the solar system.*

**★ Atwood Sphere**
*Step into North America's only walk-in planetarium, built in 1913. Light enters through the 692 holes in the surface of this huge metal ball, representing the stars in Chicago's night sky. The "stars" move across the "sky" as the sphere, powered by a motor, slowly rotates.*

**Lower Level**

## KEY TO FLOOR PLAN

- ☐ Landmark exhibition space
- ☐ Sky Pavilion exhibition space
- ☐ Sky Pavilion special exhibits
- ☐ Zeiss Sky Theater
- ☐ StarRider Theater
- ☐ Nonexhibition space

**History of Astronomy**
*Astronomical instruments, celestial charts, astrological calendars, and rare books – products of observation, speculation, and imagination – showcase a millennium of discovery.*

**Our Solar System**
*Investigate through interactive exhibits the worlds that orbit the Sun, and program a computer-activated Rover to move across simulated Martian terrain.*

**VISITORS' CHECKLIST**

1300 S Lake Shore Dr.
Map 4 F4. 922-7827.
M Roosevelt then free trolley.
12, 127, 146.
9:30am–4:30pm daily, except
1st Fri of each month
5pm–10pm. Thanksgiving,
Dec 25. (free Sep–Feb: Mon
& Tue; though there will still be
separate adm to theaters).
Lectures,
films, light shows.
W www.adlerplanetarium.org

**The Milky Way Galaxy**

★ **Milky Way Galaxy**
*Immerse yourself in a 3-D, computer-animated trip through the Milky Way.*

**Gateway to the Universe**
features interactive exhibits that explore the wonder of the universe through the scientific examination of light, gravity, motion, and energy.

**Middle Level**

**Upper Level**

★ **Space Walk**
*A mirrored, darkened room, dotted with light, simulates the exhilarating experience of stepping into infinite space.*

**Zeiss Sky Theater** is the Adler's original planetarium theater. The night heavens are cast by a modern version of the historic Zeiss projector onto a screen suspended from its dome.

**Main Entrance**

**Sky Pavilion**
*A stunning view of the city's skyline can be seen from Galileo's café, in the Sky Pavilion. This two-story 1999 addition to the east side of the landmark building also houses exhibition space and the StarRider Theater.*

**STAR FEATURES**

★ Atwood Sphere

★ Milky Way Galaxy

★ Space Walk

★ StarRider Theater

**A Chinatown grocery shop**

## Chinatown ⑰

S Wentworth Ave, south of Cermak Rd. **Map** 5 B1–C1. [C] *326-5320.* [M] *Cermak-Chinatown.* [🍽] *See* **Restaurants and Cafés** *p150.* [W] *www.chicagochinatown.org*

A RED AND GREEN gateway decorated with Chinese characters inscribed by Dr. Sun Yet-Sen, founder of the Republic of China, arches over Wentworth Avenue just south of Cermak Road. It marks the entrance to the largest China- town in the Midwest. A lively area full of Asian grocery and herbal shops, bakeries, and restaurants, this densely packed neighbor- hood of approximately 10,000 residents has been home to Chicago's highest concen- tration of Chinese people since just before World War I.

Traditional Chinese archi- tecture is evident throughout the colorful streetscape. The temple-like **Pui Tak Center** (2216 South Wentworth

**Detail of decorative tile on the Chinese Cultural Center**

Avenue) was originally the On Leong Chinese Merchants' Association Building; it is now a cultural center. Sculpted lions at the doorway guard its street-level shops; terra-cotta ornaments bedeck the walls. Modern **Chinatown Square Mall** (Archer, Cermak, 18th, and Wentworth) quarters shops and a plaza surrounded by zodiac sculptures and a mosaic mural. Annual China- town celebra- tions include the Dragon Festival in June and the Moon Festival in September.

## Illinois Institute of Technology ⑱

31st to 35th Sts, between Dan Ryan Expy & S Michigan Ave. **Map** 5 C4–D4. [C] *567-3075.* [M] *Sox-35th; 35-Bronzeville-IIT.* [🚌] *29, 35.*

T HE ILLINOIS INSTITUTE of Technology (IIT) is a world leader in engineering, technology, and architecture.

The institute is the result of the 1940 merger of Armour Institute of Technology and the technical school Lewis Institute. During the late 1940s, IIT coplanned the urban renewal of 7 sq miles (18 sq km) of the Near South Side, which helped eradicate the area's slums. IIT has played a significant role in the community ever since.

The campus is an outstanding example of the work of influential architect Ludwig Mies van der Rohe *(see p28)*, who was hired by architect John A. Holabird to direct the Armour Institute's architecture school and design the new campus.

In the campus plan, along with the 22 IIT buildings he designed, Mies expressed his modernist view that form follow function. Geometric and unadorned glass- sheathed curtain-wall structures epitomize Mies' International style. One of Mies' masterpieces is the **S.R. Crown Hall** (1956). This glass- walled pavilion is an early example of a large clear-span structure, the four exterior columns supporting the girders from which the roof is hung. The building appears to float in space. Of it, Mies said: "This is the clearest structure we have done, the best to express our philosophy."

**Alumni Memorial Hall,** Mies' first classroom building on the campus, is another notable example of structure also functioning as ornament. The steel grid of the curtain wall suggests the steel struc- ture within. In **Wishnick Hall,** the curtain wall stops short of the corner to reveal the load-bearing column.

**St. Saviour's Chapel,** waggishly known as the "God

**S.R. Crown Hall on the Illinois Institute of Technology campus**

box," is believed to be Mies' only church design.

The campus is also home to the magnificent redbrick Richardsonian Romanesque **Main Building**. Designed by Patten and Fisher (1891–3), it is IIT's most visible landmark.

The campus is explored easily on foot; maps are available at Hermann Union Hall (3241 S Federal Street).

# Pilgrim Baptist Church ⑲

3301 S Indiana Ave. **Map** 6 D4. **Church** 𝗖 842-5830; **Office** 𝗖 842-4417. Ⓜ 35-Bronzeville-IIT. ◐ during services only. ♿

BUILT IN 1890–91 and designed by Adler and Sullivan for Chicago's oldest Jewish congregation, Kehilath Anshe Ma'ariv, this building has housed the Pilgrim Baptist Church since 1926.

The magnificent arched doorway – the only surviving example of an ecclesiastical arch by Adler and Sullivan – reflects the strong masonry forms of the exterior. Terra-cotta panels of foliage designs provide ornament. The opulent interior is notable for its tunnel-vaulted ceiling and richly ornamented balcony. The church was designated a Chicago landmark in 1981.

# Calumet-Giles-Prairie District ⑳

Calumet to Prairie Aves, from 31st to 35th Sts. **Map** 6 D4. Ⓜ 35-Bronzeville-IIT.

THIS SMALL ENCLAVE of restored Victorian houses was granted national landmark status in 1980. Of particular interest is Joseph Deimel House (3141 South Calumet Avenue), designed in 1887 by Adler and Sullivan and the only remaining residential commission by the firm in this area.

The Joliet limestone row houses (3144–8 South Calumet Avenue), built in 1881, are a fine example of Victorian row-house architecture. However, only three of the original eight houses are still standing.

A block to the south are the only row houses Frank Lloyd Wright designed (1894) – the Robert W. Roloson Houses (3213–19 South Calumet Avenue). Like Robie House *(see pp102–103)*, Wright used Roman bricks for the walls, here decorated with terra-cotta panels between the upper-story windows. A trio of Richardsonian Romanesque *(see p24)* town-houses in sandstone, green-stone, and limestone are found at 3356–60 South Calumet Avenue.

**Victory monument in the Calumet-Giles-Prairie District**

**Ida B. Wells-Barnett House**

# Ida B. Wells-Barnett House ㉑

3624 S King Dr. **Map** 6 E5. Ⓜ 35-Bronzeville-IIT. ● to public.

CIVIL RIGHTS and women's suffrage advocate Ida B. Wells (1862–1931) lived in this house with her husband from 1919 to 1930. Born a slave in Mississippi, Wells became a teacher at age 14 but was dismissed for protesting segregation.

Wells' work as a columnist for *Memphis Free Speech* brought her to Chicago in 1893 to report on the lack of African-American representation at the World's Columbian Exposition. She moved to Chicago in 1895 and married Ferdinand Lee Barnett, the founder of Chicago's first Black newspaper, the *Conservator*.

Playing a key role in the 1909 founding of the National Association for the Advancement of Colored People, Wells is perhaps best known for her anti-lynching campaign, which brought national attention to the issue.

The house, designed in 1889 by Joseph A. Thain in the Romanesque style, was designated a national historic landmark in 1973 in Wells' honor. One of its most interesting features is the corner turret made of pressed metal.

**Façade of the Pilgrim Baptist Church, with its distinctive doorway**

# John G. Shedd Aquarium ⓫

NEARLY 8,000 SALTWATER and freshwater animals, representing 650 species of fish, reptiles, amphibians, invertebrates, birds, and mammals, live at the John G. Shedd Aquarium. Named after its benefactor, an influential Chicago businessman, the aquarium opened in 1930 in a Neo-Classical building designed by the firm Graham, Anderson, Probst and White. The Oceanarium and its magnificent curved wall of glass face Lake Michigan, whose water flows into its tank. This marine-mammal pavilion showcases beluga whales and dolphins. The aquarium offers various viewpoints of its exhibits, including some beneath the water.

**Aerial view of the Shedd Aquarium, looking north toward Grant Park**

**Neptune's trident atop the dome of the aquarium**

**Beluga Whales**
*Six whales live in the Oceanarium's Secluded Bay. Four are from Hudson Bay in central Canada; two were born at the aquarium.*

**The Nature Trail** leads visitors along winding paths through a re-creation of a Pacific Northwest coastal forest, complete with streams and replicas of 70 species of plants.

## KEY

☐ Aquarium

☐ Oceanarium

☐ Animal underwater viewing

☐ Special exhibits

☐ Nonexhibition space

**Sea Otter Cove**
features a Habitat Chat about these smallest of marine mammals.

## STAR EXHIBITS

★ **Amazon Rising**

★ **Caribbean Reef**

★ **Oceanarium**

**★ Oceanarium**
*Pacific white-sided dolphins, Alaskan sea otters, tidal-pool creatures, and other marine animals live in this gigantic saltwater tank, which seems to extend into Lake Michigan, a dramatic effect created by the stunning 475-ft- (145-m-) long glass wall. Watch dolphins and whales during daily educational presentations, or come face to face with them in the Underwater Viewing gallery.*

### Harbor Seals
*The seal bight is home to this vulnerable species now protected by US legislation.*

### Animals of Cold Coasts
*Creatures of the northern salt-water tide pools and oceans, such as the red-belly piranha, are exhibited here.*

### Animals of the Great Lakes Region
showcases cold water fish, including the Lake Whitefish, that dwell in the Great Lakes.

### ★ Caribbean Reef
*More than 250 tropical animals, including nurse sharks and bar-racudas, live in this reef habitat, one of the aquarium's most popular exhibits. Visitors can watch as a diver feeds the creatures.*

### ★ Amazon Rising
*Experience all four seasons affecting the floodplain forest of the mighty Amazon River, and encounter stingrays, dart frogs, lizards, and many more creatures of the Amazon.*

**Main Entrance**

### Asia, Africa, and Australia
highlights fish such as the aggressive Nile knifefish that inhabit the warm freshwaters of the eastern hemisphere.

### Central Rotunda
*Aquatic motifs on tiles, cornices, walls, and doorways grace the central rotunda of the building, designated a national historic landmark in 1987.*

# SOUTH SIDE

S ETTLED IN the mid-1800s as suburban estates, the South Side was soon transformed when the 1893 World's Fair, held in Jackson Park, brought tourists, money, and real-estate and transit development. Hyde Park in particular experienced dramatic change, as the City's preparation for the fair led to an influx of Chicago's elite. By the 1920s, however, pollution from

**St. George and the dragon, detail from the University of Chicago**

nearby industry and the encroachment of poorer neighborhoods caused the wealthy to depart. By the 1950s, Kenwood and Hyde Park were in decline. That same decade, the University of Chicago led a massive urban-renewal program. Today, the area contains many classic Prairie School homes, superb museums, and two of Chicago's largest greenspaces.

## SIGHTS AT A GLANCE

**Historic Buildings**
Robie House ❷
Rockefeller Memorial
  Chapel ❶
University of Chicago
  Quadrangles ❺

**Historic Districts**
Hyde Park ❾
Kenwood ❿

**Museums**
DuSable Museum of African
  American History ❽
*Museum of Science and
  Industry pp106–109* ⓬
Oriental Institute Museum ❸
Smart Museum of Art ❹

**Parks**
Jackson Park ⓫
Midway Plaisance ❻
Washington Park ❼

## GETTING THERE

Eight miles (13 km) south of the Loop, the South Side is accessible by car via I-94/I-55 or South Lake Shore Drive. Metra trains depart from the Randolph Street, Van Buren Street, and Roosevelt Road stations to 55th-56th-57th and 59th Street stations. CTA buses 6 and 10 offer express service to the South Side. CTA green line trains also service the area.

**KEY**

▢ Street-by-Street map
  *See pp100–101*

🚉 Metra train station

P Parking

0 meters     500
0 yards      500

◁ **Lower cloister hall in the Chicago Theological Seminary, University of Chicago**

# Street-by-Street: University of Chicago

**Angel with harp,
Bond Chapel**

THE UNIVERSITY of Chicago, founded in 1891 on land donated by Marshall Field, opened its doors to students – male and female, White and Black – in 1892. Today, it has the greatest number of Nobel laureates among faculty, alumni, and researchers of any US university and is particularly lauded in the fields of economics and physics. Over the years, John D. Rockefeller gave $35 million to the university. Henry Ives Cobb designed 18 of the university's limestone buildings before the Boston firm Shepley, Rutan and Coolidge took over as the main architects in 1901. Today, the campus boasts the designs of more than 70 architects. While large, it is easily explored on foot (for walking tours, *see pp168–9*).

**Nuclear Energy**, by sculptor Henry Moore, marks the spot where, in 1942, a team of scientists led by Enrico Fermi ushered in the atomic age with the first controlled nuclear reaction.

**Bond Chapel**
*(1926) contains beautiful stained-glass windows by Charles Connick and elaborate wood carvings.*

**Main Quadrangle**
*The university's tranquil central quadrangle is the largest of seven designed by Henry Ives Cobb* ❺

**Midway Plaisance**
*This is the site of the 1893 World's Columbian Exposition amusement park* ❻

## STAR SIGHTS

* ★ **Oriental Institute Museum**

* ★ **Robie House**

* ★ **Smart Museum of Art**

**Cobb Gate**
*was donated to the university by Henry Ives Cobb, the campus' master planner. It is ornately decorated with gargoyles.*

★ **Smart
Museum of Art**
*This light-filled,
intimate museum
offers a rich,
balanced survey of
Western art* ④

**LOCATOR MAP**
*See Street Finder maps 7 & 8*

**KEY**

--- Suggested route

**Regenstein Library,**
*the university's main library,
holds treasured rare book and
manuscript collections, along
with millions of other volumes.*

★ **Oriental Institute
Museum**
*Three millennia of
ancient Near East
civilization are
showcased at this
fascinating museum* ③

**Rockefeller Memorial
Chapel**
*Elaborate carvings and
intricate stained-glass
windows grace the interior
of this limestone-and-brick
chapel* ①

★ **Robie House**
*This Frank Lloyd Wright-designed home (1906–1909) is
a masterpiece of the Prairie School of architecture* ②

| 0 meters | 100 |
| 0 yards | 100 |

# Rockefeller Memorial Chapel ❶

5850 S Woodlawn Ave. **Map** 7 C4.
☎ *(773) 702-2100.* Ⓜ *Garfield
(green line) then bus 55.* 🚈 *11th.*
🕐 *8am–4pm daily.* ✝ *11am,
8:30pm Sun.* ♿ 🎫 *Concerts.*

Rockefeller Memorial
Chapel is Bertram G.
Goodhue's 1928 interpretation
of Gothic (see p24). The chapel
is topped with a 207-ft (63-m)
carillon tower. It is the tallest
building on campus: John D.
Rockefeller, as a condition of
his bequest, required that this
structure representing religion
be the university's most
dominant feature.

Contributing to its tradition
of musical excellence is one
of Chicago's oldest choral
ensembles, and the stunning
E.M. Skinner organ. The 72-
bell tower, the bells weighing
from 10.5 lb (5 kg) to 18.5
tons, is the second-largest
carillon in the world. The
bells ring at 6pm weekdays,
after service, and during the
annual carillon festival.

**Bust of a Man (c.1840 BC), at the Oriental Institute Museum**

# Oriental Institute Museum ❸

1155 E 58th St. **Map** 7 C4. ☎ *(773)
702-9514.* Ⓜ *Garfield (green line)
then bus 55.* 🚈 *59th.* 🕐 *10am–
4pm Tue, Thu–Sat; 10am–8:30pm
Wed; noon–4pm Sun.* ● *public
hols.* ♿ 🎫 📷 *Special events.*

The Oriental Institute
Museum is the exhibition
arm of the Oriental Institute,
its scholars having excavated
in virtually every region of

the Near East since 1919. The
museum presents the institute's famed collection of
over 100,000 artifacts from
the earliest civilizations of
the world. It is also one of
only three places in the
world where you can see a
reconstruction of an Assyrian
palace (c.721–705 BC).

Other highlights of the
museum include a monu-
mental sculpture (c.1334–25
BC) of King Tutankhamen
from a Luxor temple. At 17 ft
(5 m), it is the tallest ancient

# Robie House ❷

5757 S Woodlawn Ave. **Map** 8 D4.
☎ *(708) 848-1976.* Ⓜ *Garfield
(green line) then bus 55.* 🚈 *59th.*
🕐 *daily.* ● *Jan 1, Thanksgiving,
Dec 25.* 🎟 *(children aged under 7
free).* 🎫 *mandatory: 11am, 1pm,
3pm Mon–Fri; 11am–3:30pm every
30 minutes at weekends.* 📷

Frank Lloyd Wright's world-
famous Robie House is the
quintessential expression of
the Prairie School movement
(see p25). Designed in 1906
for Frederick Robie, a bicycle
and motorbike manufacturer,
and completed in 1909, the
home is one of Wright's last
Prairie School houses: Wright
left both his family and his
Oak Park practice during its
three-year construction.

Robie House has three
distinct parts combining to
create a balanced whole.
Two, two-story rectangular
concrete blocks sit parallel to
each other; a smaller square
third story is positioned at

**Frank Lloyd Wright-designed dining-room set from Robie House**

their junction. There is no
basement and no attic.
The exterior design of the
house perfectly captures the
prairie landscape of flat, open
fields. The roof's sweeping
planes embody the house's
aesthetic of bold rectilinear
simplicity. Steel beams,
some 60 ft (18 m) long,
support the overhanging
roof. Their use was
unorthodox in
residential architecture
at the time.

Also bold but
simple, the interior is
furnished with Wright-

**Leaded stained-glass windows and
doors,** which run the length of the
living room, allow for both privacy
and natural light.

Egyptian statue in the western hemisphere.

The museum's Egyptian collection, which includes objects of ancient Egyptian daily life and religious and funerary practices, is one of the largest in the US.

## Smart Museum of Art ❹

5550 S Greenwood Ave. **Map** 7 C4. 🅒 *(773) 702-0200.* Ⓜ *Garfield (green line) then bus 55.* ◷ *10am–4pm Tue, Wed, Fri; 10am–9pm Thu; noon–6pm Sat, Sun.* ● *public hols.* 🅰 🅿 ▣ 🄰 🅿 *Special events.*

IF YOU ARE FEELING over-whelmed by the crowds at Chicago's major museums, this is the place to come for an intimate encounter with art. Named after David and Alfred Smart, founders of *Esquire Magazine* and the museum's benefactors, the Smart Museum was established in 1974 as the art museum of the University of Chicago. It holds more than 7,500 artworks and artifacts,

**Henry Moore's** *Nuclear Energy,* **outside the Smart Museum**

including antiquities and Old Master prints, Asian paintings, calligraphies, and ceramics. By displaying its works in rotating, thematic displays, the museum ensures its collection is made available to the public.

The museum also owns important post-war Chicago artwork, furniture and glass from Robie House, and early modern and contemporary painting and sculpture.

A 1999 renovation has allowed for more comprehensive displays of the museum's collection of

important 20th century and Asian artworks.

The museum's café, with tall windows overlooking the tranquil sculpture garden, is a great spot for a quiet lunch.

## University of Chicago Quadrangles ❺

Bounded by 57th & 59th Sts, Ellis & University Aves. **Map** 7 C4. Ⓜ *Garfield (green line) then bus 55.* 🅡 *59th.*

THE CLOISTERED quadrangle plan for the University of Chicago – in the 1890s, one of the first in the US – was developed by architect Henry Ives Cobb. He patterned the unified campus after British universities Cambridge and Oxford. Despite years of development and modification, the six broken quadrangles surrounding a seventh still reflect Cobb's vision.

Cobb Gate, at the north entrance, is a gargoyled ceremonial gateway donated by Cobb in 1900.

**A huge chimney** crowns the intersection of the house's three sections, uniting the parts.

**A large hearth** is the focal point of the living room.

designed furniture. The innovative dining-room set is on view at the Smart Museum *(see above).* The house is a *Gesamtkunstwerk,* a total work of art. Every item in the house contributes to its beauty. The house is an organic whole, underscored

by the harmonious interplay between the exterior and interior and is admired by architects worldwide.

A massive restoration of Robie House was undertaken in early 2000 and is expected to take ten years. The house remains open for tours.

**The long Roman bricks** are a Wright signature.

**Main Entrance**

**Robie House Shop**

**University students playing soccer on the Midway Plaisance**

## Midway Plaisance ➏

Bounded by 59th & 60th Sts, Cottage Grove & Stony Island Aves. **Map** 7 B5–8 E5. 🚇 *59th.*

M IDWAY Plaisance, a mile- (1.6-km-) long greenway at the south end of the University of Chicago campus and the city's broadest boulevard, serves as the university's recreation grounds. The Midway is also an excellent vantage point from which to view the university's Gothic buildings.

Designed by Frederick Law Olmsted and Calvert Vaux as the link between Washington and Jackson parks, the Midway was the site of the 1893 exposition's Bazaar of Nations. It was here that the Ferris wheel – 250 ft (76m) high – made its debut.

## Washington Park ➐

Bounded by 51st & 60th Sts, Martin Luther King Jr. Dr & Cottage Grove Ave. **Map** 7 A2–A5. 🚇 *51st; Garfield (green line).*

N AMED AFTER the first US president, Washington Park was originally intended to be part of a grand South Park, comprising both Washington Park and Jackson Park, connected by a canal

running through Midway Plaisance. Landscape architects Frederick Law Olmsted and Calvert Vaux, designers of New York's Central Park, developed the South Park plan in 1871. The park commission balked at creating a canal and so the original plan was never realized in its entirety. In 1872, Horace W.S. Cleveland was hired to oversee the completion of Washington Park.

Combining expanses of meadows with borders of trees and shrubs, Washington Park's pastoral landscape also has a pond and lagoon. At the northeast end of the park is Drexel Fountain, one of the oldest fountains in Chicago. It was designed in 1881–2 by Henry Manger.

The park's most magnificent feature is the sculpture *Fountain of Time* at the south end, where Washington Park meets Midway Plaisance. Designed in 1922 by the Chicago artist Lorado Taft (1860–1936), this haunting monument depicts the cloaked figure of Time watching the endless march of humanity. It was erected to celebrate 100 years of US-British peace.

**Detail of Taft's *Fountain of Time*, Washington Park**

## DuSable Museum of African American History ➑

740 E 56th Pl. **Map** 7 B4. 🄲 *(773) 947-0600.* Ⓜ *Garfield (green line) then bus 55.* 🚌 *4, 10.* 🕙 *10am–5pm Mon–Sat; noon–5pm Sun & major public hols.* ⏺ *Thanksgiving, Dec 25, Jan 1.* 🎟 *(children under 6 free; free Sun).* 🅰 🎥 *book in advance.* 🄰 **P** *Lectures, films.*

A S PART OF ITS mission to celebrate the rich and diverse history and culture of African Americans and their contributions to the nation, the DuSable Museum highlights accomplishments of the

ordinary and extraordinary alike. Founded in 1961, the museum is the oldest such institution in the US.

The museum's permanent exhibit "Songs of My People" brings together diverse images by Black photojournalists of African-American lives.

Memorabilia from the life and political career of Chicago's first Black mayor, Harold Washington, make up the "Harold Washington in Office" exhibit.

Disturbing pop-culture materials are collected in "Distorted Images: Made in USA?," an exhibit focusing on contrived and demeaning images of African Americans. "Africa Speaks" presents art from Africa, much of which has a functional purpose. Handcrafted door panels, for example, are given to a Nigerian bride on her wedding day so she may close her boudoir while decorating it. The ritual masks from closed West African societies are particularly striking.

## Hyde Park ➒

Bounded by Hyde Park Blvd, 61st St, Washington Park, & Lake Michigan. **Map** 8 D3. 🚇 *53rd; 55th-56th-57th; 59th.* 🄲 *call 922-3432.* 🍴 🄰

H YDE PARK is one of Chicago's most pleasant neighborhoods. The University of Chicago's presence contributes a collegiate atmosphere, while the many shops, restaurants, theaters, and galleries provide a broad array of attractions.

The area was open countryside in 1853 when Chicago lawyer Paul Cornell established the community on a swath of lakeside property.

**Unruly gardens characteristic of the Rosalie Villas, in Hyde Park**

**Isidore Heller House, in Hyde Park, by Frank Lloyd Wright**

The quiet suburb was transformed by three events: its 1889 annexation by the City of Chicago, the 1890 founding of the University of Chicago, and the 1893 World's Columbian Exposition. Many of the houses from this 1890s spurt of development survive. Isidore Heller House (5132 South Woodlawn Avenue) is a Frank Lloyd Wright design (1897) that precedes his celebrated Robie House *(see pp102–103)* by a decade yet reveals his characteristic Prairie style.

Rosalie Villas (Harper Avenue, from 57th to 59th), designed by Solon S. Beman between 1884 and 1890, was Hyde Park's first planned community. It consists of about 50 Queen Anne-style residences, each unique in architectural detail.

The retail heart of Hyde Park is 53rd Street, while ethnic restaurants cluster on 55th Street. Bookstores thrive in Hyde Park; it has been called the largest center for books in the Midwest.

## Kenwood ⑩

Bounded by 47th St, Hyde Park & Drexel Blvds, & Blackstone Ave. **Map** 7 C1. Ⓜ *47th (green line) then bus 28.* 🚉 *47th.* 📞 *call 922-3432.* 🔟 🅿

HISTORIC KENWOOD was established in 1856 when dentist Jonathan A. Kennicott bought and subdivided a large plot of land near 43rd Street. During the next three decades, it became one of the most fashionable South Side communities. In the 1920s, many middle-class African

Americans moved to the area, but the late 1940s saw a period of decline. A massive urban renewal project, led by social planners from the University of Chicago, was begun in the early 1950s.

The neighborhood has some of the finest mansions constructed in Chicago, along with many Prairie School *(see p25)* homes. Two commissions Frank Lloyd Wright undertook while working for Adler and Sullivan include the George W. Blossom House (4858 Kenwood Avenue) and the Warren McArthur House (4852 Kenwood Avenue).

Noteworthy are the mansions on Greenwood Avenue between 49th and 50th, in particular the elegant Prairie style of the Ernest J. Magerstadt House (4930 South Greenwood Avenue), designed in 1908 by George W. Maher, as well as the ornate houses lining South Kimbark Avenue. One of Chicago's largest single-family homes is the Julius Rosenwald House (4901 South Ellis Avenue), built for the Sears, Roebuck magnate.

## Jackson Park ⑪

Bounded by 57th & 67th Sts, Stony Island Ave & Lake Michigan. **Map** 8 E5. 🚉 *59th; 63rd.* 📞 *call 922-3432; bird walk, call (773) 493-7058.*

JACKSON PARK was designed by Frederick Law Olmsted and Calvert Vaux in 1871 as part of the unrealized South Park plan *(see p104)*. Even though the park was redesigned after being chosen as the main site for the 1893 World's Fair, and again in 1895, its original aquatic theme is still evident.

Osaka Garden is a re-creation of the Japanese garden built for the fair. This serene spot on Wooded Island has a pavilion, waterfall, and gorgeous cherry trees. The island is considered the best place in Chicago for bird-watching: more than 120 species of birds have been sighted here.

In the center of the park, a smaller, gilded replica of the 65-ft-(20-m-) statue *The Republic* celebrates the fair's 25th anniversary.

There are also two beaches and several sports facilities.

**Jackson Park's "Golden Lady," a replica of Daniel Chester French's *The Republic***

**The contemplative Osaka Garden in Jackson Park**

# Museum of Science and Industry ⑫

A carved stone figure over the north portal

THE MUSEUM OF SCIENCE AND INDUSTRY celebrates the scientific and technological accomplishments of humankind, with an emphasis on achievements of the 20th century. Originally called the Rosenwald Industrial Museum, after the museum's benefactor, its name was soon changed at Julius Rosenwald's urging, who said that the museum belonged not to him but to the people. While the building, a monumental Neo-Classical structure dominating Jackson Park, is a nod to history *(see p109)*, the museum within has been the North American leader in modern, interactive displays, making the exploration of science and technology an accessible experience.

**Colleen Moore's Fairy Castle**
*This 9-sq-ft (0.8-sq-m) dollhouse is complete with miniature furniture and working electricity and plumbing.*

**Apollo 8 Command Module**
*This historic spacecraft played an important role in early US lunar missions, which culminated in the landing on the moon.*

**U-505 Submarine,** a World War II U-Boat, sank eight allied ships before being captured on the high seas by the US Navy, in 1944.

Main Floor
Ground Floor
Crown Entrance
Great Hall

**Circus**
*Roland Weber, a railroad worker, spent 33 years carving and casting the 22,000 figures that come to life in this tiny, animated circus.*

**STAR EXHIBITS**

★ All Aboard the Silver Streak

★ The Heart

★ Take Flight

★ **All Aboard the Silver Streak**
*Climb aboard the record-breaking 1930s train that revolutionized industrial design.*

### ★ Take Flight
*Explore the inner workings of a 727 jetliner, cantilevered to the museum's balcony, then experience a simulated San Francisco-to-Chicago flight.*

**Coal Mine**
transports visitors through a reproduction of an early Illinois coal mine so realistic its walls are made of coal.

**AIDS: The War Within**
explores the life cycle of HIV and scientific advances in the battle against the deadly virus.

**Balcony**

**Foucault's Pendulum**
*This pendulum is modeled on the one invented by the French physicist in 1851 to prove that the Earth rotates.*

**Virtual Reality**
places visitors in a virtual world.

**North Entrance**

### ★ The Heart
*Walk through this 16-ft- (5-m-) tall replica of a human heart, which would, if real, be suitable for a person 28 stories tall. Learn about heart-healthy practices and take a journey via computer through the circulatory system.*

**Flight Simulators**
take visitors on an exhilarating F-14 Tomcat bombing mission.

**Main Entrance**, accessed from the three-level parking garage.

### MUSEUM GUIDE
*The museum's Great Hall houses the museum shop, information desk, and Silver Streak train exhibit. Space Exploration exhibits are on the ground floor; Computer Technology on the main. All other exhibits are displayed throughout the ground floor, main floor, and balcony. Each floor has a color-coded staircase on each corner facilitating navigation of the building. Each staircase itself features an intriguing exhibit. The Omnimax Theater is in the Henry Crown Space Center. Cafés are on the ground and main floors.*

### KEY
- ☐ Space exploration
- ☐ Transportation
- ☐ The human body
- ☐ Computer technology
- ☐ Energy and environment
- ☐ Permanent exhibitions
- ☐ Temporary exhibitions
- ☐ Nonexhibition space

# Exploring the Museum of Science and Industry

**Caryatids grace the museum's exterior**

THE MUSEUM OF SCIENCE and Industry, with its more than 800 exhibits and 2,000 interactive displays, encompasses everything from basic science to advanced technology. Space exploration and transportation are particularly strong areas. A few exhibits, such as the Circus, fall outside the museum's defined focus, but prove to be enduring crowd pleasers. With more than 350,000 sq ft (32,500 sq m) of exhibition space, there's more than enough to keep visitors of all ages engaged for a full day of investigation and discovery.

**View of the Museum of Science and Industry from across Columbia Basin**

## SPACE EXPLORATION

THE HENRY CROWN Space Center is the epicenter of the museum's excellent display on space exploration. Here, you can view the Apollo 8 Command Module – the first manned spacecraft to circle the moon, orbiting ten times in December 1968. Less than 13 ft (4 m) in diameter and weighing 13,100 lb (6,000 kg), the cramped vessel still bears the scars of its epic journey on its pitted exterior.

The exhibit includes a replica of NASA's Apollo Lunar Module Trainer, which is used for astronaut training, and a 6.5-oz (185-g) piece of moon rock retrieved by the Apollo 17 mission.

The Space Center is also home to the Aurora 7 Mercury Space Capsule, one of the earliest manned

**Henry Crown Space Center, showcasing US space exploration**

spacecrafts to orbit the Earth – doing so four times consecutively in May 1962.

A 20-minute movie simulating the experience of blasting off in a space shuttle, complete with shaking seats, allows viewers to feel like astronauts, if only briefly.

## TRANSPORTATION

PICK A MODE of transport – from train, plane, to automobile – and you can be sure the museum has an outstanding example, ready for visitors to climb aboard.

Train-nostalgia buffs will enjoy the All Aboard the Silver Streak exhibit, which showcases the first diesel-electric passenger train in America, the Pioneer Zephyr. Built in 1934, the Zephyr was the swiftest, sleekest train in the US, initiating the conversion from steam to diesel-electric locomotion and ushering in the era of luxury passenger rail travel. The Zephyr's interior was dramatically different from the opulent Pullman cars in use at the time *(see p119)* yet just as elegant in its simplicity. Visitors can get behind the

controls and pretend they are driving this historic train.

The museum also has one of the largest train models in the world. The 3,000-sq-ft (280-sq-m) model highlights the role of the railroad in the US economy.

The history of aviation is well represented in the museum's transportation zone. Look up to the balcony and you will see a rare Boeing 40B-2 airplane suspended from the ceiling.

Nearby is Take Flight, an exhibit explaining the scientific principles behind the wonder of flight, such as radar, aerodynamics, and engine and wing construction. This exhibit contains one of the museum's largest attractions, a cantilevered United Airlines Boeing 727. Visitors can board the aircraft to explore, and watch from the balcony its seven-minute simulated flight.

Adjacent to the Boeing 727 is Designed to Fly, an exhibit tracing the history of humans' efforts to fly, from the 15th century to the Wright Brothers' first successful powered flight, in 1903.

Another popular attraction is the U-505 Submarine, a World War II German submarine captured by US naval forces off the west coast of Africa in 1944. Tour this cramped, 252-ft- (77-m-) long vessel, now a memorial to

**The Great Hall, the popular Silver Streak train in the background**

Navy war veterans, in which sailors could not be taller than 5.5 ft (1.7 m) if they wished to stand upright.

Directly above, on the main floor, is the NAVY: Technology at Sea exhibit, where a high-tech flight simulator replicates a take-off and landing on the back of an aircraft carrier.

**Fast machines in the museum's transportation zone**

Closer to earth is the Auto Gallery's Spirit of America, the first car to break the 500 mph (800 kph) land speed barrier. On October 15, 1964, Craig Breedlove became the "fastest man on wheels" when he piloted this missile-like vehicle to spectacular speeds.

## THE HUMAN BODY

UNDOUBTEDLY the weirdest and most compelling exhibit in the museum (for the strong of stomach only) is the Anatomical Slices, located on the blue staircase between the main floor and balcony. In the 1940s, the corpses of a man and woman who died of natural causes were frozen and then cut into 0.5-inch (1.25-cm) sections – the man, horizontally, and the woman, vertically – and preserved in fluid between glass. These unique displays allow you to look right inside the human body – in all its queasiness-inducing glory.

Equally dramatic – but less gory – is The Heart, a 16-ft- (5-m-) tall replica of a human heart. Walk through the model to see the heart from the perspective of a blood cell. Then check your blood pressure and calculate the number of times your heart has beaten since birth.

AIDS: The War Within is the world's first permanent museum exhibit on AIDS and HIV. It explores, in part through bold comic-book

## FROM PLASTER TO STONE

Architect Charles B. Atwood *(see p28)* based his design of this majestic building – built as a temporary structure for the 1893 World's Fair and, today, the only surviving building from the fair – on classical Greek models. Over 270 columns and 24 caryatids, weighing 6 tons each, grace the exterior. Covered in plaster, with a roof of skylights, the building deteriorated badly after the fair. The Field Museum *(see pp86–9)* occupied it briefly, until 1920. The building then sat in a state of disrepair until the mid-1920s, when Julius Rosenwald, chairman of Sears, Roebuck and Co., campaigned to save it and founded the museum, donating millions of dollars to a massive reconstruction effort. Exterior plaster was replaced with 28,000 tons of limestone and marble in an 11-year renovation. The Museum of Science and Industry opened in 1933, in time for the Century of Progress World's Exposition.

**The original building during the 1893 World's Columbian Exposition**

artwork, the nine stages of the AIDS virus and the efforts of scientists to control it. Interactive displays encourage visitors to learn about viruses, the ecology of disease, and the human immune system.

## COMPUTER TECHNOLOGY

ALTHOUGH the museum makes effective use of computers in its many interactive displays, relatively little space is devoted specifically to the subject of computer technology. A fascinating exception is Imaging; The Tools of Science. This installation explores computer-imaging procedures such as MRIs (which produce the image of a cross-section of an object) and CT scans (soft-tissue X-rays). Visitors can delve into radiosurgery and forensic science through hands-on exhibits.

Don goggles in the main floor's Virtual Reality exhibit and become part of an environment created by computer technology. A video camera, real-time digitizer,

**Bronze plaques on the main doors honor the sciences**

and recorded images will place you in a virtual world, where you can "play" a drum or "bounce" a ball.

## ENERGY AND ENVIRONMENT

ONE OF THE MUSEUM'S most popular exhibits is Coal Mine. It is worth waiting for in the inevitable lineup. This re-creation of a 1933 Illinois coal mine is remarkably life-like. The 20-minute tour begins at the top of a mineshaft, where an elevator takes visitors down in semi-darkness to a bituminous coal seam and a fascinating demonstration of coal-mining machinery. A short ride on a mine train ends this unique, if somewhat claustrophobic, experience. Environmental issues are front and center at the Reusable City. Interactive displays encourage visitors to learn more about the Earth's ozone layer, climate change, and pollution. A periscope allows visitors to see inside a "landfill," down to its decades-old contents.

# FARTHER AFIELD

HICAGO'S OUTLYING areas offer a wealth of sight-seeing opportunities. For lovers of architecture, Oak Park is a must-see for its Frank Lloyd Wright designs. Other Chicago neighborhoods, such as Wicker Park and Lakeview, each with its own distinct character, are ideal day-trip destinations. Pullman is one of the US's best-preserved

**Mexican sugar skull, Pilsen**

19th-century neighborhoods. A little farther is Brookfield Zoo, renowned for its realistic animal habitats. Walking paths lead through varied landscapes at Morton Arboretum. Visitors with more time can traverse the canal corridor, which runs alongside the 1848 historic canal and encompasses extensive recreational trails and several fine museums.

## SIGHTS AT A GLANCE

**Historic Buildings, Districts, and Canals**
Hull-House **7**
Illinois and Michigan Canal National Heritage Corridor **11**
Oak Park **5**
Pullman Historic District **12**

**Neighborhoods**
Lakeview and Wrigleyville **2**

Lower West Side **8**
Near West Side **6**
Wicker Park **3**

**Zoos and Botanic Gardens**
Brookfield Zoo **9**
Garfield Park Conservatory **4**
*Lincoln Park Zoo pp112–13* **1**
Morton Arboretum **10**

**KEY**

| | |
|---|---|
| | Urban area |
| | Interstate highway |
| | State highway |
| | Major road |

**5 miles = 8 km**

◁ **Pink flamingos at Lincoln Park Zoo**

# Lincoln Park Zoo ❶

ESTABLISHED IN 1868 with the gift of two swans from New York's Central Park, Lincoln Park Zoo is the US's oldest free public zoo. Today, more than 1,000 mammals, reptiles, and birds from around the world live here, in realistic habitats. The zoo's status as a world leader in wildlife conservation is evident in its educational exhibits, as well as in its many international efforts to save endangered species. Although it is not Chicago's largest zoo (see Brookfield Zoo *p117*), Lincoln Park Zoo, in the heart of Lincoln Park, is easily accessible from the Downtown Core. The park, Chicago's largest, offers walking and biking paths that wind along groves of native trees, paddle-boating ponds, lagoons, and sandy beaches.

**Statue of Abraham Lincoln in Lincoln Park**

**West Entrance**

**Lincoln Park Conservatory**
*This stunning conservatory (1890–95), designed by architect Joseph L. Silsbee, houses many exotic plants, including orchids. Thousands of flowers for use in the park are grown here.*

**★ Regenstein Small Mammal-Reptile House**
*This exhibit show-cases 40 species, including African Dwarf crocodiles.*

STOCKTON DRIVE

**Waterfowl Lagoon**
*Flamingos and other water-fowl find refuge in this peaceful lagoon, one of the zoo's earliest features.*

**Café Brauer** was designed in 1908 by Dwight Perkins, a leading architect of the Prairie School. The building was restored in 1989. Its Great Hall has spectacular chandeliers and a skylight.

## STAR FEATURES

★ Farm in the Zoo

★ Lester E. Fisher
Great Ape House

★ Regenstein Small
Mammal-Reptile
House

**★ Farm in the Zoo**
*The five barns of this working farm shelter cows, horses, chickens, and pigs. Children especially enjoy the daily milking in the Dairy Barn and horse-grooming demonstrations.*

**VISITORS' CHECKLIST**

2200 N Cannon Dr. 742-2000. M Clark/Division. 22, 36, 135, 136, 145, 146, 147, 151. **Zoo grounds** 9am–6pm daily, except May–Sep: 9am–7pm Sat, Sun & holidays. P on N Cannon Dr. **Workshops** (call 742-2053), **special events** (call 742-2283). W www.lpzoo.com

### McCormick Bear and Wolf Habitat
*The zoo's polar bear pool is one of the largest in the world.*

**East Entrance**

**Gateway Building**, at the zoo's main east entrance, houses the information and security desk.

### Kovler Lion House
*Rare cats, including Siberian tigers, inhabit this 1912 historic building.*

### ★ Lester E. Fisher Great Ape House
*The zoo's collection of lowland gorillas is one of the largest in the US – testimony to the zoo's extraordinarily successful breeding program.*

### Antelope and Zebra Area
*Various hoofed animals live in 11 outdoor habitats by the zoo's south pond, including the threatened Grevy's zebra from Africa and the endangered Bactrian camel from Mongolia, as well as rare gazelles, antelopes, deer, and alpacas.*

CANNON DRIVE

**South Entrance**

0 meters 100

0 yards 100

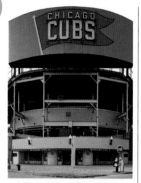

**Wrigley Field baseball stadium, home of the famous Chicago Cubs**

# Lakeview and Wrigleyville ❷

West of Lake Michigan to Ashland Ave, from Diversey Ave to W Irving Park Rd. **M** *Belmont (red, brown, purple lines).* 🚌 *8, 22, 36.* 🎟 *See Entertainment p163.*

LAKEVIEW AND Wrigleyville make up one of Chicago's most colorful neighborhoods. Now a cultural melting pot, the area was settled by German immigrants in the 1830s. Farms dotted the landscape until the mid-1800s, when the area began to develop as a residential neighborhood of working-class Swedish immigrants. After annexation by the City in 1889, a spurt of development established the area as one of the liveliest in Chicago – a distinction it continues to hold today.

Wrigleyville, the northern half of Lakeview, is named after Wrigley Field, home of the famous Chicago Cubs baseball team. This charming stadium, designed by Zachary Taylor Davis in 1914, is the oldest National League ballpark. The community resisted electric lighting of the stadium into the late 1980s.

Lakeview hosts a thriving theater scene and excellent restaurants, coffeehouses, bars, specialty shops, and bookshops. Trendy boutiques line Belmont Avenue between Halsted and Sheffield Streets. Lakeview is also the heart of Chicago's gay community.

To sample Lakeview's architectural heritage, visit

**Alta Vista Terrace**, between Grace and Byron Streets. This block of turn-of-the-century row houses was designed by Joseph C. Brompton in 1904 and was the first area in Chicago to be designated a historic district. Hawthorne Place, north of Belmont Avenue, east of Broadway, is a rare surviving Victorian-era residential design typical of the area's early development.

Beautiful tombstones mark the resting places of Chicago's notables in **Graceland Cemetery** (4001 North Clark Street), just north of Lakeview. Buried here are Louis Sullivan *(see p28)* and George Pullman *(see p119),* among others. A site map is available at the cemetery's office; call 922-8687 for tour information.

**Rapp House, one of Wicker Park's architectural gems**

# Wicker Park ❸

Bounded by Schiller & Leavitt Sts, Damen & Milwaukee Aves. **M** *Damen (blue line).* 🚌 *56.* 🎟 *Around the Coyote (Sep).*

IF YOU ARE LOOKING for the trendy area of Chicago, Wicker Park is it. It is brimming with galleries, boutiques, coffeehouses, restaurants, and nightclubs.

In the late 1800s, German and Scandinavian immigrants built mansions here and many of them remain, making Wicker Park a great place for an architectural tour. Of particular interest are Caton Street, Leavitt Street, Pierce Avenue, and John Rapp House (1407 North Hoyne Avenue.

# Garfield Park Conservatory ❹

300 North Central Park Ave. **📞** *(312) 746-5100.* **M** Central Park Dr. (green line). 🕐 *9am–5pm daily.* **Plants Alive!**: *12am–5pm Mon–Fri; 9am–5pm Sat–Tue.* 🎫 *available to members.* 🎁 ♿ 🅿. 🌐 *www.garfield-conservatory.org.*

DESIGNED BY Jens Jensen, (who was known as "the dean of Prairie landscape") in 1906, the spectacular Garfield Park Conservatory is a two-acre enclosed garden which houses the world's largest public horticultural collection under glass. Shows and events are held throughout the year. Children are well catered for, in particular with the Plants Alive! garden, with exhibits showing how plants grow and reproduce.

# Oak Park ❺

Bounded by N Chicago Ave, S Randolph St, E Harlem & W East Aves. **ℹ** *(708) 848-1500.* **M** *Oak Park (green line); Harlem/Lake (green line).* 🚆 *Oak Park (Union Pacific/West line).* **Visitors' center**: *158 N Forest Ave.* 🕐 *10am–4pm daily.* ⬤ *Jan 1, Thanksgiving, Dec 25.* 🎫 🎁 **Frank Lloyd Wright Home and Studio Foundation**: *951 Chicago Ave.* **📞** *(708) 848-1978.* 🎫 🌐 *www.wrightplus.org*

IN 1889, FRANK LLOYD Wright moved to Oak Park, at the age of 22. During the next 20 years here, he created many groundbreaking buildings in his legendary Prairie School style evolved. This community is home to 25 Wright buildings – the largest grouping of his work anywhere. Oak Park is

**Frank Lloyd Wright's Home and Studio, his residence for 20 years**

Unity Temple, Frank Lloyd Wright's "little jewel"

also known for its literary association: famed American writer Ernest Hemingway *(see p29)* was born here in 1899.

The best place to feast on Wright's achievement is the **Frank Lloyd Wright Home and Studio**. Designed by Wright in 1889, the superbly restored residence and workspace is where the architect developed his influential Prairie style.

Nearby are two private homes that reveal Wright's versatility. The **Arthur Heurtley House** (1902: 318 Forest Ave) is typically Prairie style, with its row of windows spanning the low roofline and its simple but elegant entrance arch. The **Moore-Dugal**

**House** (1895: 333 Forest Ave) is a hybrid of styles, with Tudor Revival and Gothic elements.

At the southern end of Oak Park is the masterful **Pleasant Home** (217 Home Ave), a 30-room Prairie-style mansion designed in 1897 by George W. Maher. The house contains extraordinary art glass (designed panels of leaded glass), intricate woodwork, and decorative motifs, as well as a display on the area's history.

Wright was particularly proud of **Unity Temple** (875 Lake St.), his design for the Unitarian Universalist Congregation. He called this church, one of his most important designs, his first expression of an "entirely new architecture."

It was built between 1906 and 1908 using a then-unusual technique of poured reinforced concrete, in part because of a budget of only $45,000. Unity Temple is a masterpiece of powerful simplicity wedded with functional ornamentation.

Ernest Hemingway lived in Oak Park until the age of 18. The **Ernest Hemingway Birthplace** (339 North Oak Park Ave) a grand Victorian home with turn-of-the-century furnishings, has displays on this Nobel Prize winner's life. The **Ernest Hemingway Museum** (200 North Oak Park Ave) features artifacts from Hemingway's early life, including a childhood diary.

**The Victorian house in which Ernest Hemingway was born**

## OAK PARK

Arthur Heurtley House ②
Ernest Hemingway
  Birthplace ⑥
Ernest Hemingway
  Museum ⑦
Frank Lloyd Wright Home
  and Studio ①
Moore-Dugal House ③
Pleasant Home ④
Unity Temple ⑤

0 meters    400

0 yards    400

## KEY

| | |
|---|---|
| Ⓜ | CTA train station |
| 🚉 | Metra train station |
| P | Parking |
| i | Tourist information |

Map labels:
CHICAGO AVENUE
SUPERIOR STREET
ERIE STREET
ONTARIO STREET
LAKE STREET
NORTH BOULEVARD
SOUTH BOULEVARD
PLEASANT STREET
HARLEM AVENUE
FOREST AVENUE
KENILWORTH AVENUE
OAK PARK AVENUE

**Jane Addams' Hull-House Museum, seen from the courtyard**

# Near West Side ❻

Bounded by Chicago River, 16th & Kinzie Sts, & Ogden Ave. **Map** 3 A1–A5. **M** UIC-Halsted. 🚌 8, 60.

OVER THE YEARS, Chicago's Near West Side has experienced waves of successive immigrant settlement. Today, it is one of the best places to experience the city's many ethnic communities.

It was settled in the 1840s and 1850s by working-class Irish immigrants. The Great Chicago Fire of 1871 began here, on DeKoven Street (No. 558), in the O'Leary barn. Appropriately (or ironically, depending on how you look at it), the **Chicago Fire Academy** is now located on the site. An arresting bronze sculpture of flames marks the spot where the devastating fire reportedly began.

Following the fire, Russian and Polish Jews settled the area in the 1890s, while to the north, a lively Greek Town developed, centered along Halsted Street, between Madison and Van Buren Streets. To the west, Little Italy, centered around Taylor Street at Halsted Street, flourished.

**Egon Weiner's sculpture at the Chicago Fire Academy**

The **University of Illinois at Chicago** holds a prominent position in the area. Walter A. Netsch Jr. designed the university in the 1960s, in

the modern style known as Brutalism. The campus is characterized by unadorned concrete buildings with rows of narrow vertical windows.

# Hull-House ❼

800 S Halsted St. 📞 413-5353. **Map** 3 A3. **M** UIC-Halsted. 🚌 7, 8, 60. ⬤ Thanksgiving, Dec 25, Jan 1. 🎥 📷 mandatory: 10am–4pm weekdays; noon–5pm Sun. 🅿

JANE ADDAMS' Hull-House Museum, now part of the University of Illinois campus, celebrates the work of Addams (see p29), who won the 1931 Nobel Peace Prize for her social-justice work and advocacy and became perhaps the most famous woman in the US. In her pioneering work with the poor, Addams fought for child-labor laws, a minimum wage, and better public sanitation, among other social causes.

It was in this 1856 mansion in the then industrial center of Chicago that Addams and Ellen Gates Starr established, in 1889, a settlement house to provide social services to immigrants, the poor, and the dispossessed. The house's interior has been restored to look as it did in its early days, with original furnishings. Exhibits document the history of the settlement and the work of its residents.

# Lower West Side ❽

Bounded by Chicago River, 16th St, & Pulaski Rd. **M** 18th. 🚌 9, 18, 60.

THE LOWER WEST SIDE, like the Near West Side, developed as an industrial, working-class neighborhood after the 1871 fire. Immigrants from Bohemia were the first to arrive, in the 1870s, followed in the early 20th century by Germans, Poles, and Yugoslavians. In the 1950s, an influx of Mexican and Puerto Rican immigrants brought a Hispanic flavor to the community.

Today, the neighborhood of Pilsen, centered along 18th Street between South Damen Avenue and South Halsted Street, is home to many fine Mexican restaurants, bakeries, and specialty shops. The sounds of salsa are everywhere, the inviting scent of corn tortillas emanates from tortillerias, and colorful murals brighten the streetscape. Artists, lured here by low rents in the 1980s, contribute a touch of eclecticism to the area.

The best way to experience this vibrant district is to stroll along 18th Street, admire the late-19th-century buildings – one of the most interesting is the Romanesque-style Thalia Hall at the corner of Allport Street – and perhaps stop at a street vendor for a tasty cob of roasted corn.

For more substantial fare, one of the best restaurants in Pilsen is Nuevo León (No. 1515), where the food is tasty and the portions huge. Café Jumping Bean (No. 1439) exhibits work by local artists

**Café Jumping Bean on Chicago's Lower West Side**

and serves up delicious snacks. Panaderia El Paraiso (No. 1156) is an excellent local bakery.

The cultural heart of Pilsen is the **Mexican Fine Arts Center Museum** (1852 West 19th Street; 738-1503; 10am–5pm Tue–Sun), the largest Mexican arts institution in the US. The museum rotates a broad range of exhibitions, covering subjects as diverse as ancient Mexico and young avant-garde artists. The more than 1,500 works in the permanent collection include Mexican masters such as Diego Rivera.

A Capuchin monkey at Tropic World watching visitors

Signs for Mexican bakeries and eateries lining the streets of Pilsen

## Brookfield Zoo ⑨

First Ave & 31st St, Brookfield.
**C** (708) 485-0263. **R** Hollywood (Burlington Northern Santa Fe line).
**B** 304, 311. ☐ Memorial Day–Labor Day: 9:30am–6pm daily. Labor Day–Memorial Day: 10am–5pm daily. (free Jan–Mar, Oct–Dec: Tue, Thu; separate adm to some exhibits). ◙ ⚒ ⚐ ⅱ ▤ ◙ ◙ P
Lectures, daily special events.
W www.brookfieldzoo.org

BROOKFIELD ZOO, opened in 1934, is one of the largest zoos in the US. More than 2,800 animals representing approximately 450 species, gathered from around the world, roam realistic habitats.

Many of the animal exhibits are outdoors, along the zoo's 15 miles (24 km) of trails, but there are also a number of fascinating indoor displays, such as the Living Coast and Tropic World.

The Fragile Kingdom comprises two indoor exhibits – an African desert and an Asian rainforest, with indigenous bats, squirrels, and foxes – and an outdoor display featuring large cats, including a Siberian tiger.

Nearby is the 2,000-seat Dolphinarium. Shows featuring Atlantic bottlenose dolphins are offered here daily. To the north of the Dolphinarium is the Seven Seas Seascape: outdoor pools containing sea lions, harbor seals, and walruses.

At the southeast corner of the grounds is the Children's Zoo, where kids can pet barnyard animals and watch cow and goat milking.

Another children's favorite is Tropic World, one of the largest indoor mixed-species exhibits in the world. Here, rainforest creatures and primates from South America, Asia, and Africa swing through trees and wander the forest floor while visitors watch from the observation deck. The Brazilian tapir, with a flexible snout; the giant anteater, with a 2-ft- (0.6-m-) long tongue; and Ramar, the 365-lb (165-kg) silverback gorilla, are particularly impressive.

Close by is the Swamp, an indoor re-created cypress swamp with egrets, storks, and a 10-ft- (3-m-) long American alligator, which sleeps with its eyes open.

The Living Coast features three habitats of South America's western coast: open ocean, near-shore waters, and rocky shores. Jellyfish, turtles, and penguins are just a few of the creatures to be found here.

At the interactive Be a Bird exhibit, visitors can learn about bird anatomy and behavior, and test their own ability to fly.

One of the most spectacular exhibits is Habitat Africa! This re-created savanna is complete with giraffes and wild dogs. A "danger game" trail allows visitors to pretend they're thirsty animals walking to a waterhole, their steps activating taped sounds of predators.

Along the zoo's northern boundary are enclosures for large animals, including the unusual Grevy's zebras. To the south, near Roosevelt Fountain, is Pachyderm House, home to elephants, rhinos, and hippos.

A hippopotamus grazing in the Pachyderm House

# Morton Arboretum ⓾

4100 Illinois Route 53, Lisle.
☎ (630) 719-2400. 🚉 Lisle
(Burlington Northern Santa Fe line).
🕐 Apr–Oct: 7am–7pm daily;
Nov–Mar: 7am–5pm daily. 🏷
(discount Wed). 🅾 ♿ 🍴 🏠
🅿 **Workshops, library**.

MORTON ARBORETUM is home to more than 3,600 species of trees, shrubs, and flowers from around the world. Eight lakes and ponds dot this 2.5-sq-mile (6.5-sq-km) outdoor museum, providing wonderful picnic settings.

Founded in 1922 by Joy Morton of the Morton Salt Company, the arboretum's mission is educational. It conducts scientific research as well as providing informative public displays. Collections are grouped according to plant families and habitats, allowing visitors to learn about each species' unique features and to compare related plants.

The arboretum's Daffodil Glade is particularly stunning in spring. Its Schulenberg Prairie, radiant in summer, is a pioneering landscape restoration begun in the early 1960s by Ray Schulenberg. The prairie is admired throughout the Midwest as a fine re-creation of this now-endangered prairie that covered the region before settlement. The maples are dramatic in the fall; the ever-green trees striking in winter.

If you do not have time to hike along any of the 12 miles (19 km) of trails, you can drive through the arboretum in about 50 minutes via 11 miles (18 km) of one-way roads. Open-air tram tours are offered daily.

Begin your visit at the visitors' center, located near the entrance. The center lists daily events and seasonal bloom information. It also has an excellent bookstore.

The arboretum's Thornhill Education Center (open weekdays) houses displays about Joy Morton and the Morton family. The Sterling Morton Library has a wide range of publications on plants, gardening and landscaping, and natural history. The library's holdings also include rare botanical books and prints.

# Illinois and Michigan Canal National Heritage Corridor ⓫

From Chicago's south branch of
Chicago River to LaSalle-Peru.
☎ (815) 942-0796. See **The History
of Chicago** p15. 🆆 www.canalcor.org

THE FIRST EUROPEANS to explore the Chicago region – Louis Jolliet and Father Jacques Marquette – urged, in their 1673 expedition report, the building of a canal to connect Lake Michigan to the Des Plaines and Illinois Rivers.

**St. James of the Sag, burial place
of many canal laborers**

They believed that such a transportation link would be of great economic benefit to the region. It took a century and a half for their prediction to come true, and the loss of many – mostly Irish – canal laborers to diseases such as dysentery and cholera, but when the Illinois and Michigan (I&M) Canal opened in 1848, it did indeed transform the area's economy. It also established Chicago as the transportation center of the Midwest.

As the use of rail to transport freight became increasingly popular, however, canal traffic declined. Carrying waste away from Chicago became the canal's primary purpose, until the Sanitary and Ship Canal took over this function, in 1914. The I&M Canal, with its 15 locks, was abandoned entirely in 1933 when the Illinois Waterway replaced it as a connection between the Great Lakes and Mississippi River.

Fifty years later, in 1984, the canal was designated a national heritage corridor. Today, with almost 100 miles (160 km) of multiuse trails running alongside the canal, the canal route offers abundant recreational opportunities, from bird-watching to biking, hiking, and canoeing. The route passes through more than 40 towns and cities, sites of historic buildings and fascinating museums.

A good place to begin your exploration is the town of Lockport, 30 miles (48 km) southwest of Chicago. During

**Lush trees reflected in one of Morton Arboretum's several lakes**

the canal's heyday, this town thrived as the center of the boat-building and -repair trades. The visitors' center (200 West 8th Street) in Lockport's historic Gaylord Building, the oldest industrial structure along the waterway, offers maps and information. Adjacent to the center is a restored pioneer settlement, its buildings characteristic of those built during the development of the canal.

Will County Historical Society Museum is located in Lockport's scenic 1837 canal headquarters building. Tour guides tell stories of the canal and explain historic artifacts.

# Pullman Historic District

Bounded by 111th & 115th Sts, Ellis & Cottage Grove Aves. **M** *95/Dan Ryan then bus 111.* **R** *111th St (Electric District line).* **i** *11141 S Cottage Grove Ave.* **C** *(773) 785-3828.* **O** *noon–2pm Mon–Fri; 11am–2pm Sat; noon–3pm Sun.* **✦** *May–Oct 12:30pm, 1:30pm 1st Sun of month; call (773) 785-3828.* **P** **W** *www.lincolnnet.net/users/lrhpf*

PULLMAN HISTORIC District, one of Chicago's best-preserved 19th-century communities, is the site of a fascinating – if ultimately unsuccessful – experiment. The town, the first of its kind in the US, was built by George M. Pullman, founder of the luxury rail-carriage manufacturer Pullman Palace Car Company, to house his employees. In 1879, Pullman

**Interior of Hotel Florence, typical of the town's Queen Anne-style elegance**

purchased 6.25 sq miles (16 sq km) of marshland in Chicago's far south side, 14 miles (22.5 km) south of downtown Chicago. He hired architect Solon S. Beman and landscape architect Nathan F. Barrett to plan the company town. Most of the more than 1,700 row houses and apartment units were constructed between 1880 and 1885.

Workers rented the living quarters from Pullman, who expected to realize a 6 percent profit by collecting rent on all the buildings, including the church and library. This was the first development to offer the working class indoor plumbing, gas, and recreational facilities.

The experiment ended in acrimony when Pullman laid off workers and cut wages without lowering rents during the 1893 depression. A huge

**Ornate west window of Greenstone Church**

strike, which eventually spread across the entire nation, ensued. The US government intervened, sending in federal troops. The workers lost the seven-week strike, but Pullman's experiment was tainted with failure. He died three years later, in 1897, still resentful. By 1907, all the houses in Pullman had been sold to private buyers.

Plans in 1960 to demolish the area's buildings and create an industrial park were defeated by residents. The district of Pullman was designated a national landmark in 1971. Today, many of the row houses have been restored. The town is easily explored in an afternoon; maps are available at the visitors' center.

Hotel Florence (11111 S Forestville Ave), named for Pullman's favorite daughter, is a superb 1881 example of Queen Anne style. Now a museum housing artifacts from the town's labor struggles, it is undergoing a $3-million renovation.

The mansions lining 111th and 112th Streets were built for Pullman executives; the Pullman colors of maroon and green frame the windows and doors. The Greenstone Church and the curved Beman-designed Colonnade Apartments and Town Houses by Market Hall are also worth a look. The apartments (1892) were bachelor units.

**Building once housing several Pullman Palace Car Company workers**

# BEYOND CHICAGO

# Exploring Beyond Chicago

Visitors eager to discover more of Illinois won't be disappointed by the rich mix of historical sights, recreational activities, and picturesque countryside Chicago's environs have to offer. Excursions to the attractive North Shore towns of Evanston, Wilmette, Glencoe, and Lake Forest will take you along the shoreline of Lake Michigan, affording stunning views.

For those wishing to venture farther, the resort area of Lake Geneva awaits just across the Wisconsin state line. The delightful, historic town of Galena lies near the Iowa border, a three-and-a-half hour drive west of Chicago. The drive to both leads through rural farmland dotted with small towns and state parks. The typically flat Midwestern terrain gives way to rolling hills just outside Galena.

**A picturesque circular barn near Highway 20, West Galena**

## Sights at a Glance

## Getting Around

Chicago has excellent Metra commuter rail links to the northern suburbs. The Union Pacific/North line, departing from the Ogilvie Transportation Center, services Evanston, Wilmette, Glencoe, and Lake Forest, with frequent trains during rush hour and every one to three hours at other times. The CTA purple line also services Evanston. You will need a car to reach Lake Geneva and Galena. Highway I-94 leads north from Chicago; I-90 is the western route.

**Galena's Belvedere Mansion** *(see p128)*

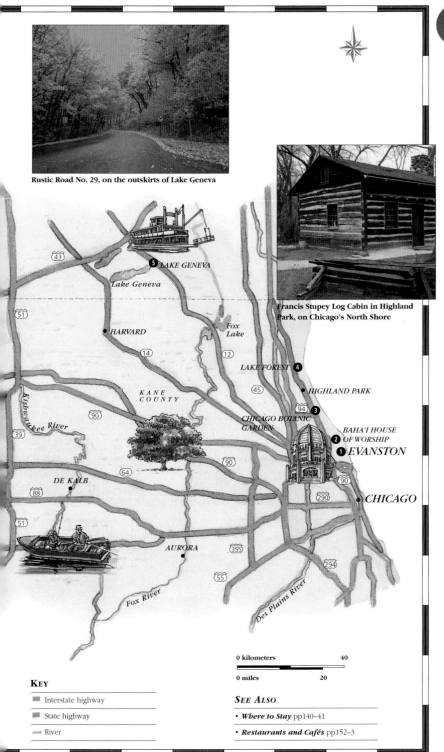

Rustic Road No. 29, on the outskirts of Lake Geneva

Francis Stupey Log Cabin in Highland Park, on Chicago's North Shore

43

LAKE GENEVA

Lake Geneva

51

HARVARD

Fox
Lake

14

12

LAKE FOREST

KANE
COUNTY

45

HIGHLAND PARK

Kishwaukee River

90

94

CHICAGO BOTANIC
GARDEN

39

BAHA'I HOUSE
OF WORSHIP

EVANSTON

64

90

DE KALB

88

90

CHICAGO

51

290

AURORA

355

294

55

Fox River

Des Plains River

0 kilometers          40

0 miles          20

**KEY**

■ Interstate highway

■ State highway

〰 River

**SEE ALSO**

• **Where to Stay** pp140–41

• **Restaurants and Cafés** pp152–3

# Evanston ●

E VANSTON, ON THE SHORES of Lake Michigan, 14 miles (22 km) north of Chicago, offers stunning beaches, charming boutiques and restaurants, and exciting museums, art galleries, and theater. Originally known as Ridgeville, it began as a community of farmers from New England, and Irish and German immigrants. In 1850, a group of Chicago Methodists bought a large tract of lakefront land, opening Northwestern University five years later. Ridgeville changed its name to Evanston in 1857 to honor John Evans, one of the university's founders. By the 1870s, wealthy Chicagoans, is search of cleaner neighborhoods, were moving to Evanston. Many of their mansions still stand.

Charles Gates Dawes House, overlooking Lake Michigan

## Exploring Evanston

Many of Evanston's attractions, including shops, restaurants, and art galleries, are concentrated in the historic downtown around Grove Street and Sherman Avenue, an area easily explored on foot. Other interesting districts include that at Central Street, and at Chicago Avenue and Dempster Street. The large lakefront university campus, the buildings of which reflect widely varied architectural styles, provides greenspace ideal for strolling. Or you can saunter along Forest Avenue to see the historic mansions built for Chicago's wealthy.

### 🚩 Charles Gates Dawes House

225 Greenwood St. 📞 1-847 475-3410. ◯ 1–5pm Thu–Sun. ● major public hols. 🈺 (children under 6 free). 📷 mandatory. 🚻

This massive Chateauesque mansion was designed in 1894 by Henry Edwards-Ficken for Robert Sheppard, treasurer of Northwestern University. Sheppard sold it in 1909 to Charles Gates Dawes, who went on to become US vice-president under Calvin Coolidge. The restored 28-room house, home to the Evanston Historical Society, showcases the period 1925–9.

### 🚩 Rest Cottage

1730 Chicago Ave. 📞 1-847 864-1396. ◯ Mar–Dec: 1–4pm 1st Sun of month or by appt. ● major public hols. 🈺 📷 mandatory. 🚻

Pioneering suffragist and Women's Christian Temperance Union (WCTU) activist Frances Willard lived at Rest Cottage from 1865 until her death in 1898.

This quaint, Gothic-style (see p24) cottage, built by Willard's father in 1865, is now a museum devoted to Willard's life and the history of the WCTU. The world's oldest voluntary, non-sectarian women's organization, the WCTU is best known for its campaign against alcohol.

### 🏛 Block Sculpture Garden

1967 S Campus Dr. 📞 1-847 491-4000/4002. ● summer, except for guided tours Jul–Aug Sun.

The Block Museum's sculpture garden showcases 20th-century sculpture. Among the garden's treasures are two large, bronze abstract sculptures by British artist Barbara Hepworth (1903–1975) and an intriguing movable bronze sculpture by Spanish artist Joan Miró (1893–1983).

### 🏛 Mary and Leigh Block Museum of Art

1967 S Campus Dr. 📞 1-847 491-4000. ◯ 10am–5pm Tue, Wed, Fri, Sat; 10am–8pm Thu; noon–5pm Sun. ● summer, major hols. 🚻 📷 call for details. **Lectures, films, concerts**.

Artwork from the 14th century onward and thematic historical displays are featured at this art museum of Northwestern University, one of the US's top university museums. Major national exhibits also often stop here.

### 🚩 Grosse Point Light Station

2601 Sheridan Rd. 📞 1-847 328-6961. ● hol weekends. 🈺 📷 mandatory: Jun–Sep: 2, 3, 4pm Sat, Sun.

This lighthouse was built in 1873 in response to one of the worst maritime disasters on the Great Lakes – the 1860 sinking of the paddle wheeler *Lady Elgin*, in which nearly 300 people died.

During the summer, visitors can climb to the top of the lighthouse for wonderful views of the town and lake.

A maritime museum is on the lower floor. Plants native to Illinois are grown in the Wildflower Trail Garden, on the grounds of the station.

Grosse Point Light Station, guiding ships since 1873

Interior of the Mitchell Museum of the American Indian

**VISITORS' CHECKLIST**

M *Davis.* R *Davis (Union Pacific/North line).* i *1560 Sherman Ave.* ( *1-847 328-1500.* W *www.evanston-illinois.org.* ☆ *Ethnic Arts (Jul); Lakeshore Arts (Aug); Jump & Verve Jazz Festival (Sep).*

## 🏛 Evanston Art Center

2603 Sheridan Rd. ( *1-847 475-5300.* ⬭ *9am–5pm, 7–10pm, Mon–Thu; 9am–5pm Fri; 9am–4pm Sat; 1–4pm Sun.* ● *major public hols & 4th Thu evening of month.* ☒ *by donation.* ▣ ♿ *1st-floor gallery.* ✦ P *Lectures, workshops.*

Housed in a 1926 mansion, the gallery of this community art center exhibits regional contemporary artwork by both established and emerging artists. Gallery talks by exhibiting artists are offered regularly. The center's annual spring art auction is a great opportunity to acquire work by Midwest artists.

The lovely grounds of the center were designed by the Prairie School-influenced landscape architect Jens Jensen, designer of several parks in Chicago, including Columbus Park and the conservatory in Garfield Park, on Chicago's west side.

## 🏛 Mitchell Museum of the American Indian

2600 Central Park Ave. ( *1-847 475-1030.* ⬭ *10am–5pm Tue, Wed, Fri, Sat; 10am–8pm Thu; noon–4pm Sun.* ● *major public hols, last two weeks Aug.* ☒ *by donation.* ▣ ♿ ✦ P i *Lectures, concerts, films.*

The Mitchell Museum showcases North American Indian cultures from prehistoric to contemporary times. More than 6,000 domestic objects, including pottery, baskets, clothing, and textiles, are on display. The Mitchell is particularly rich in artifacts of Indians of the Midwest. Temporary exhibitions at the museum highlight ancient and present-day Native crafts.

---

### EVANSTON

Block Sculpture Garden ③
Charles Gates Dawes
  House ①
Evanston Art Center ⑤
Grosse Point Light Station ⑥

Mary and Leigh Block
  Museum of Art ④
Mitchell Museum of the
  American Indian ⑦
Rest Cottage ②

### KEY

M CTA train station

R Metra train station

P Parking

i Tourist information

## Baha'i House of Worship ❷

100 Linden Ave, Wilmette. **C** *1-847 733-3469.* **M** *Linden.* **R** *Wilmette (Union Pacific/North line) then bus 421, 422.* ◻ *May 1–Sep 30: 10am–10pm daily. Oct 1–Apr 30: 10am–5pm daily.* **Devotions:** *12:15pm Mon–Sat; 1:15pm Sun.* **&** **P** **W** *www.us.bahai.org*

T HE BAHA'I HOUSE of Worship, gleaming like a white beacon, is the North Shore's most striking building. There are seven major Baha'i houses of worship in the world; this is the only major one in North America. The Baha'i faith, based on the teachings of the 19th-century Persian prophet Baha'u'llah, promotes unity among all people and religions.

Construction of the house, which began in 1920, wasn't completed until 1953. Adhering to Baha'i requirements, there are nine sides to this building designed by French-Canadian architect Louis Bourgeois. An entrance door is on each side. Quotations from Baha'u'llah are carved into the stone, one above each entrance and each of the nine alcoves. Elaborate filigree-like carvings adorn the exterior. A dramatic dome of quartz and white cement rises 135 ft (41 m) above the central auditorium, which seats almost 2,000 people. The colorful, symmetrical gardens are lovely to stroll in.

A short video at the visitors' center introduces the Baha'i faith and the house's history.

**The Baha'i House of Worship, with its beautifully filigreed dome**

**Fountains and pools dot the serene grounds of the Chicago Botanic Gardens**

## Chicago Botanic Garden ❸

1000 Lake Cook Rd, Glencoe. **C** *1-847 835-5440.* **R** *Braeside; Glencoe (Union Pacific/North line) then bus 213.* ◻ *8am–sunset daily.* ● *Dec 25.* ◙ **&** **✔** ▢ **▯** **P** **Lectures, exhibits.** **W** *www.chicago-botanic.org*

T HE CHICAGO Botanic Garden, 25 miles (40 km) north of downtown Chicago, is dazzling with its 20 themed gardens and 3 native habitats of flowers, vines, shrubs, and trees. Opened in 1972, the Garden contains 1.5 million specimens representing 8,000 plant families from around the world. Eight lagoons and nine islands dot the Garden's attractive grounds.

The audiovisual presentation at Gateway Center is a useful introduction to the Garden. The center, which is near the entrance, also leads to the main island, the site of the majority of themed gardens.

The English Walled Garden consists of a secluded enclosure with six garden "rooms," each reflecting a

**Chicago Botanic Garden banners**

different English gardening style. The Heritage Garden is modeled after Europe's first botanical garden. Intoxicating scents of the Rose Garden's 5,000 rose bushes accompany the colorful blooms.

Unsurprisingly, the jewel of the Waterfall Garden is a 45-ft (14 m) waterfall. Sansho-En, or "garden of three islands," reflects the tranquil minimalism of Japanese garden design. One of the islands is tantalizingly out of reach.

The Botanic Garden's mission of conservation is well represented in the Endangered Species Garden; native plants threatened with extinction thrive here.

The Garden's three natural habitat areas (an oak woodland, a prairie, and a riverscape) offer wonderful walking trails through secluded sections of the grounds.

## Lake Forest ❹

**R** *Lake Forest (Union Pacific/North line).* ▤ *472.* **Deer Path Golf Course** *500 W Deerpath Rd.* **C** *1-847 615-4290.* **Forest Park Beach** **C** *1-847 615-4284.*

L AKE FOREST is one of Chicago's most affluent suburbs, about 30 miles (48 km) north of Chicago's Downtown Core.

The town was established in the 1850s by a group of Presbyterians who planned to build a college. The St. Louis landscape architect hired to plan the town took advantage of the area's beautiful prairie lands, ravines, and hills, designing streets to follow the natural curves of the landscape. Presbyterian Lake Forest College, established in 1857, has many grand, late-1800 buildings. The Romanesque-style Hotchkiss Hall was designed by Henry Ives Cobb *(see p24)* in 1890 and named after the town's planner.

The First Presbyterian Church (700 N Sheridan Rd) was designed by Charles Frost in 1887. The church's unusual design is an adaptation of the New England cottage style, known as Shingle style.

Market Square, in downtown Lake Forest, is one of the first planned suburban shopping centers in the US. Designed in 1916 by Howard Van Doren Shaw, this pleasant town square has a quaint English character.

**Belle of the Lake**, a reproduction of a Mississippi paddle wheeler

**The charming Market Square in Lake Forest**

The best way to experience Lake Forest is to drive on meandering Sheridan Road. Along the route are many beautiful homes on spacious, landscaped grounds.

Golfers can take advantage of Deer Path Golf Course, while at Forest Park Beach, beachgoers can enjoy the cooling waters of Lake Michigan during the summer heat.

## Lake Geneva ❺

🅸 201 Wrigley Dr, WI. 🅲 (262) 248-4416, 800-345-1020.
🅞 9am–5pm Mon–Fri; 10am–4pm Sat, Sun. 🄶 🄸 🄳
🅦 www.lakegenevawi.com

LAKE GENEVA, 70 miles (113 km) north of Chicago, nestles on the shores of a spring-fed lake of the same name. There is much to keep you occupied for a weekend in this picturesque resort town and its surrounding rural communities. Boating on the wide lake, hiking, and ballooning are just a few of the possibilities.

Lake Geneva is also a shopper's and diner's paradise. Many of the charming boutiques and antique stores are in turn-of-the-century buildings. Several of the town's restaurants, particularly those along Wrigley Drive, provide spectacular views of the lake.

In autumn, the countryside is ablaze with fall foliage. It is an ideal backdrop to the 21-mile (34-km) trail encircling the lake, a trail that once connected Indian camps. On the western edge of town is a state-designated "Rustic Road," an ideal route for a leisurely drive through the country. In winter, skiing and snowmobiling are popular activities. However, accommodations fill up quickly in summer and traffic is heavy.

Lake Geneva has a rich history. The Oneota tribes of the now-extinct Hopewell Culture Indians, an agricultural people, lived in the area as long ago as 1000 BC. In 1836, the local Potawatomi tribe was evicted from the area, and pioneer Christopher Payne built the first log cabin in town. The site is marked with a plaque on Center Street, north of White River.

The town, laid out in 1837, was originally a sawmill town. Following the Civil War, it became a resort for wealthy Chicagoans, who built their homes on the lakefront.

One of the best ways to see these mansions is by boat. Geneva Lake Cruise Line's fleet of ships includes replicas of a Southern paddle wheeler and a turn-of-the-century lake steamer. The *Walworth II* operates as a US mail boat, one of the last in service. A mail carrier delivers mail during the tour.

Geneva Lake Area Museum of History (818 Geneva Street) displays interesting historical photographs and artifacts.

**Riviera Docks, departure point for Lake Geneva boat cruises**

# Galena ❻

The old town hall, built in 1872, in historic East Galena

A VISIT TO GALENA, "the town that time forgot," is like stepping into a bygone era. More than 85 percent of this town, in Jo Daviess County, is on the National Register of Historic Places. Its architectural gems, museums, and unique landscape make Galena a great weekend destination.

As early as the 1600s, Indians were mining the area's rich deposits of lead and ore. In the 1820s, as prospectors flocked to Galena, the town became one of the US's most important mining centers. By the mid-1800s, it was a major Mississippi River port. But as rail displaced shipping as the mode of freight transportation, the town went into decline. The expense of tearing down the old buildings ensured that its historic core remained intact.

**Statue of Ulysses S. Grant**

### Exploring Galena
The best way to explore Galena is on foot or by trolley tour. Downtown parking is limited; it is best to park at the lot by the visitors' center at the old railroad depot.

Galena has a number of noteworthy historic churches. The **Union Baptist Church** (1854) features a Romanesque Revival doorway, whereas the

**A trolley tour is one of the best ways to explore Galena**

enchanting **First Presbyterian Church** (1838) has a Georgian spire. The 1838 Erban organ is still played at the Gothic Revival-style *(see p24)* **Grace Episcopal Church**.

The **Galena post office** (1857–9) is the second-oldest continuously operating post office in the US.

### 🅷 Old Illinois Central Railroad Depot
101 Bouthillier St. ☎ *(815) 777–4390.* ◷ *9am–5pm Mon–Thu; 9am–7pm Fri, Sat; 10am–5pm Sun.* ♿
Originally Galena's station for passenger rail service, it was from here that former US president Ulysses S. Grant departed for war while a Civil War colonel. The 1857 Italianate *(see p24)* building now houses the Visitor Information Center; watch its informative video on the town's history.

### 🅣 Belvedere Mansion
1008 Park Ave. ☎ *(815) 777-0747.* ◷ *11am–4pm Sun–Fri; 11am–5pm Sat.* ◉ *Oct–Memorial Day.* 📷 🎫 *mandatory.*
Built in 1857 for J. Russell Jones, a steamship owner and US ambassador to Belgium, the Italianate-style Belvedere Mansion is the largest house in Galena.

Completely restored to its original condition, the 22 rooms contain Victorian furnishings. Pieces include furniture once belonging to former US president Theodore Roosevelt, and a gold-painted cabinet once owned by entertainer Liberace.

### 🅣 Washburne House
908 Third St. ☎ *(815) 777-3310.* ◷ *10am–4pm (closed noon–1pm) Fri–Sun.* ◉ *Jan 1, Thanksgiving, Dec 25.* 📷 🎫 *mandatory: on the hour and half-hour.* ♿
A stunning example of Greek Revival architecture, this house was built in 1843 for prominent Galena attorney

and later US congressman Elihu Washburne (1816–87). Washburne was a comrade of Abraham Lincoln and a strong supporter of the career of Ulysses S. Grant. It was in the library of Washburne's home that Grant first heard the news that he had won the 1868 US presidential election.

The restored interior of the house reflects Victorian middle-class elegance.

### 🅣 Ulysses S. Grant Home
500 Bouthillier St. ☎ *(815) 777-3310.* ◷ *9am–4:45pm daily.* ◉ *major public hols.* 📷 🎫 *mandatory.* ♿
This two-story, brick Italianate *(see p24)* house designed by William Dennison was constructed in 1860. It was given to returning Civil War hero General Ulysses S. Grant by a group of prominent Galena citizens in 1865.

Even though Grant spent little time in the house after being elected US president in 1868, it has been restored to its 1870s appearance and contains furnishings used by the Grant family. Costumed guides lead visitors through the house while telling Grant's story.

**The Old Illinois Central Railroad Depot now housing Galena's visitors' center**

**View of Galena looking northeast from the pedestrian bridge**

### 🏛 Dowling House
220 Diagonal St. 📞 (815) 777-
1250. 🕐 May–Oct: 10am–5pm
Sun–Fri; 10am–6pm Sat. Apr, Nov,
Dec: 10am–4pm Fri–Sun. 📷
🎫 mandatory.

This 1826 example of
vernacular architecture is
Galena's oldest house. Built
of limestone, it originally
served as a miner's trading
post and rather crude residence. It has been restored
to reflect the era of Galena's
early pioneers.

### 🏛 DeSoto House Hotel
230 S Main St. 📞 (815) 777-0090,
800-343-6562. ♿ 🍴 🍸 🅿
This hotel was considered the
largest, most luxurious hotel
west of New York City when
it opened its doors in 1855. It
was built by Galena mer-
chants in preparation for the
boom that accompanied the
1854 arrival of Illinois Central
Railroad service in Galena.

Many famous Americans,
including writer Mark Twain,
have stayed here. Abraham
Lincoln made a speech from
its balcony in 1856, and it was
from the DeSoto House Hotel
that Ulysses S. Grant ran his
1868 presidential campaign.

### 🏛 Old Market House
123 N Commerce St. 📞 (815) 777-
3310. 🕐 9am–5pm Thu–Mon.
● Jan 1, Thanksgiving, Dec 25. 📷
🎫 mandatory. ♿
The recently restored Greek
Revival-style Market House
was built by the City of
Galena in 1846. One of the
Midwest's oldest extant market houses, it was buzzing
with activity until the early
1900s. Farmers sold produce
inside and out, city offices
were on the second floor, and
the city jail was in the basement. Today, a first-floor exhibition space is dedicated to
displays of historical interest.

### 🏛 Galena/Jo Daviess County Historical Society and Museum
211 S Bench St. 📞 (815) 777-9129.
🕐 9am–4:30pm daily. ● Jan 1,
Thanksgiving, Dec 25. 📷 (children
under 10 free). 🅿
🌐 www.galenahistorymuseum.org
This 1858 Italianate mansion,
designed by William Dennison, was built for merchant
Daniel Barrows. It is now
occupied by a museum spe-
cializing in the area's history.

The creation of the stunning
geology of Jo Daviess County
– rugged hills, rocky bluffs,
and riveting vistas – is
depicted in a large landform
model, which shows how Ice
Age glaciers detoured around
the land, sparing this hilly
part of Illinois.

A display on the Galena
River tells the story of the
Army Corps of Engineers'
building of the town's flood
dike and massive gate.

**GALENA CITY CENTER**

Belvedere Mansion ②
DeSoto House Hotel ⑤
Dowling House ⑦
Galena/Jo Daviess County
 Historical Society and Museum ⑥
Old Illinois Central Railroad
 Depot ①
Old Market House ⑧
Ulysses S. Grant Home ④
Washburne House ③

0 meters 500

0 yards 500

**KEY**

🅿 Parking

ℹ Tourist information

# TRAVELERS' NEEDS

# WHERE TO STAY

CHICAGO HAS A ROOM for every taste and budget. The top hotels are good value by international standards. For those travelers on a budget, there are many inexpensive and comfortable hotels and youth hostels in the city. Two-room suites are suitable for families, and some have kitchenettes, for those visitors who want to do their

**A friendly doorman**

own cooking. Bed-and-breakfasts, often located in charming Victorian houses in residential areas, are also a good option for visitors to Chicago. The listings in *Choosing a Hotel,* on pages 134–41, will help you narrow down the numerous choices. We have selected 86 places to stay that represent the best of their kind, in all price ranges.

**Hotel Burnham's lobby, modeled on the 1891 original *(see p134)***

## WHERE TO LOOK

MOST OF CHICAGO's hotels are clustered in two areas: the Downtown Core and the North Side. Many are both good and moderately priced. Downtown hotels are particularly convenient for visitors interested in Chicago's cultural sights such as the Chicago Art Institute, the Museum Campus, and the theater district, as well as those attending conventions at McCormick Place. This area can become quiet at night, though. By contrast, hotels on the North Side, just north of the Loop, are in one of the liveliest areas of the city. Many of the city's finer hotels are on the Magnificent Mile and the Gold Coast.

Business travelers often favor the chain hotels near O'Hare and Midway airports. Bed-and-breakfasts are scattered throughout the city.

Contact the **Illinois Bureau of Tourism** or the **Chicago Convention and Tourism Bureau** for information.

## FACILITIES

AIR-CONDITIONING and cable TV are both standard in Chicago hotels. Fax and photocopy service, computer modem hook-up, in-room speaker-phones, exercise facilities, and a swimming pool are amenities to inquire about. Be sure you understand the charges; some hotels offer these facilities for free, other hotels will charge handsomely for them.

The many conventions and trade shows held in the city provide Chicago's hotels with a major part of their business, so most hotels offer an array of business meeting rooms.

## HOTEL RATES AND DISCOUNTS

HOTEL PRICES in Chicago are competitive, but keep in mind when booking that hotels charge a steep 14.9 percent room tax.

Some hotels offer discounts to visitors attending a convention or major exhibition. Hotels may also offer corporate rates and discounts to persons in

the military, senior citizens, teachers, automobile-club members, and frequent flyers. Business travelers often leave the city on weekends, and hotels will offer special weekend rates to encourage more business. Be sure to ask.

Hotels in Chicago do not usually include meals in the room rate, though meal plans are sometimes available.

Two notable discount reservation agencies in Chicago are **Hot Rooms** and **Hotel Reservations Network**. Both charge a fee if you cancel for any reason.

## HIDDEN COSTS

ROOM RATES are usually quoted assuming double occupancy. But always ask; some hotels quote single-occupancy rates and charge as much as $35 per night for a second person.

Keep in mind, too, that a room with a view will likely come at a premium.

Convenience costs money. Parking at your hotel can add as much as $30 a day to your bill. You will also pay a steep

**Guests relaxing in their suite at Palmer House Hilton *(see p134)***

Lobby of Hotel Allegro, inspired by the building's 1920 design *(see p134)*

premium for any drinks and snacks you take from the room's mini-bar.

A telephone call made from your room will cost substantially more than a telephone call made from the pay phone in the hotel lobby.

## HOW TO RESERVE

IF THERE IS one secret to finding a good room, it is planning. Reserve as far in advance as possible. Hotels can fill up quickly when a convention is in town.

Reservations usually require a deposit by credit card. You will be given a confirmation or reservation number when you book. Always confirm your reservation before arriving at the hotel.

If you have special requirements, such as a quiet room away from busy streets, elevators, and ice machines, make these known when booking a room.

Notify the hotel if you expect to arrive later than 5 pm, or you may lose your reservation. If you need to cancel your reservation, it is advisable to record the cancelation number you are given, in case you are later charged for the room. Most hotels do not charge a cancelation fee if you give 24 or 48 hours' notice. Without sufficient notice, you may be charged for the room.

## TRAVELERS WITH DISABILITIES

HOTELS IN THE US are by law required to provide facilities for wheelchair-bound persons (some older properties are exempt). Most establishments are eager to provide rooms and assistance to travelers with disabilities. Persons with visual impairments may bring guide dogs into hotels.

## TRAVELING WITH CHILDREN

CHILDREN ARE WELCOME in all Chicago hotels, and few charge extra when one or two children under 12 stay in their parent's room. Ask about family rates when making reservations, and make sure the room is suitable. The hotel may offer a room with two beds or a sofa that easily converts to a bed. Many hotels will provide a cot for an additional $15 to $35 a night. Suite hotel rooms are also a good option.

French Deco living room, Hotel Monaco *(see p134)*

## BED-AND-BREAKFASTS

A BED-AND-BREAKFAST is a charming alternative to a hotel. Primarily in residential neighborhoods, such accommodations range from rooms in Victorian homes to rooms in high-rise buildings. Some have private bathrooms. In general, bed-and-breakfasts are very reasonably priced. For information call **Bed and Breakfast Chicago**.

# Choosing a Hotel

THESE HOTELS HAVE BEEN SELECTED across a wide price range for their good value, facilities, and location. Rooms have private bath, TV, and air-conditioning, and are wheelchair accessible unless otherwise noted. Fitness facilities and pool may be off-site. Some hotels are pet-friendly; ask when making a reservation. Hotels are listed by area, starting with downtown. For map references, see pages 190–97.

| | | NUMBER OF ROOMS | BUSINESS FACILITIES | RESTAURANT | CONCIERGE |
|---|---|---|---|---|---|

## DOWNTOWN CORE

**TRAVELODGE DOWNTOWN CHICAGO. Map 4 D3.** ⑤ | 250 | | ■ | |
65 E Harrison St, Chicago, IL 60605. 📞 427-8000 or (800) 525-9055. 📠 427-8261.
🔲 www.travelodge.com This budget hotel offers all the conveniences of downtown: within walking distance of shopping in the Loop, theaters, and museums. The hotel is not fully wheelchair accessible. 🗲 🅿 🏃 🍸 🥢

**HOTEL ALLEGRO. Map 3 C1.** ⑤⑤⑤ | 483 | ● | ■ | ●
171 W Randolph St, Chicago, IL 60601. 📞 236-0123 or (800) 643-1500. 📠 236-3440.
@ reservations@allegro.com 🔲 www.allegrochicago.com This Art Deco hotel, part of the Kimpton chain, is located in Chicago's theater district. Live music in the lobby accompanies the nightly wine reception. Ask about weekend specials that include tickets to local shows. 🗲 🅿 🏃 🍸 🍴 🥢

**HOTEL BURNHAM. Map 3 C1.** ⑤⑤⑤ | 122 | | ■ | ●
1 W Washington St, Chicago, IL 60602. 📞 782-1111 or (877) 294-9712. 📠 782-0899.
🔲 www.burnhamhotel.com Originally designed by Daniel Burnham in 1895 (see p50), the remodeled steel-and-glass Reliance Building is just minutes from the theater district. This Kimpton hotel is pet-friendly. 🗲 🅿 🏃 🍸 🍴 🥢

**PALMER HOUSE HILTON. Map 3 C2.** ⑤⑤⑤ | 1639 | ● | ■ | ●
17 E Monroe St, Chicago, IL 60603. 📞 726-7500 or (800) 445-8667. 📠 917-1707.
🔲 www.hilton.com Exquisite paintings on the ceiling complete the rich decor in this upscale hotel's lobby. Rooms are pleasant but not quite as splendid. Minutes from the Art Institute of Chicago and Grant Park. 🗲 🅿 🏃 🍸 🍴 ♒ 🥢

**RENAISSANCE CHICAGO HOTEL. Map 3 C2.** ⑤⑤⑤ | 553 | ● | ■ | ●
1 W Wacker Dr, Chicago, IL 60601. 📞 372-7200 or (800) 228-9290. 📠 795-3474.
🔲 www.renaissancehotels.com Friendly service and richly appointed rooms overlooking the river. The fee for Club Level, which includes complimentary breakfast and evening hors d'oeuvres, is worth it. 🗲 🅿 🏃 🍸 🍴 ♒ 🥢

**SWISSOTEL CHICAGO. Map 4 E1.** ⑤⑤⑤ | 632 | ● | ■ | ●
323 E Wacker Dr, Chicago, IL 60601. 📞 565-0565 or (800) 637-9477. 📠 565-0540.
@ emailus.chicago@swissotel.com 🔲 www.swissotel.com This hotel has a handsome wood-trimmed lobby and oversized luxury rooms with breathtaking views of Lake Michigan or Grant Park. 🗲 🅿 🏃 🍸 🍴 ♒ 🥢

**EXECUTIVE PLAZA. Map 4 D1.** ⑤⑤⑤⑤ | 421 | ● | ■ | ●
71 E Wacker Dr, Chicago, IL 60601. 📞 346-7100 or (800) 621-4005. 📠 346-1721.
🔲 www.executive-plaza.com This hotel overlooking the Chicago River offers comfort, location, and convenience, close to Michigan Avenue. Guests staying in the hotel's tower are treated to many extras. 🗲 🅿 🏃 🍸 🍴 🥢

**FAIRMONT HOTEL. Map 4 D1.** ⑤⑤⑤⑤ | 692 | ● | ■ | ●
200 N Columbus Dr, Chicago, IL 60601. 📞 565-8000 or (800) 866-5577. 📠 861-3656.
@ chicago@fairmont.com 🔲 www.fairmont.com Contemporary rooms with large bathrooms and all the extras. Guests may use the Illinois Center Athletic Club for a fee. Room rates may be lower on the weekend. 🗲 🅿 🍸 🍴 ♒ 🥢

**HOTEL MONACO. Map 4 D1.** ⑤⑤⑤⑤ | 192 | | ■ | ●
225 N Wabash Ave, Chicago, IL 60601. 📞 960-8500 or (866) 610-0081. 📠 960-1883.
🔲 www.monaco-chicago.com The front desk, modeled after a steamer trunk, epitomizes the travel theme of this Kimpton-chain hotel. Goldfish are available to keep you company in your room; wine is served in the evening. The hotel's limited business facilities include a meeting room. 🗲 🅿 🏃 🍸 🍴 🥢

**HYATT REGENCY CHICAGO. Map 4 D5.** ⑤⑤⑤⑤ | 2019 | ● | ■ | ●
151 E Wacker Dr, Chicago, IL 60601. 📞 565-1234 or (800) 233-1234. 📠 565-2966.
🔲 www.hyatt.com/usa This hotel offers immaculate, contemporary rooms in a spectacular downtown setting. Its beautiful atrium contains a sparkling fountain surrounded by ficus trees. 🗲 🅿 🍸 🍴 🥢

| | | | | |
|---|---|---|---|---|
| **Price categories** for a standard double room per night, including tax and service (prices will fluctuate depending on arrival date and availability):<br><br>⑤ under $100<br>⑤⑤ $100–$180<br>⑤⑤⑤ $180–$260<br>⑤⑤⑤⑤ over $260 | **BUSINESS FACILITIES**<br>Message service; desk and telephone in each room; meeting room, Internet access, and fax and copy machine within the hotel.<br>**RESTAURANT**<br>Hotel restaurant or dining room, usually also open to nonresidents.<br>**CONCIERGE**<br>Available to advise, make reservations, secure tickets. | NUMBER OF ROOMS | BUSINESS FACILITIES | RESTAURANT | CONCIERGE |

| Hotel | | Rooms | Bus. | Rest. | Conc. |
|---|---|---|---|---|---|
| **THE SILVERSMITH**. Map 4 D2.<br>10 S Wabash Ave, Chicago, IL 60603. 📞 372-7696 or (800) 227-6963. FAX 372-7320.<br>@ crowneplazachicago@att.net ⓦ www.sixcontinentshotels.com This Arts-and-Crafts-style Crowne Plaza hotel, in a historic landmark building, offers comfort and excellent service. Rooms have high windows and ceilings. 🚭 P ♿ 🍴 📺 ✉ | ⑤⑤⑤⑤ | 143 | ● | ■ | ● |
| **W CHICAGO CITY CENTER**. Map 3 C2.<br>172 W Adams St, Chicago, IL 60603. 📞 332-1200 or (800) 621-2360. FAX 917-5771.<br>ⓦ www.starwood.com/whotels Formerly the Midland Hotel, this hotel's recent refurbishing offers guests spacious, comfortable rooms, some with velvet chaise longues. The day spa provides pampering, for a fee. 🚭 P ♿ 🍴 📺 ⚊ ✉ | ⑤⑤⑤⑤ | 390 | ● | ■ | ● |

## NORTH SIDE

| Hotel | | Rooms | Bus. | Rest. | Conc. |
|---|---|---|---|---|---|
| **CASS HOTEL**. Map 2 D4.<br>640 N Wabash Ave, Chicago, IL 60611. 📞 787-4030 or (800) 227-7850. FAX 787-8544.<br>ⓦ www.casshotel.com This hotel, dating from 1927, offers reasonably priced rooms. Rooms with a sink and refrigerator are handy for families. Data ports in rooms; parking next door. Not fully wheelchair accessible. 🚭 P ♿ 🍴 ✉ | ⑤ | 155 | | ■ | |
| **OHIO HOUSE MOTEL**. Map 1 C5.<br>600 N LaSalle St, Chicago, IL 60610. 📞 943-6000. FAX 943-6063.<br>This 1950s-style hotel, located in one of the most popular areas of the city, near Magnificent Mile shopping, is a true gem for the price. Rooms are clean, if plain; the staff helpful. Not wheelchair accessible. Free guest parking. 🚭 P ♿ ✉ | ⑤ | 50 | | ■ | ● |
| **BEST WESTERN INN OF CHICAGO**. Map 2 D5.<br>162 E Ohio St, Chicago, IL 60611. 📞 787-3100 or (800) 557-2378. FAX 573-3136.<br>ⓦ www.bestwestern.com This hotel, a member of the famous Best Western chain, offers comfortable rooms just one block from the Magnificent Mile and shopping splendor. Also close to nightlife and Navy Pier. 🚭 P ♿ 🍴 📺 ✉ | ⑤⑤ | 354 | ● | ■ | ● |
| **BEST WESTERN RIVER NORTH HOTEL**. Map 2 D5.<br>125 W Ohio St, Chicago, IL 60610. 📞 467-0800 or (800) 727-0800. FAX 467-1665.<br>ⓦ www.bestwestern.com Clean, comfortable accommodation in the heart of the city. Rooms have tiled bathrooms and floor-to-ceiling windows that open; beds have cozy duvets and four pillows each. The rooftop sundeck offers a fantastic view of the city. Free parking for guests. 🚭 P ♿ 🍴 📺 ⚊ ✉ | ⑤⑤ | 150 | | ■ | ● |
| **GOLD COAST GUEST HOUSE**. Map 1 C3.<br>113 W Elm St, Chicago, IL 60610. 📞 337-0361. FAX 337-0362. ⓦ www.bbchicago.com Located in an 1873 townhouse, this guest house is quaint and comfortable. A secluded garden, living room, and dining room provide quiet elegance. Complimentary continental breakfast. Not wheelchair accessible. 🚭 P ✉ | ⑤⑤ | 4 | ● | | ● |
| **HOLIDAY INN CHICAGO CITY CENTER**. Map 2 E5.<br>300 E Ohio St, Chicago, IL 60611. 📞 787-6100 or (800) 465-4329. FAX 787-6259.<br>@ info@chicc.com ⓦ www.sixcontinentshotels.com/holiday-inn This hotel offers clean rooms and one of the finest hotel-connected spa and sports clubs in the city. It tends to cater to business travelers during the week, to tourists on the weekends. Minutes to Navy Pier. 🚭 P ♿ 🍴 📺 ⚊ ✉ | ⑤⑤ | 500 | ● | ■ | ● |
| **HOWARD JOHNSON INN**. Map 1 C4.<br>720 N LaSalle St, Chicago, IL 60610. 📞 664-8100 or (800) 446-4656. FAX 664-2365.<br>ⓦ www.hojo.com This classic two-story Howard Johnson is perfect for those adverse to high prices and tall buildings. Some business facilities in suites; limited free guest parking available. 🚭 P ♿ ✉ | ⑤⑤ | 71 | | ■ | |
| **OLD TOWN BED AND BREAKFAST**. Map 1 C1.<br>1442 N North Park Ave, Chicago, IL 60610. 📞 440-9268. FAX 440-2378.<br>ⓦ www.oldtownchicago.com This B & B, in an Art Deco mansion on a tree-lined street, is close to shops and the beach. It has hypoallergenic facilities. Free guest parking but no wheelchair access. 🚭 P 📺 ✉ | ⑤⑤ | 4 | | | |

For key to symbols see back flap

| | | | |
|---|---|---|---|
| **Price categories** for a standard double room per night, including tax and service (prices will fluctuate depending on arrival date and availability):<br><br>⑤ under $100<br>⑤⑤ $100–$180<br>⑤⑤⑤ $180–$260<br>⑤⑤⑤⑤ over $260 | **BUSINESS FACILITIES**<br>Message service; desk and telephone in each room; meeting room, Internet access, and fax and copy machine within the hotel.<br><br>**RESTAURANT**<br>Hotel restaurant or dining room, usually also open to nonresidents.<br><br>**CONCIERGE**<br>Available to advise, make reservations, secure tickets. | | |

| | | NUMBER OF ROOMS | BUSINESS FACILITIES | RESTAURANT | CONCIERGE |
|---|---|---|---|---|---|
| **RED ROOF INN – CHICAGO DOWNTOWN**. Map 2 D4.<br>162 E Ontario St, Chicago, IL 60611. ☎ 787-3580 or (800) 733-7663. FAX 787-1299.<br>W www.redroof.com Excellent value and comfort for the price; kids stay free with adult. The rooms are not fancy, but the motel is in a good location, close to Michigan Avenue and Navy Pier. 🎫 P 🏃 🅿 | ⑤⑤ | 191 | | ■ | |
| **SENECA HOTEL**. Map 2 D4.<br>200 E Chestnut St, Chicago, IL 60610. ☎ 787-8900 or (800) 800-6261. FAX 988-4438.<br>W www.senecahotel.com Originally an apartment complex, the building housing this hotel boasts spacious deluxe rooms and suites, each with a kitchen or kitchenette. Excellent personal service, and conveniently located between Water Tower Place and the John Hancock Center. 🎫 P 🏃 Y 🍴 🅿 | ⑤⑤ | 130 | ● | ■ | ● |
| **AMBASSADOR WEST**. Map 1 C2.<br>1300 N State Pkwy, Chicago, IL 60610. ☎ 787-3700 or (866) 229-3272. FAX 640-2967.<br>Although not quite as upscale as the Omni Ambassador East (see p137), to which it is connected by a walkway, the Ambassador West offers a charming old-world atmosphere and elegance. 🎫 P 🏃 Y 🍴 🅿 | ⑤⑤⑤ | 219 | | ■ | ● |
| **CLARIDGE HOTEL**. Map 1 C1.<br>1244 N Dearborn Pkwy, Chicago, IL 60610. ☎ 787-4980 or (800) 245-1258. FAX 266-0978.<br>W www.claridgehotel.com This hotel, on a tree-lined street, is a short walk from the best shopping, dining, and nightlife Chicago has to offer. Comfortable, elegant rooms. Complimentary continental breakfast. 🎫 P 🏃 Y 🍴 🅿 | ⑤⑤⑤ | 161 | ● | ■ | ● |
| **COURTYARD BY MARRIOTT CHICAGO DOWNTOWN**. Map 2 D5.<br>30 E Hubbard St, Chicago, IL 60611. ☎ 329-2500 or (800) 321-2211. FAX 329-0293.<br>W www.courtyard.com Large, comfortable rooms, each with desk, work chair, and data ports, provide space to work or plan the next day's sightseeing. Located on a quiet street in the busy River North neighborhood, the hotel is close to Navy Pier and the Magnificent Mile. 🎫 P Y 🍴 ♒ 🅿 | ⑤⑤⑤ | 334 | ● | ■ | ● |
| **FITZPATRICK CHICAGO HOTEL**. Map 2 D4.<br>166 E Superior St, Chicago, IL 60611. ☎ 787-6000 or (800) 367-7701. FAX 787-6133.<br>@ reservations@fitzpatrickhotels.com W www.fitzpatrickhotels.com This elegant boutique hotel has authentic Irish furnishings (from Waterford crystal chandeliers to an Irish pub) and an intimate atmosphere. 🎫 P 🏃 Y 🍴 ♒ 🅿 | ⑤⑤⑤ | 143 | ● | ■ | ● |
| **HILTON GARDEN INN CHICAGO DOWNTOWN NORTH**. Map 2 D5.<br>10 E Grand Ave, Chicago, IL 60611. ☎ 595-0000 or (800) 445-8667. FAX 595-0955.<br>W www.hilton.com Opened in 1999, this hotel features a 24-hour business center. Rooms have oversized desks and two telephones, as well as a refrigerator and microwave. Near the Magnificent Mile. 🎫 P 🏃 Y 🍴 ♒ 🅿 | ⑤⑤⑤ | 363 | ● | ■ | ● |
| **HOUSE OF BLUES HOTEL**. Map 1 C5.<br>333 N Dearborn St, Chicago, IL 60610. ☎ 245-0333 or (877) 569-3742. FAX 923-2444.<br>W www.loewshotels.com/houseofblueshome.html The eclectically designed Moroccan-style rooms come with many extras, including stereo systems and VCRs. The hotel is connected to a bowling alley with 36 lanes and to the House of Blues music hall (see p165). 🎫 P 🏃 Y 🍴 🅿 | ⑤⑤⑤ | 367 | ● | ■ | ● |
| **LENOX SUITES**. Map 2 D4.<br>616 N Rush St, Chicago, IL 60611. ☎ 337-1000 or (800) 445-3664. FAX 337-7217.<br>W www.lenoxsuites.com Each suite has a kitchen. Fine accommodations for the price, in an excellent location. Complimentary morning muffin and juice. The hotel is not fully wheelchair accessible. 🎫 P 🏃 Y 🍴 🅿 | ⑤⑤⑤ | 324 | ● | ■ | ● |
| **MARRIOTT RESIDENCE INN**. Map 2 D3.<br>201 E Walton Pl, Chicago, IL 60611. ☎ 943-9800 or (800) 331-3131. FAX 943-8579.<br>W www.Residenceinn.com Close to Chicago's top tourist destinations, here you'll find comfortable, clean rooms, each with a kitchen. Meals on demand from local restaurants; complimentary continental breakfast.<br>🎫 P 🏃 🍴 ♒ 🅿 | ⑤⑤⑤ | 221 | ● | | |

**MILLENNIUM KNICKERBOCKER HOTEL.** Map 2 D3. $$$ | 305
163 E Walton Pl, Chicago, IL 60611. 751-8100 or (866) 866-8086. FAX 751-9205.
www.millennium-hotels.com Luxurious rooms and personalized pampering are just two of the features of this hotel, which also claims to serve the best martini in town. Located near fashionable Oak Street.

**OMNI AMBASSADOR EAST.** Map 1 C2. $$$ | 285
1301 N State Pkwy, Chicago, IL 60610. 787-7200 or (800) 843-6664. FAX 787-4760.
www.omnihotels.com This hotel, in a national historic landmark building, recently underwent a $20-million restoration and has some of the most lavish rooms in Chicago. A favorite of celebrities and authors.

**PARK HYATT CHICAGO.** Map 2 D4. $$$ | 203
800 N Michigan Ave, Chicago, IL 60611. 335-1234 or (800) 233-1234. FAX 239-4000.
www.hyatt.com/usa The rooms in this new European-style hotel, the Park Hyatt's flagship, boasts custom-designed furniture, including the BRNO chair by Ludwig Mies van der Rohe. Other details reflect the styles of 20th-century architects Frank Lloyd Wright and Le Corbusier.

**RAPHAEL HOTEL.** Map 2 D3. $$$ | 172
201 E Delaware Pl, Chicago, IL 60622. 943-5000 or (800) 983-7870. FAX 943-9483.
www.raphaelchicago.com This elegant hotel offers old-world charm and superb service. Guests may use the fitness center at the nearby Tremont Hotel (see p137).

**TALBOTT HOTEL.** Map 2 D3. $$$ | 149
20 E Delaware Pl, Chicago, IL 60611. 944-4970 or (800) 223-5652. FAX 944-7241.
www.talbotthotel.com Converted in the late 1970s from a 1920s apartment building to an upscale hotel, the Talbott, on a pleasant tree-lined street in the heart of the Gold Coast, is a soothing oasis in the city. All extras, such as nightly turn-down and morning paper, are included.

**TREMONT HOTEL.** Map 2 D4. $$$ | 130
100 E Chestnut St, Chicago, IL 60611. 751-1900 or (800) 621-8133. FAX 751-8691.
www.tremonthotel.com Located just off Michigan Avenue, this European-style hotel offers cozy, comfortable lodgings. The lobby, with its carved-wood ceiling, has an English-country atmosphere. The hotel is not fully wheelchair accessible.

**ALLERTON CROWNE PLAZA.** Map 2 D4. $$$$ | 443
701 N Michigan Ave, Chicago, IL 60611. 440-1500 or (800) 227-6963. FAX 440-1819.
@ info@allertoncrowneplaza.com www.allertoncrowneplaza.com Following a $39-million restoration, this hotel, in a historic building on the Magnificent Mile, features European decor and luxurious amenities.

**CHICAGO MARRIOTT DOWNTOWN.** Map 2 D5. $$$$ | 1192
540 N Michigan Ave, Chicago, IL 60611. 836-0100 or (800) 228-0265. FAX 836-6139.
www.marriott.com This hotel, on the Magnificent Mile, is ideally situated for shopping and visiting many of Chicago's major attractions. Great views of Lake Michigan from the upper floors.

**DOUBLETREE GUEST SUITES.** Map 2 D3. $$$$ | 345
198 E Delaware Pl, Chicago, IL 60611. 664-1100 or (800) 222-8733. FAX 664-8627.
www.doubletree.com Your stay at this hotel begins with warm chocolate-chip cookies upon check-in. Each room is wired and furnished for business. Located across the street from John Hancock Center.

**DRAKE HOTEL.** Map 2 D3. $$$$ | 537
140 E Walton Pl, Chicago, IL 60611. 787-2200 or (800) 553-7253. FAX 787-1431.
www.hilton.com From your first step into the lobby, it is apparent that the Drake lives up to its reputation for service and luxury. Each spacious room is individually designed and offers an excellent view.

**EMBASSY SUITES CHICAGO.** Map 2 D4. $$$$ | 358
600 N State St, Chicago, IL 60610. 943-3800 or (800) 362-2779. FAX 943-7629.
@ info@embassysuiteschicago.com www.embassysuiteschicago.com Handsome Biedermeier furnishings in each of the two-room suites. Not fully wheelchair accessible.

**FOUR SEASONS HOTEL.** Map 2 D3. $$$$ | 343
120 E Delaware Pl, Chicago, IL 60611. 280-8800 or (800) 332-3442. FAX 280-1748.
www.fourseasons.com The Four Seasons Hotel provides unparalleled service and accommodations. This location has the only hotel outdoor rooftop jogging track in the city.

For key to symbols see back flap

<table>
<tr><td>

**Price categories** for a standard double room per night, including tax and service (prices will fluctuate depending on arrival date and availability):

$ under $100
$$ $100–$180
$$$ $180–$260
$$$$ over $260

</td><td>

**BUSINESS FACILITIES**
Message service; desk and telephone in each room; meeting room, Internet access, and fax and copy machine within the hotel.
**RESTAURANT**
Hotel restaurant or dining room, usually also open to nonresidents.
**CONCIERGE**
Available to advise, make reservations, secure tickets.

</td></tr>
</table>

| | NUMBER OF ROOMS | BUSINESS FACILITIES | RESTAURANT | CONCIERGE |
|---|---|---|---|---|
| **HOTEL INTER-CONTINENTAL CHICAGO. Map 2 D5.** $$$$ <br> 505 N Michigan Ave, Chicago, IL 60611. **(** 944-4100 or (800) 628-2112. FAX 944-1320. <br> @ chicago@interconti.com W www.chicago.interconti.com The South Tower, the epitome of historic elegance, features a bar with a 1920s atmosphere (see p62). The rooms in the rather nondescript North Tower have excellent views. ⚡ P ♿ Ⓨ 📺 ♨ 🍴 | 807 | ● | ■ | ● |
| **OMNI CHICAGO HOTEL. Map 2 D4.** $$$$ <br> 676 N Michigan Ave, Chicago, IL 60611. **(** 944-6664 or (800) 843-6664. FAX 266-3015. <br> W www.omnihotels.com Mahogany and imported marble accentuates the vaulted ceilings and Art Deco furnishings in this hotel's common areas. Each room includes a parlor separated from the bedroom by French doors. Complimentary hors d'oeuvres and weekday bar buffet. ⚡ P ♿ Ⓨ 📺 ♨ 🍴 | 347 | ● | ■ | ● |
| **RITZ-CARLTON CHICAGO. Map 2 D4.** $$$$ <br> 160 E Pearson St, Chicago, IL 60611. **(** 266-1000 or (800) 621-6906. FAX 266-1194. <br> W www.fourseasons.com Located above Water Tower Place, Ritz-Carlton (owned by the Four Seasons chain) provides the service and satisfaction one expects from a world-renowned hotel company. ⚡ P ♿ Ⓨ 📺 ♨ 🍴 | 435 | ● | ■ | ● |
| **SHERATON CHICAGO HOTEL AND TOWERS. Map 2 E5.** $$$$ <br> 301 E North Water St, Chicago, IL 60611. **(** 464-1000 or (877) 242-2558. FAX 329-6929. <br> W www.sheratonchicago.com Ideally situated, this hotel has beautifully appointed guest rooms overlooking the Chicago River and Lake Michigan. Tower guests receive deluxe treatment. ⚡ P ♿ Ⓨ 📺 ♨ 🍴 | 1209 | ● | ■ | ● |
| **SUTTON PLACE HOTEL. Map 2 D3.** $$$$ <br> 21 E Bellevue Pl, Chicago, IL 60611. **(** 266-2100 or (800) 606-8188. FAX 266-2141. <br> @ info@chi.suttonplace.com W www.suttonplace.com This hotel's stunning Art Deco interior features original prints by American photographer Robert Mapplethorpe. ⚡ P ♿ Ⓨ 📺 🍴 | 246 | ● | ■ | ● |
| **W CHICAGO LAKESHORE. Map 2 E4.** $$$$ <br> 644 N Lake Shore Dr, Chicago, IL 60611. **(** 943-9200 or (800) 621-2360. FAX 255-4411. <br> W www.whotels.com One of latest offerings from the W chain, this luxurious hotel offers breathtaking views of Chicago's skyline or lakefront from all the rooms. Within walking distance of the lake and Navy Pier. ⚡ P ♿ Ⓨ 📺 ♨ 🍴 | 556 | ● | ■ | ● |
| **WESTIN MICHIGAN AVENUE. Map 2 D3.** $$$$ <br> 909 N Michigan Ave, Chicago, IL 60611. **(** 943-7200 or (800) 228-3000. FAX 397-5580. <br> W www.westinmichiganave.com Providing all the comforts of home, this hotel recently renovated all its rooms. The beds have been upgraded to feature "heavenly" 1-foot- (30-cm-) thick mattresses. ⚡ P ♿ Ⓨ 📺 🍴 | 751 | ● | ■ | ● |
| **WESTIN RIVER NORTH. Map 1 C5.** $$$$ <br> 320 N Dearborn St, Chicago, IL 60610. **(** 744-1900 or (877) 866-9216. FAX 527-2650. <br> W www.westinrivernorth.com All rooms have an elegant, residential atmosphere. The large marble bathrooms include hair driers, magnifying mirrors, robes, and exclusive toiletries. Gourmet coffee in all rooms. ⚡ P ♿ Ⓨ 📺 🍴 | 424 | ● | ■ | ● |
| **WHITEHALL HOTEL. Map 2 D3.** $$$$ <br> 105 E Delaware Pl, Chicago, IL 60611. **(** 944-6300 or (800) 948-4255. FAX 944-8552. <br> W www.whitehallchicago.com Following an extensive renovation, this hotel offers technological conveniences along with old-world charm and excellent service. Not fully wheelchair accessible. ⚡ P ♿ Ⓨ 📺 🍴 | 221 | ● | ■ | ● |

## SOUTH LOOP AND NEAR SOUTH SIDE

| | | | | |
|---|---|---|---|---|
| **BEST WESTERN GRANT PARK HOTEL. Map 4 D4.** $$ <br> 1100 S Michigan Ave, Chicago, IL 60605. **(** 922-2900 or (800) 472-6875. FAX 922-8812. <br> W www.bestwestern.com The prime location of this older high-rise hotel allows for easy access to Grant Park, as well as to the Museum Campus and McCormick Place. Data ports in each room. ⚡ P ♿ 📺 ♨ 🍴 | 172 | ● | ■ | |

**CONGRESS PLAZA HOTEL. Map 4 D3.** 🅢🅢 | 852
520 S Michigan Ave, Chicago, IL 60605. 🎧 427-3800 or (800) 635-1666. ᖴᴀX 427-3307.
🆆 www.congressplazahotel.com This hotel has much of the same charm it had
when it was built in 1893 for the World's Fair. Rooms are large, some with views
of Grant Park and the lake. Not fully wheelchair accessible. 🔁 🅟 🕴 🍸 🍴 🌀

**ESSEX INN. Map 4 D3.** 🅢🅢 | 255
800 S Michigan Ave, Chicago, IL 60605. 🎧 939-2800 or (800) 621-6909. ᖴᴀX 939-0526.
🆆 www.sagehospitality.com An intimate, informal hotel near Grant Park. Many
rooms have an excellent view of the city and lake. Courtesy shuttle bus to
the Loop, Magnificent Mile, and State Street shops. 🔁 🅟 🕴 🍸 🍴 ♒ 🌀

**HILTON CHICAGO. Map 4 D3.** 🅢🅢🅢 | 1544
720 S Michigan Ave, Chicago, IL 60605. 🎧 922-4400 or (800) 445-8667. ᖴᴀX 922-5240.
🆆 www.chicagohilton.com The Hilton provides spacious rooms and excellent
service. Executive class rooms come with many extras worth the higher price.
Located close to museums and nightlife. 🔁 🅟 🍸 🍴 ♒ 🌀

**HYATT ON PRINTER'S ROW. Map 3 C3.** 🅢🅢🅢 | 161
500 S Dearborn St, Chicago, IL 60605. 🎧 986-1234 or (800) 233-1234. ᖴᴀX 939-2468.
🆆 www.hyatt.com Large, comfortable rooms in a national historic landmark building that was once a print shop. Business travelers receive excellent extras for
a small fee. Its Prairie restaurant (see p150) is award winning. 🔁 🅟 🕴 🍸 🌀

**HYATT REGENCY MCCORMICK PLACE. Map 5 E2.** 🅢🅢🅢 | 800
2233 S Martin Luther King Jr. Dr, Chicago, IL 60616. 🎧 567-1234 or (800) 233-1234.
ᖴᴀX 528-4189. 🆆 www.hyatt.com/usa This hotel is connected to McCormick
Place via a walkway that leads to all the exposition buildings. Fifty rooms
have telescopes for great views of the lake and skyline. 🔁 🅟 🕴 🍸 🍴 ♒ 🌀

## SOUTH SIDE

**RAMADA INN LAKE SHORE. Map 7 E1.** 🅢🅢 | 184
4900 S Lake Shore Dr, Chicago, IL 60615. 🎧 (773) 288-5800 or (800) 228-2828.
ᖴᴀX (773) 288-5745. 🆆 www.the.ramada.com/chicago00538 Newly renovated
rooms provide comfort and convenience at an affordable price. Courtesy
shuttle bus to popular sights; free guest parking. 🔁 🅟 🕴 🍸 ♒ 🌀

**WOODED ISLE SUITES. Map 7 F5.** 🅢🅢 | 13
5750 Stony Island Ave, Chicago, IL 60637. 🎧 (773) 288-6305 or (800) 290-6844. ᖴᴀX (773)
288-8972. 🅐 reserve@woodedisle.com 🆆 www.woodedisle.com Vintage-style suites with
kitchenettes; free street parking. Not wheelchair accessible. 🔁 🕴 🌀

## FARTHER AFIELD

**LAKEVIEW: Best Western Hawthorne Terrace.** 🅢🅢 | 59
3434 N Broadway St, Chicago, IL 60657. 🎧 (773) 244-3434 or (888) 675-2378.
ᖴᴀX (773) 244-3435. 🆆 www.bestwestern.com The fireplace in the Colonial-style
lobby warms up guests after a day of touring. Standard rooms, many with micro-
wave and refrigerator. Complimentary continental breakfast. 🅟 🕴 🍸 🍴 🌀

**LAKEVIEW: City Suites.** 🅢🅢 | 45
933 W Belmont Ave, Chicago, IL 60657. 🎧 (773) 404-3400 or (800) 248-9108. ᖴᴀX (773)
404-3405. 🆆 www.cityinns.com This Neighborhood Inn of Chicago (one of
three) has been restored to Art Deco style. Data ports in rooms;
complimentary continental breakfast. Not wheelchair accessible. 🔁 🅟 🕴 🌀

**LAKEVIEW: House of Two Urns.** 🅢🅢 | 5
1239 N Greenview Ave, Chicago, IL 60622. 🎧 (773) 235-1408 or (877) 896-8767.
ᖴᴀX (773) 235-1410. 🅐 twourns@earthlink.net 🆆 www.twourns.com This B & B
offers cozy rooms decorated with antiques and artworks. Shared bathroom;
complimentary continental breakfast. Not wheelchair accessible. 🔁 🅟 🕴 🌀

**LAKEVIEW: Majestic Hotel.** 🅢🅢 | 52
528 W Brompton Ave, Chicago, IL 60657. 🎧 (773) 404-3499 or (800) 727-5108. ᖴᴀX (773)
404-3495. 🆆 www.cityinns.com This English-style Neighborhood Inn (one of
three) provides comfort at a reasonable price. Data ports in rooms;
complimentary continental breakfast. Not wheelchair accessible. 🔁 🅟 🌀

**LINCOLN PARK: Arlington House International Hostel and Hotel.** 🅢 | 250
616 W Arlington Pl, Chicago, IL 60614. 🎧 (773) 929-5380 or (800) 467-8355. ᖴᴀX (773)
665-5485. 🆆 www.arlingtonhouse.com Both dormitory and private rooms are
available at this hostel, which offers 24-hour check-in, linen rental, and
luggage storage. Hostel membership may be required for discount. 🔁 🌀

For key to symbols see back flap

| | | | |
|---|---|---|---|
| **Price categories** for a standard double room per night, including tax and service (prices will fluctuate depending on arrival date and availability):<br><br>⑤ under $100<br>⑤⑤ $100–$180<br>⑤⑤⑤ $180–$260<br>⑤⑤⑤⑤ over $260 | **BUSINESS FACILITIES**<br>Message service; desk and telephone in each room; meeting room, Internet access, and fax and copy machine within the hotel.<br>**RESTAURANT**<br>Hotel restaurant or dining room, usually also open to nonresidents.<br>**CONCIERGE**<br>Available to advise, make reservations, secure tickets. | | |

| | | NUMBER OF ROOMS | BUSINESS FACILITIES | RESTAURANT | CONCIERGE |
|---|---|---|---|---|---|
| **LINCOLN PARK:** *City Scene Bed and Breakfast.* ⑤⑤<br>2101 N Clifton Ave, Chicago, IL 60614. **(** *(773) 549-1743.* **FAX** *(773) 529-4711.* **@** *cityscene@aol.com* **w** *www.cityscenebb.com* This B & B, in a Victorian building, offers one eclectically furnished suite, rented as either a one or two bedroom (shared bath). Not wheelchair accessible. 🛇 **P** | | 2 | | | |
| **LINCOLN PARK:** *Comfort Inn of Lincoln Park.* ⑤⑤<br>601 W Diversey Pkwy, Chicago, IL 60614. **(** *(773) 348-2810 or (800) 228-5150.* **FAX** *(773) 348-1912.* **w** *www.choicehotels.com* An affordable, clean inn. Breezes from the lake provide the only air-conditioning. Complimentary continental breakfast is a pleasant start to a day of touring. 🛇 **P** 🛉 🌀 | | 74 | | | |
| **LINCOLN PARK:** *Days Inn Lincoln Park North.* ⑤⑤<br>644 W Diversey Pkwy, Chicago, IL 60614. **(** *(773) 525-7010 or (888) 576-3297.* **FAX** *(773) 525-6998.* **w** *www.daysinn.com* This winner of the Days Inn Chairman's Award for consistent quality has been recently remodeled and finely appointed. Complimentary continental breakfast. 🛇 **P** 🛉 ⏻ 🍴 ♒ 🌀 | | 130 | ● | ■ | |
| **LINCOLN PARK:** *The Willows.* ⑤⑤<br>555 W Surf St, Chicago, IL 60657. **(** *(773) 528-8400 or (800) 787-3108.* **FAX** *(773) 528-8483.* **w** *www.cityinns.com* The floral decor of this Neighborhood Inn (one of three) exudes 19th-century French-country charm. Data ports in rooms; complimentary continental breakfast. Not wheelchair accessible. 🛇 **P** 🛉 🌀 | | 55 | | | ● |
| **LINCOLN PARK:** *Belden-Stratford Hotel.* ⑤⑤⑤<br>2300 N Lincoln Park W, Chicago, IL 60614. **(** *(773) 281-2900 or (800) 800-8301.* **FAX** *(312) 787-0573.* **@** *info@beldenstratford.com* **w** *www.beldenstratford.com* This hotel has a vintage façade and a dramatic two-story lobby. Located across from Lincoln Park Zoo and close to the theater district. Rooms come with data ports. Not fully wheelchair accessible. 🛇 **P** 🛉 ⏻ 🍴 🌀 | | 30 | | ■ | |
| **LINCOLN PARK:** *Windy City Bed and Breakfast Inn.* ⑤⑤⑤<br>607 W Deming Pl, Chicago, IL 60614. **(** *(773) 248-7091 or (877) 897-7091.* **FAX** *(773) 529-4123.* **w** *www.chicago-inn.com* Windy City combines Victorian details, such as fireplaces in some rooms (and no TVs), with modern luxury, such as whirlpool baths. The inn is not wheelchair accessible. 🛇 **P** 🌀 | | 8 | ● | | ● |
| **OAK PARK:** *Carleton of Oak Park Hotel.* ⑤⑤<br>1110 Pleasant St, Oak Park, IL 60302. **(** *(708) 848-5000 or (888) 227-5386.* **FAX** *(708) 848-0537.* **@** *info@carletonhotel.com* **w** *www.carletonhotel.com* Pleasant hotel minutes from specialty shops and boutiques. Conference facilities and complimentary use of a nearby health club. Free guest parking. 🛇 **P** 🛉 ⏻ 🍴 🌀 | | 154 | | ■ | ● |

## BEYOND CHICAGO

| | | NUMBER OF ROOMS | BUSINESS FACILITIES | RESTAURANT | CONCIERGE |
|---|---|---|---|---|---|
| **EVANSTON:** *Homestead Hotel.* ⑤⑤<br>1625 Hinman Ave, Evanston, IL 60201. **(** *1-847 475-3300.* **FAX** *(847) 570-8100.* **w** *www.thehomestead.net* Built in 1927 in the Williamsburg Colonial style, this hotel, near Northwestern University, offers genuine hospitality. Complimentary continental breakfast and guest parking. Not wheelchair accessible. 🛇 **P** 🌀 | | 91 | | ■ | |
| **EVANSTON:** *Margarita European Inn.* ⑤⑤<br>1566 Oak Ave, Evanston, IL 60201. **(** *1-847 869-2273.* **FAX** *(847) 869-2353.* **w** *www.margaritainn.com* Friendly, cozy accommodations in a Georgian mansion. Relax in the library or on the rooftop deck, with its great view of downtown, and enjoy the award-winning restaurant, Va Pensiero *(see p153).* Complimentary continental breakfast. Some rooms with shared bathroom. 🛇 **P** 🌀 | | 44 | ● | ■ | |
| **EVANSTON:** *Omni Orrington Hotel.* ⑤⑤⑤<br>1710 Orrington Ave, Evanston, IL 60201. **(** *1-847 866-8700 or (800) 843-6664.* **FAX** *(847) 866-8724.* **w** *www.omnihotels.com* An upscale hotel near public transit. Services at a health club and spa located at Northwestern University are available to guests but will cost extra. 🛇 **P** 🛉 ⏻ 🍴 ♒ 🌀 | | 277 | ● | ■ | ● |

**GALENA:** *Best Western Quiet House and Suites.* ⓢⓢ 42
9915 Route 20 E, Galena, IL 61036. 📞 *(815) 777-2577 or (800) 528-1234.*
📠 *(815) 777-0584.* 🌐 *www.bestwestern.com* This Best Western offers oversized rooms and suites with theme decors ranging from northwest frontier to high tech. Free parking for guests. ⮔ P 🏃 ▾ ♨ ✦

**GALENA:** *Chestnut Mountain Resort.* ⓢⓢ 120
8700 W Chestnut Rd, Galena, IL 61036. 📞 *(815) 777-1320 or (800) 397-1320.*
📠 *(815) 777-1068.* @ *reservations@chestnutmtn.com* 🌐 *www.chestnutmtn.com* A resort 8 miles (13 km) southeast of Galena, overlooking the Mississippi River. Prime skiing with 17 runs, and ski apparel and equipment rental. ⮔ P 🏃 ▾ ♨ ✦

**GALENA:** *Early American Settlement Log Cabin Lodging.* ⓢⓢ 12
9401 Hart John Rd, Galena, IL 61036. 📞 *(815) 777-4200 or (800) 366-5647.* 🌐 *www. easll.com* Replica one-room log cabins with period decor are situated on lovely grounds. Each cabin has a gas fireplace, VCR, refrigerator, and adjacent modern bathroom. Two cabins are wheelchair accessible. Free guest parking. P 🏃 ✦

**GALENA:** *Stoney Creek Inn.* ⓢⓢ 76
940 Galena Square Dr, Galena, IL 61036. 📞 *(815) 777-2223 or (800) 659-2220.*
📠 *(815) 777-6762.* 🌐 *www.stoneycreekinn.com* This inn offers charming, rustic lodgings. Children under 18 stay free with adult. Complimentary continental breakfast, free parking, and shuttle service for guests. ⮔ P 🏃 ▾ ♨ ✦

**GALENA:** *Eagle Ridge Inn and Resort.* ⓢⓢⓢ 470
444 Eagle Ridge Dr, Galena, IL 61036. 📞 *(815) 777-2444 or (800) 892-2269.* 📠 *(815) 777-5609.* 🌐 *www.eagleridge.com* A favorite destination in northern Illinois, 6 miles (10 km) east of Galena, this resort offers cross-country skiing, and golf on its award-winning courses. Free guest parking. ⮔ P 🏃 ▾ ♨ ✦

**LAKE GENEVA:** *Budget Host Diplomat Motel.* ⓢ 23
1060 Wells St, Lake Geneva, WI 53147. 📞 *(262) 248-1809 or (800) 264-5678.* 📠 *(262) 248-2455.* @ *rooms@budgethost-lakegeneva.com* 🌐 *www.budgethost-lakegeneva.com* Recreation grounds include volleyball, badminton, and picnicking areas. First floor is wheelchair accessible. Free guest parking. ⮔ P 🏃 ♨ ✦

**LAKE GENEVA:** *Best Western Harbor Shores.* ⓢⓢ 108
300 Wrigley Dr, Lake Geneva, WI 53147. 📞 *(262) 248-9181 or (888) 746-7371.*
📠 *(262) 248-1885.* 🌐 *www.bestwestern.com* Enjoy a fabulous view from one of the lakefront rooms or relax by the lobby's fireplace after a day of activities. Complimentary continental breakfast; free guest parking. ⮔ P 🏃 ▾ ♨ ✦

**LAKE GENEVA:** *Geneva Inn.* ⓢⓢ 37
N2009 State Rd 120, Lake Geneva, WI 53147. 📞 *(262) 248-5680 or (800) 441-5881.*
📠 *(262) 248-5685.* 🌐 *www.genevainn.com* An intimate inn with English charm. Cognac and chocolates with nightly turn-down are part of the personal service. Complimentary continental breakfast; free guest parking. ⮔ P 🏃 ▾ ✦

**LAKE GENEVA:** *Pederson Victorian Bed and Breakfast.* ⓢⓢ 4
1782 Highway 120 N, Lake Geneva, WI 53147. 📞 *(262) 248-9110 or (888) 764-9653.*
📠 *(262) 249-9830.* @ *pederson@pedersonvictorian.com* 🌐 *www.pedersonvictorian.com* This Victorian home whisks visitors back to the 1880s with its vintage furnishings (and no TVs or telephones). Some rooms with shared bathroom; free guest parking. Not wheelchair accessible. ⮔ P ✦

**LAKE GENEVA:** *Grand Geneva Resort and Spa.* ⓢⓢⓢ 355
7036 Grand Geneva Way, Lake Geneva, WI 53147. 📞 *(262) 248-8811 or (800) 558-3417.*
📠 *(262) 249-4763.* @ *grandgeneva.info@grandgeneva.com* 🌐 *www.grandgeneva.com* After skiing at this upscale resort's Mountain Top ski slopes or shopping in town, relax in the spacious lobby, complete with fireside bar. Weekend packages are available. Free parking for guests. ⮔ P 🏃 ▾ ♨ ✦

**LAKE GENEVA:** *Lake Lawn Resort.* ⓢⓢⓢ 284
2400 E Geneva St, Delavan, WI 53115. 📞 *(262) 728-7950 or (800) 338-5253.* 📠 *(262) 728-2347.* 🌐 *www.lakelawnresort.com* You will find rustic luxury at this resort, a 90-minute drive north of Chicago. Its spa offers packages designed to indulge the body and spirit, and its wooded grounds alongside Lake Delavan are ideal for a scenic hike. Free guest parking. ⮔ P 🏃 ▾ ♨ ✦

**LAKE GENEVA:** *T.C. Smith Inn Bed and Breakfast.* ⓢⓢⓢ 8
834 Dodge St, Lake Geneva, WI 53147. 📞 *(262) 248-1097 or (800) 423-0233.* 📠 *(262) 248-1672.* 🌐 *www.tcsmithinn.com* This inn, in a historic downtown building, offers elegant theme rooms, many with fireplace and whirlpool bath. Breakfast buffet; free parking. Not wheelchair accessible. ⮔ P 🏃 ✦

# RESTAURANTS AND CAFÉS

CHICAGO IS A BIG CITY and many establishments, from coffee shops to four-star restaurants, ask big-city prices. However, with thousands of places to eat and drink in Chicago, competition between restaurants is fierce, and visitors *can find great food at reasonable prices*. The city's immigrant roots mean you can sample dishes from around the world, from Greek and Italian dishes to Vietnamese and Korean specialties. If you're in Chicago during the annual Taste of Chicago festival *(see p31)*, you will be able to sample cuisine from dozens of Chicago's restaurants. Those in our listings, *Choosing a Restaurant* (pages 146–53), have been selected as the best Chicago offers.

**A waiter serving champagne**

## CHICAGO'S RESTAURANTS

CHICAGO restaurants represent the many cultures that make up the city. Some ethnic restaurants are clustered together, such as those in Chinatown *(see p94)* or on Greek Town's Halsted Street. Italian eateries abound on Taylor Street between Halsted and Western Avenues.

However, restaurants on the city's major streets offer a broad range of cuisine. Those in the Loop tend to cater to office workers, though many are staying open later as the area's theater district blossoms. River North is home to many of the city's premier restaurants. Numerous restaurants are situated farther north along Wells Street in Old Town and along nearby Lincoln and Halsted Avenues.

Although there are few strictly vegetarian restaurants in Chicago, most establishments offer vegetarian dishes. The menus at Amitabul *(see p151)* and Chicago Diner *(see p151)*, however, exclusively focus on vegetarian dishes.

Many restaurants are wheelchair accessible *(see p169)*.

## RESTAURANT MENUS

MOST MENUS offer three courses: appetizer (starter), entrée (main course), and dessert. Almost all restaurants, except fast-food, serve bread and butter at no charge. Water glasses are filled with (free) tap water; bottled water is usually available.

Most Italian menus list pasta as a first course before a main course of meat or fish, but many restaurants also treat pasta as an entrée.

Coffee and dessert conclude the meal. If you have coffee, your cup may be refilled until you refuse any more.

## OTHER PLACES TO EAT

DELICATESSENS offering soups, salads, and sandwiches are mostly found downtown. Hotdog stands

**The handsome bar at the Omni Ambassador East Hotel** *(see p137)*

and no-frills lunch counters are a quick, inexpensive alternative to restaurants.

Most malls have food courts, selling a variety of dishes. Some don't rise above fast-food fare, but a few are excellent, notably Foodlife at Water Tower Place, and 7 on Seven at Marshall Field's.

Brew pubs are popular in Chicago. They serve beer brewed on site, as well as "pub grub" such as hamburgers or fish and chips. Many taverns that appear to be only bars serve steaks, pasta, fish, and sandwiches.

## ALCOHOL

THE LEGAL DRINKING age in Chicago is 21 and is strictly enforced. Alcohol is served until 2am most days. Some bars have late-night licenses and pour until 4am. On Sunday, alcohol is not served before 11am.

**The grand mahogany and crystal Pump Room** *(see p150)*

The Berghoff restaurant, family operated since 1898 *(see p146)*

## HOURS AND PRICES

THE CITY OPENS early: coffee shops and diners at 6am. Coffee and a roll costs about $3.50. A breakfast of bacon and eggs is about $5 in diners and twice that in hotel restaurants. Sunday brunch, served between 11am and 2pm, costs about $20 per person.

Lunch is offered between 11am and 2pm. Restaurants catering to office workers may offer weekday lunch specials in the $5 to $8 range.

Most restaurants open for dinner at 5:30pm. Kitchens close once business tapers, around 10pm on weekdays, later on weekends. The most difficult time to secure a table is from 7:30pm to 9:30pm.

Salads and appetizers generally cost between $5 and $8 each, entrées between $9 and $25. Many restaurants offer superb wines by the glass for between $5 and $9.

Ethnic restaurants offer good value for the money. Mexican and Thai restaurants are always a good bet, as are pizzerias. Indian and Greek food is often a good bargain.

Some restaurants, especially Thai ones, let you "bring your own bottle" of wine, which can cut costs dramatically. A corkage fee is unlikely unless the restaurant has a bar.

Valet parking, offered by many restaurants, costs between $6 and $8.

## PAYING AND TIPPING

THE CHECK will be brought to the table after you have finished eating. This is not meant to hurry you. Nearly all restaurants accept major credit cards. Traveler's checks are accepted with appropriate identification. Personal checks are not welcome. *(See p172.)*

A sales tax of 9.75 percent will be added to meal checks in downtown Chicago; 8.75 percent in surrounding areas.

**Sign for a Mexican restaurant specializing in seafood**

You are expected to tip servers 15 percent for average service, 18 to 20 percent for excellent service. Calculate the tip before tax. The gratuity is usually added to the check for parties of six or more.

An especially helpful wine steward may be tipped $2 or $3. There is no need to tip the host or hostess. Nor will slipping him or her money get you a better table or position on the waiting list.

## DRESS CODES

FEW RESTAURANTS have dress codes. Some hotel and country-club establishments expect men to wear a jacket and tie, and women to be dressed-up. At trendier spots, diners are expected to be fashionably attired. Inquire when making reservations.

## RESERVATIONS

TRY TO MAKE a reservation at any restaurant you plan to eat at unless it's fast-food. If booking more than a day in advance, confirm the booking on the day of your reservation. Some restaurants will not accept reservations for parties of less than six.

Even with a reservation, expect to wait up to an hour at the bar for your table at the most popular restaurants. You may be seated sooner by accepting a table in the smoking section *(see p168)*.

## CHILDREN

ALL RESTAURANTS in the city are happy to serve well-behaved children. Many are particularly kid-friendly, supplying high chairs and offering children's portions or menus. However, you may feel uncomfortable bringing children to some of the more fashionable spots. In general, Italian, Greek, Mexican, and chain restaurants are more family-oriented. Children may accompany adults to taverns and pubs if food is ordered.

Goose Island Clybourn Brewpub, brewing beer on the premises *(see p165)*

# What to Eat and Drink in Chicago

GOOD FOOD is something that Chicago takes pride in. Whether it's pizza or martinis, the mention of food or drink will always spark lively debate about who makes it the best. The city's immigrant roots mean you can sample delicacies from around the world, ranging from authentic Chinese *dim sum* to back-country barbecue. The highest-quality regional ingredients are brought to Chicago restaurant kitchens every day, as is fresh produce and seafood from both US coasts. And while Chicagoans are concerned with health, it's a democratic city: you are likely to find fried chicken on the same menu as delicate, low-calorie creations.

**Classic martini**

**Pancakes**, *made of batter that has been fried until thick and fluffy, are served with whipped butter and maple syrup for breakfast. Fruit such as blueberries may be mixed into the batter before cooking.*

**Bacon and eggs** *is a classic Chicago breakfast dish. Eggs are prepared in a variety of styles, shown here "over easy," and served with sausage or bacon, home fries, and toast.*

**Waffles**, *made of batter baked in a waffle iron, are topped with fresh berries and whipped cream, with syrup on the side. They are offered on breakfast and brunch menus.*

**Deli sandwiches** *are custom-made from a large choice of breads and fillings, such as meat and cheese. They are available at most delicatessens.*

Meat and vegetable toppings

Cheese

Spiced tomato sauce

Thick, deep crust

**Mixed green salad** *is made of fresh lettuce and a variety of garnishes, such as feta cheese and tomatoes. The choice of dressings includes oil-and-vinegar and Italian.*

**Fried calamari** *are tender deep-fried rings of squid. They are served with fresh lemon wedges and tangy tartar, yogurt, or seafood-cocktail sauce.*

## Deep-dish pizza

*Created in Chicago, deep-dish pizza satisfies the hungriest. The high crust creates a perfect container for layers of mozzarella and Parmesan cheese, spiced tomato sauce, vegetables such as mushrooms and olives, and sausage. Topped with olive oil, it is then baked in a hot oven.*

**Thai green curry**, *chicken and rich coconut milk mixed with spices and basil, is a Chicago favorite.*

**Hot dog**, *the archetypical American dish, as well as other types of sausages, such as Polish, are sold by street vendors all over the city. Garnishes include sauerkraut, pickles, and onions.*

**Charbroiled steak**, *flame-grilled Midwest beef, some of the most tender meat in the world, is served with French fries or a baked potato.*

**Quesadillas** *are a Mexican dish of grilled corn or wheat tortillas, stuffed with cheese or other filling such as chicken, beef, or seafood.*

**Sushi** *is a Japanese specialty consisting of fresh raw fish on cakes of vinegar-flavored cold rice. Pickled ginger and fiery wasabi complement the dish.*

**Burger with fries** *is popular pub food. The ground-beef burger, with various garnishes, may also be served with salad.*

**Spaghetti all'Amatriciana** *is a tasty pasta dish made with bacon, tomatoes, and onion, and topped with cheese.*

**Dim sum**, *served for brunch, consists of a variety of steamed Chinese dumplings stuffed with seafood, meat, or vegetables.*

**Nachos**, *a Mexican snack of fried corn chips covered with melted cheese, is typically accompanied by salsa, a spicy chunky tomato sauce.*

**Cheesecake**, *a rich baked dessert, may be served plain or topped with strawberries or other fruit. Flavored varieties are also widely available.*

**Tiramisù**, *consisting of layers of ladyfingers, coffee, and mascarpone sprinkled with chocolate, is a delightful traditional Italian dessert.*

## COCKTAILS AND DRINKS

The dry martini remains a favorite, though designer martinis are very fashionable. Mimosas, orange juice with champagne, are popular at brunch, while the lime-and-tequila margarita is a happy-hour favorite. Manhattans, made of whiskey and red vermouth, are a classic. Local breweries provide superb beers, and excellent wines from the western states are on good wine lists. Italian coffee drinks and artificially flavored regular coffees are popular.

**Espresso**   **Cappuccino**   **Caffe latte**   **Iced cola**

**Beer**   **Mimosa**   **Manhattan**   **Margarita**

# Choosing a Restaurant

T HESE RESTAURANTS have been selected across a wide price range for their good value, facilities, and location. They are listed area by area, starting with Chicago's Downtown Core and moving on to restaurants farther outside the center. Most restaurants are wheelchair accessible and provide nonsmoking seating areas. For map references, see pages 190–97.

| | VEGETARIAN SPECIALTIES | GOOD WINE LIST | OUTDOOR SEATING | LIVE MUSIC |
|---|---|---|---|---|
| **DOWNTOWN CORE** | | | | |
| **HEAVEN ON SEVEN. Map 4 D1.** $ | ● | | | ▨ |
| Garland Building, 111 N Wabash Ave (7th Fl), Chicago, IL 60602. *263-6443.* A spicy tingle in your mouth on your first bite is a good indication that you're in for real Cajun cooking here. Lunch daily; call for dinner hours. ● *Sun.* | | | | |
| **MILLER'S PUB. Map 3 C2.** $ | | | | |
| 134 S Wabash Ave, Chicago, IL 60603. *263-4988.* The high ceilings and paintings on the wall lend this pub a comfortable saloon-like atmosphere. Canadian baby back ribs and the Diamond Jim Brady cut of prime rib are on the menu. | | | | |
| **POTBELLY SANDWICH WORKS. Map 2 D3.** $ | ● | | | |
| 520 N Michigan Ave, Chicago, IL 60603. *528-1405.* Made-to-order sandwiches, hand-dipped shakes and malts, and homemade desserts in a comfortable, entertaining atmosphere. One of nine locations. | | | | |
| **TAZA. Map 4 D2.** $ | ● | | | |
| 39 S Wabash Ave, Chicago, IL 60603. *425-9988.* Serving perhaps the best cafeteria food you'll ever taste, Taza's is a good alternative to the usual fast-food outlets. Closes at 7pm. ● *Sun.* | | | | |
| **THE BERGHOFF. Map 3 C2.** $$ | ● | | | |
| 17 W Adams St, Chicago, IL 60603. *427-3170.* Owned by the same family for more than 100 years, serving delectable schnitzel, grilled fish, and pasta, and its own beer and draft root beer. ● *Sun.* | | | | |
| **LA CANTINA ENOTECA. Map 3 C2.** $$ | ● | ▨ | | |
| 71 W Monroe St, Chicago, IL 60603. *332-7005.* This cozy spot is the first in a trilogy of Italian restaurants at this location known as Italian Village. The kitchen specializes in fresh seafood and hearty traditional Italian dishes. Not wheelchair accessible. ● *Sun.* | | | | |
| **THE VILLAGE. Map 3 C2.** $$ | ● | ▨ | | |
| 71 W Monroe St, Chicago, IL 60603. *332-7005.* One of three restaurants at Italian Village. Twinkling lights and cozy alcoves complement a traditional Italian menu. Not wheelchair accessible. | | | | |
| **ATWOOD CAFÉ.** $$$ | ● | ▨ | ● | |
| W Washington St, Chicago, IL 60601. *368-1900.* Located in the historic Reliance Building *(see p50)*, serving breakfast, lunch, and dinner. The food is American "comfort" and café cuisine. | | | | |
| **RED LIGHT. Map 3 B1.** $$$ | ● | ▨ | ● | |
| 820 W Randolph St, Chicago, IL 60607. *733-8880.* Unique cuisine with beverages carefully paired with the food. Unusual and stunning interior. | | | | |
| **RHAPSODY. Map 4 D2.** $$$ | ● | ▨ | ● | |
| 65 E Adams St, Chicago, IL 60603. *786-9911.* This spacious room with its understated elegance is a great place to dine before the symphony. ● *dinner Sun & Mon, Jun–Sep.* | | | | |
| **TRATTORIA NO. 10. Map 3 C1.** $$$ | ● | | | |
| 10 N Dearborn St, Chicago, IL 60602. *984-1718.* A stylish, subterranean spot with an unusual and interesting variety of ravioli and northern Italian dishes. Convenient before a show downtown. ● *Sun.* | | | | |
| **VIVERE. Map 3 C2.** $$$ | ● | ▨ | | |
| 71 W Monroe St, Chicago, IL 60603. *332-4040.* Another in the trilogy of restaurants at Italian Village, Vivere features upscale regional Italian cooking. ● *Sun.* | | | | |

**Price categories** for a three-course evening meal and a half bottle of house wine, including taxes and service:
$ under $30
$$ $30–$45
$$$ $45–$65
$$$$ $65–$90
$$$$$ over $90

**VEGETARIAN SPECIALTIES**
Denotes a vegetarian restaurant, or restaurant with vegetarian selections.

**GOOD WINE LIST**
Denotes a wide range or specialized selection of wines.

**OUTDOOR SEATING**
Facilities for eating on a terrace, or in a garden or courtyard.

**LIVE MUSIC**
Indicates live music, usually piano or small jazz ensembles, during dinner on weekends, sometimes on weeknights.

| | Price | Vegetarian Specialties | Good Wine List | Outdoor Seating | Live Music |
|---|---|---|---|---|---|
| **MARCHÉ. Map 3 B1.** 833 W Randolph St, Chicago, IL 60607. ( 226-8399. Striking and colorful interior with sculpted wrought iron and eclectic paintings. The excellent food is French brasserie. ✚ ✉ | $$$$ | ● | ■ | ● | |
| **RUSSIAN TEA TIME. Map 4 D2.** 77 E Adams St, Chicago, IL 60603. ( 360-0000. The red decor exudes luxury while the menu reflects the best of Soviet regional cuisine. A popular destination before or after the symphony. ✚ ❱ ✉ | $$$$ | ● | | | |
| **EVEREST. Map 3 C2.** One Financial Plaza, 440 S LaSalle St, Chicago, IL 60605. ( 663-8920. On the 40th floor, the chef's talents at preparing continental cuisine provide what many rank as one of the best, and most expensive, meals they have ever eaten. Notable is a pre-theater tasting menu. Dinner only. ● *Sun, Mon.* ✚ ✉ | $$$$$ | | ■ | | |

## NORTH SIDE

| | Price | Vegetarian Specialties | Good Wine List | Outdoor Seating | Live Music |
|---|---|---|---|---|---|
| **CORNER BAKERY. Map 1 C5.** 516 N Clark St, Chicago, IL 60610. ( 644-8100. When Corner Bakery first opened, it sold European breads off racks. As the menu expanded to include breakfast and lunch items, so did the number of locations. Alert staff keep the cafeteria-style line moving. No bar. ✉ | $ | ● | | | |
| **ED DEBEVIC'S. Map 1 C4.** 640 N Wells St, Chicago, IL 60610. ( 664-1707. The menu, from meatloaf to milkshakes, is painted on the wall outside. Inside, there is plenty of fun. A disc jockey spins 1950s tunes while costumed wait staff sing, dance, and dish out sassy attitude with the fries. ✚ ❱ ✉ | $ | ● | | | |
| **EDWARDO'S. Map 1 C3.** 1212 N Dearborn St, Chicago, IL 60610. ( 337-4490. This upscale chain is known for its award-winning stuffed pizza, baked with lots of cheese and topped with premier tomatoes, served hot from the oven. ✚ ✉ | $ | ● | | | |
| **FLAT TOP GRILL. Map 1 C1.** 319 W North Ave, Chicago, IL 60610. ( 787-7676. Asian ingredients and sauces that customers have chosen from a self-serve bar are stir-fried on a flat top grill. All you can eat. Reservations are accepted, or arrive early to avoid waiting in line. One of five locations. ✚ ❱ ✉ | $ | ● | | | |
| **GIORDANO'S. Map 2 D4.** 730 N Rush St, Chicago, IL 60611. ( 951-0747. A pizzeria with a wholesome, collegiate atmosphere. Some claim Giordano's has the best pizza in town. One of many locations. ✚ ❱ ✉ | $ | ● | | | |
| **MR. BEEF. Map 1 B3.** 666 N Orleans St, Chicago, IL 60610. ( 337-8500. Famous for serving the best Italian beef sandwich in Chicago. There are chairs and stools but most people eat standing up. It is said that it is a favorite of celebrities such as Jay Leno and Jerry Springer. | $ | ● | | | |
| **MITY NICE GRILL. Map 2 D4.** Water Tower Place, 835 N Michigan Ave, Chicago, IL 60611. ( 335-4745. This cozy 1940s-style diner serves burgers, turkey burgers, grilled flatbread, and a low-fat Enlightened Caesar salad, among other items. ✚ ✉ | $ | ● | | | |
| **NOOKIES. Map 1 C1.** 1746 N Wells St, Chicago, IL 60614. ( 337-2454. The original Nookies, like Nookies Too and Nookies Tree, is a clean, upbeat neighborhood restaurant where you can order breakfast all day, a good sandwich, or simply a cup of coffee. Bring your own wine. ✚ | $ | ● | | ● | |

| | VEGETARIAN SPECIALTIES | GOOD WINE LIST | OUTDOOR SEATING | LIVE MUSIC |
|---|---|---|---|---|

**Price categories** for a three-course evening meal and a half bottle of house wine, including taxes and service:
Ⓢ under $30
ⓈⓈ $30–$45
ⓈⓈⓈ $45–$65
ⓈⓈⓈⓈ $65–$90
ⓈⓈⓈⓈⓈ over $90

**VEGETARIAN SPECIALTIES**
Denotes a vegetarian restaurant, or restaurant with vegetarian selections.
**GOOD WINE LIST**
Denotes a wide range or specialized selection of wines.
**OUTDOOR SEATING**
Facilities for eating on a terrace, or in a garden or courtyard.
**LIVE MUSIC**
Indicates live music, usually piano or small jazz ensembles, during dinner on weekends, sometimes on weeknights.

---

**OLD JERUSALEM. Map 1 C2.**  Ⓢ
1411 N Wells St, Chicago, IL 60610. 944-0459.
This Old Town establishment draws a varied crowd, but everyone agrees that this is how falafel is supposed to taste. Bring your own wine. 🚶 🍴

| | ● | | ● | |

**CARSON'S FOR RIBS. Map 1 C4.**  ⓈⓈ
612 N Wells St, Chicago, IL 60610. 280-9200.
Famous nationwide for its ribs, Carson's also offers outstanding Greek chicken, steak, and pork chops. Seating is ample and comfortable. 🚶 🍴

| | | ■ | | |

**FIREPLACE INN. Map 1 C2.**  ⓈⓈ
1448 N Wells St, Chicago, IL 60610. 664-5264.
For 33 years, people have been returning to this Old Town institution for ribs and a lodge-like atmosphere. 🚶 🍽 🍴

| | | | ● | |

**HEAVEN ON SEVEN ON RUSH. Map 2 D4.**  ⓈⓈ
600 N Michigan Ave, Chicago, IL 60611. 280-7774.
This restaurant serves up the same fiery Cajun food as its sister restaurant in the Downtown Core (see p146). Weekend brunch. 🚶 🍴

| | ● | | | |

**PAPAGUS GREEK TAVERNA. Map 1 C4.**  ⓈⓈ
620 N State St, Chicago, IL 60610. 642-8450.
The restaurant team of Lettuce Entertain You has created an interesting and fun environment at this rustic taverna. A wide selection of delicious *mezedes* (appetizers), as well as lamb, seafood, and pasta entrées. 🚶 🍽 🍴 P

| | ● | | ● | |

**PIZZERIA UNO. Map 2 D4.**  ⓈⓈ
29 E Ohio St, Chicago, IL 60611. 321-1000.
This is the home of Chicago-style pizza, also known as deep-dish pizza. A plaque at the door tells the whole story. Not wheelchair accessible. 🚶 🍽 🍴

| | ● | | ● | |

**TWIN ANCHORS. Map 1 B1.**  ⓈⓈ
1655 N Sedgwick St, Chicago, IL 60614. 266-1616.
Arrive at this neighborhood bar and restaurant early or be prepared for a long wait. Not wheelchair accessible. 🚶 🍽 🍴

| | | | ● | |

**BISTRO 110. Map 2 D4.**  ⓈⓈⓈ
110 E Pearson St, Chicago, IL 60611. 266-3110.
Standard bistro fare and daily specials that go a little out of bistro bounds, but deliciously so. A good Sunday brunch with live jazz. 🍴

| | ● | | ● | ■ |

**BRASSERIE JO. Map 1 C5.**  ⓈⓈⓈ
59 W Hubbard St, Chicago, IL 60610. 595-0800.
Reminiscent of elegant train-station dining rooms in days of old. The menu offers delicious, hearty Alsatian food, such as *choucroute garnie* or steak *frites*, as well as custom-brewed beer. Surprising touches in the service. 🚶 🍴

| | ● | ■ | ● | |

**CAFÉ LUCIANO. Map 2 D3.**  ⓈⓈⓈ
871 N Rush St, Chicago, IL 60611. 266-1414.
Beautiful antiques create a comfortable setting in which to enjoy authentic Italian dishes such as *giambotta* (a hearty stew of vegetables, chicken, and sweet sausage). Cigar lounge upstairs. Not wheelchair accessible. 🚶 🍴

| | | | ● | ■ |

**CAFÉ SPIAGGIA. Map 2 D3.**  ⓈⓈⓈ
980 N Michigan Ave, Chicago, IL 60611. 280-2755.
The Italian food here is simpler and less expensive than at Spiaggia next door (see p150), but the decor, preparation, and service remain exceptional. 🍴

| | ● | | | |

**CAPITAL GRILLE. Map 2 D4.**  ⓈⓈⓈ
633 N St. Clair St, Chicago, IL 60611. 337-9400.
With its tasteful decor of antiques, hand-crafted woodwork, and leather furnishings, this steakhouse provides the perfect setting in which to entertain clients or celebrate special occasions. 🚶 🍴 P

| | ● | ■ | | |

**CARMINE'S. Map 2 D3.** $$$
1043 N Rush St, Chicago, IL 60610. 988-7676.
This classy Italian restaurant serves huge portions of steaks, chops, seafood, and pasta. There is a piano bar downstairs, a dining room more conducive to conversation upstairs. Carmine's is very popular on weekends.

**CENTRO RISTORANTE. Map 1 C4.** $$$
710 N Wells St, Chicago, IL 60610. 988-7775.
The plush, comfortable dining room isn't stuffy, though it can be very busy, and the traditional Italian menu has something for everyone. Specialties include lamb chops and chicken Vesuvio. Large portions.

**LE COLONIAL. Map 2 D3.** $$$
937 N Rush St, Chicago, IL 60611. 255-0088.
With its ceiling fans whirling above the rattan furniture and palm trees, Le Colonial has the elegant, sultry atmosphere of 1920s French Colonial Vietnam. Dishes have the flavors of Asia crafted with French finesse. Food is also served in the intimate upstairs lounge. Business casual.

**ELI'S THE PLACE FOR STEAK. Map 2 D4.** $$$
215 E Chicago Ave, Chicago, IL 60611. 642-1393.
Opened in 1966, this has become a Chicago institution and a favorite of celebrities, from athletes to politicians (Frank Sinatra often came here). It has a piano bar in a cozy lounge area.

**FRONTERA GRILL. Map 1 C5.** $$$
445 N Clark St, Chicago, IL 60610. 661-1434.
Less expensive than Topolobampo at the same address *(see p150)*, Frontera Grill has earned a national reputation for its commitment to fine Mexican cuisine. Even the tortillas are made from scratch daily. The dining room is decorated with museum-quality folk art. *Sun, Mon.*

**GIBSON'S STEAKHOUSE. Map 1 C3.** $$$
1028 N Rush St, Chicago, IL 60611. 266-8999.
A popular restaurant with the city's business elite, as well as with local celebrities, Gibson's is a handsome restaurant that serves strong drinks and good steaks in a stylish atmosphere. Dinner only; reservations required.

**ROSEBUD ON RUSH. Map 2 D4.** $$$
720 N Rush St, Chicago, IL 60611. 266-6444.
Visit this classy Italian restaurant when in need of some Frank Sinatra music and a great *marinara*. The upstairs dining room is romantic and cozy; the bar and dining area downstairs has live entertainment. Not wheelchair accessible.

**SALPICÓN. Map 1 C2.** $$$
1252 N Wells St, Chicago, IL 60610. 988-7811.
Colorful paintings by local artists set an upbeat atmosphere for contemporary cooking that reflects the various regions of Mexico. Dishes include beef in spicy *tomatilla* sauce, and shrimp with fresh mango. Dinner only.

**SHAW'S CRAB HOUSE. Map 1 C5.** $$$
21 E Hubbard St, Chicago, IL 60611. 527-2722.
In the main dining room of this restaurant, you'll find fresh seafood, served in a pleasant, formal atmosphere. The adjoining Blue Crab Lounge, offering a lighter menu, provides a casual atmosphere with booth seating.

**ZINFANDEL. Map 1 C5.** $$$
59 W Grand Ave, Chicago, IL 60611. 527-1818.
Everything at this restaurant is American, even the vodka. The menu offers a survey of regional American cuisine, featuring monthly regional menus, cooked with care and presented with flair. The decor is fun, ranging from petroglyphs to model airplanes. *Sun.*

**COCO PAZZO. Map 1 C5.** $$$$
300 W Hubbard St, Chicago, IL 60610. 836-0900.
A loft space with dark blue curtains and track lighting makes for a stylish dining room equally suited for talking business or romance. The staff is not overly friendly, but the Tuscan cooking is pure and simple.

**PUMP ROOM. Map 1 C2.** $$$$
Omni Ambassador East Hotel, 1301 N State Pkwy, Chicago, IL 60610. 266-0360.
One of the great classic dining rooms in Chicago, with a fine continental menu. Its mahogany-toned decor is accented with lush greenery and crystal chandeliers. Live jazz nightly and a secluded dance floor. Jacket required.

For key to symbols see back flap

<table>
<tr><td>

**Price categories** for a three-course evening meal and a half bottle of house wine, including taxes and service:
⑤ under $30
⑤⑤ $30–$45
⑤⑤⑤ $45–$65
⑤⑤⑤⑤ $65–$90
⑤⑤⑤⑤⑤ over $90

</td><td>

**VEGETARIAN SPECIALTIES**
Denotes a vegetarian restaurant, or restaurant with vegetarian selections.

**GOOD WINE LIST**
Denotes a wide range or specialized selection of wines.

**OUTDOOR SEATING**
Facilities for eating on a terrace, or in a garden or courtyard.

**LIVE MUSIC**
Indicates live music, usually piano or small jazz ensembles, during dinner on weekends, sometimes on weeknights.

</td></tr>
</table>

| | VEGETARIAN SPECIALTIES | GOOD WINE LIST | OUTDOOR SEATING | LIVE MUSIC |
|---|---|---|---|---|
| **THE SIGNATURE ROOM. Map 2 D4.** ⑤⑤⑤<br>875 N Michigan Ave, 95th Floor John Hancock Bldg, Chicago, IL 60611. 787-9596.<br>This restaurant is worth the visit just for the stunning views through the floor-to-ceiling windows. Not surprisingly it is very popular with tourists. The food is contemporary American; noted for its Sunday brunch. | ● | ■ | | ■ |
| **SPIAGGIA. Map 2 D3.** ⑤⑤⑤⑤<br>980 N Michigan Ave, Chicago, IL 60611. 280-2750.<br>There is not a bad seat in the house at Spiaggia. The tiered dining room and floor-to-ceiling windows afford views of Michigan Avenue, Oak Street Beach, and Lake Michigan. Perhaps the best Italian food in town. | ● | ■ | | |
| **TOPOLOBAMPO. Map 1 C5.** ⑤⑤⑤⑤<br>445 N Clark St, Chicago, IL 60610. 661-1434.<br>Sharing the same address with Frontera Grill *(see p149)*, Topolobampo features Mexican cuisine in a beautiful, semi-formal setting. ● *Sun, Mon.* | ● | ■ | ● | |
| **TRU. Map 2 D4.** ⑤⑤⑤⑤⑤<br>676 N St. Clair St, Chicago, IL 60611. 202-0001.<br>A new entry on the ultra-chic dining scene. Every detail here is thoughtfully considered. The cuisine is progressive French, with frequent Italian and Asian influences. Reservations and jacket required. ● *Sun.* | ● | ■ | | |
| **SOUTH LOOP AND NEAR SOUTH SIDE** | | | | |
| **EMPEROR'S CHOICE. Map 5 C2.** ⑤<br>2238 S Wentworth Ave, Chicago, IL 60616. 225-8800.<br>The decor at this, one of Chinatown's most elegant restaurants, reflects an emperor motif. The owner is exceptionally helpful. | ● | | | |
| **HONG MIN. Map 5 C1.** ⑤<br>221 W Cermak Rd, Chicago, IL 60616. 842-5026.<br>This Chinatown spot may not have much atmosphere, but dip into the hot-and-sour soup and ambiance won't matter. Bring your own wine. | ● | | | |
| **PHOENIX. Map 5 B2.** ⑤<br>2131 S Archer Ave, Chicago, IL 60616. 328-0848.<br>The spacious and modern second-floor Chinatown restaurant draws a large crowd for *dim sum* (small brunch dishes, served from passing trolleys), especially on weekends. Ask for jasmine or chrysanthemum tea. | ● | | | |
| **CHICAGO FIREHOUSE RESTAURANT. Map 4 D5.** ⑤⑤⑤<br>1401 S Michigan Ave, Chicago, IL 60605. 786-1401.<br>This restaurant inside a converted firehouse offers creative American fare, such as coriander-crusted salmon, in a restrained, tasteful setting. | | | ● | ■ |
| **PRAIRIE. Map 3 C3.** ⑤⑤⑤<br>Hyatt on Printer's Row Hotel, 500 S Dearborn St, Chicago, IL 60605. 663-1143.<br>Prairie proves that Midwest cooking is much more than meat and potatoes. The spare, elegant dining room was inspired by Frank Lloyd Wright. | ● | | | |
| **PRINTER'S ROW. Map 3 C3.** ⑤⑤⑤<br>550 S Dearborn St, Chicago, IL 60605. 461-0780.<br>This restaurant is notable for its innovative American dishes, such as maple-glazed pork chop served with herbed spaetzle, smoked bacon greens, and bourbon-molasses sauce. ● *Sun.* | ● | ■ | | |
| **SOUTH SIDE** | | | | |
| **CAFFE FLORIAN. Map 8 D4.** ⑤<br>1450 E 57th St, Chicago, IL 60637. (773) 752-4100.<br>A café popular with university students. Though not a culinary destination, it is a good neighborhood spot for a sandwich. Bring your own wine. | ● | | | |

**DIXIE KITCHEN AND BAIT SHOP. Map 8 D2.**  ⑤
5225 S Harper Ave, Chicago, IL 60615. 📞 *(773) 363-4943.*
This roadhouse is small and busy, with decor that is a caricature of a 1930s
Carolina kitchen and bait shop. Southern favorites such as the starter cornmeal
johnnycakes are always superb. One of two locations *(see p152).* 🏃 ✍

**MEDICI. Map 8 D4.**  ⑤
1327 E 57th St, Chicago, IL 60637. 📞 *(773) 667-7394.*
This café caters to university students and Hyde Park locals who appreciate
items such as "Family Garbage Pizza." Bring your own wine. 🏃 ✍

**LA PETITE FOLIE. Map 7 B3.**  ⑤⑤⑤
1504 E 55th St, Chicago, IL 60615. 📞 *(773) 493-1394.*
A sophisticated and well-regarded restaurant, serving unpretentious classic
French cuisine in an intimate and quiet atmosphere. It is close to the
University and the Museum of Science and Industry. ✍

## FARTHER AFIELD

**LAKEVIEW:** *Ann Sather.*  ⑤
929 W Belmont Ave, Chicago, IL 60657. 📞 *(773) 348-2378.*
This is considered something of a Chicago institution (of which there are four
other outlets). A popular place for breakfast or brunch, they serve food such
as Swedish pancakes, Swedish meatballs, hot and cold sandwiches, fresh fish,
and baked goods such as cinnamon rolls. 🏃 ✍

**LAKEVIEW:** *Chicago Diner.*  ⑤
3411 N Halsted St, Chicago, IL 60657. 📞 *(773) 935-6696.*
The wooden booths and counter suggest a roadside diner rather than a
vegetarian restaurant. The menu offers vegan and wheat-free items, as well as
beer, wine, and cocktails. Low-energy service. Not wheelchair accessible. 🏃 ✍

**LAKEVIEW:** *Mia Francesca.*  ⑤⑤
3311 N Clark St, Chicago, IL 60657. 📞 *(773) 281-3310.*
A line for this restaurant often forms before it even opens, thanks to its no-
reservations policy. Black-and-white photographs decorate the simple dining
room. Large portions of good Italian food keep the place packed and noisy
year after year. One of several locations. Dinner only. 🏃 ✍

**LAKEVIEW:** *erwin.*  ⑤⑤⑤
2925 N Halsted St, Chicago, IL 60657. 📞 *(773) 528-7200.*
A seasonal menu that emphasizes regional American ingredients, particularly
those of the Midwest, produces such sensations as pork chop and basil sausage
and pasta with rabbit and greens. Great burgers, too. ● *Mon.* 🏃 ◗ ✍

**LINCOLN PARK:** *Café Ba-Ba-Reeba!*  ⑤
2024 N Halsted St, Chicago, IL 60614. 📞 *(773) 935-5000.*
The *tapas* menu (offering appetizer-size portions of everything from garlic
potato salad to baked goat cheese to grilled squid) is a grazer's paradise;
order several and share. The Spanish cooking is good, and the vivacious staff
keep things lively. The best patio in Chicago. 🏃 ◗ ✍

**LINCOLN PARK:** *Red Lion Pub.*  ⑤
2446 N Lincoln Ave, Chicago, IL 60614. 📞 *(773) 348-2695.*
Red Lion is a down-to-earth pub. The bar TV is more likely to be showing
documentaries or old movies than sports. Cornish pasties, bangers and mash,
and steak-and-kidney pie are all on the menu. 🏃 ◗ ✍

**LINCOLN PARK:** *Vinci.*  ⑤⑤
1732 N Halsted St, Chicago, IL 60614. 📞 *266-1199.*
Rustic Italian cooking is to be found here, in a setting evocative of an Italian
villa. Located in the heart of the Lincoln Park theater district, this restaurant
can be very busy; reservations are recommended. ● *Mon.* 🏃 ◗ ✍

**LINCOLN PARK:** *Aubriot.*  ⑤⑤⑤
1962 N Halsted Ave, Chicago, IL 60614. 📞 *(773) 281-4211.*
Small, bustling Aubriot serves excellent French cooking, presented with flair.
The long, cherry-wood room is inviting. ● *Mon.* 🏃 ✍

**LINCOLN PARK:** *Geja's Café.*  ⑤⑤⑤
340 W Armitage Ave, Chicago, IL 60614. 📞 *(773) 281-9101.*
A unique experience, where you can sit in candlelight in a curtained booth
and dip pieces of meat into sizzling oil and dripping cheese while watching a
musician perform. Intimate and romantic. ✍

| | | VEGETARIAN SPECIALTIES | GOOD WINE LIST | OUTDOOR SEATING | LIVE MUSIC |
|---|---|---|---|---|---|

**Price categories** for a three-course evening meal and a half bottle of house wine, including taxes and service:

$ under $30
$$ $30–$45
$$$ $45–$65
$$$$ $65–$90
$$$$$ over $90

**VEGETARIAN SPECIALTIES**
Denotes a vegetarian restaurant, or restaurant with vegetarian selections.

**GOOD WINE LIST**
Denotes a wide range or specialized selection of wines.

**OUTDOOR SEATING**
Facilities for eating on a terrace, or in a garden or courtyard.

**LIVE MUSIC**
Indicates live music, usually piano or small jazz ensembles, during dinner on weekends, sometimes on weeknights.

---

**LINCOLN PARK:** *North Pond Café.*                                          $$$
2610 N Cannon Dr, Chicago, IL 60614. *(773) 477-5845.*
Both the regional American cuisine, inspired by locally grown products, and the decor reflect the philosophy of the Arts and Crafts movement: simplicity and respect for quality craftsmanship. Excellent weekend brunch. ● *Mon.* 🚹 📧

| | | | ● | |

---

**LINCOLN PARK:** *Ambria.*                                          $$$$
2300 N Lincoln Park West, Chicago, IL 60614. *(773) 472-5959.*
The kitchen at Ambria, one of the finest restaurants in the city, melds Spanish and French cooking techniques to create luxurious, intricate dishes, served in an Art Nouveau dining room. Excellent presentation and service. ● *Sun.* 🚹 📧

| ● | ■ | | |

---

**LINCOLN PARK:** *Charlie Trotter's.*                                          $$$$$
816 W Armitage Ave, Chicago, IL 60614. *(773) 248-6228.*
A modest townhouse is home to this American culinary destination. Two tasting menus, each consisting of six to eight seasonal dishes, are offered. Impeccable service; reservations and jacket required. ● *Sun, Mon.* 🎵 📧

| ● | ■ | | |

---

**NORTHWEST SIDE:** *Eli's Cheesecake World.*                                          $
6701 W Forest Preserve, Chicago, IL 60634. *(773) 205-3800 (308-7000 for the tour).*
This is a bakery, café, and retail store. There are over 30 different flavors of cheesecake on sale. A fascinating tour of the bakery is also available, but you must call ahead to make reservations. 🚹 📧

---

**NORTHWEST SIDE:** *Lutz Café and Konditorei.*                                          $
2458 W Montrose Ave, Chicago, IL 60618. *(773) 478-7785.*
This is Chicago's first authentic German konditorei and has been in this location since 1948. The interior is very much in the old European style and there is a lovely garden with tables and chairs. 🚹 📧

| | | ● | |

---

**NORTHWEST SIDE:** *Arun's.*                                          $$$$$
4156 N Kedzie Ave, Chicago, IL 60618. *(773) 539-1909.*
An award-winning four-star Thai restaurant of national renown. The elegant interior has intimate nooks and small rooms with antiques, rich woods, paintings and artworks (some by the chef and his brother). 📧

| ● | ■ | | |

---

**NEAR WEST SIDE:** *Greek Islands.*                                          $
200 S Halsted St, Chicago, IL 60661. *782-9855.*
This Greek restaurant, the liveliest in Greektown, has several small dining rooms, each with its own ambiance, such as a bustling garden room. 🚹 🎵 📧

| ● | ■ | ● | |

---

**NEAR WEST SIDE:** *Parthenon.*                                          $
314 S Halsted St, Chicago, IL 60661. *726-2407.*
As at any self-respecting Greek restaurant, here you'll find *moussaka,* *pastitsio,* and *saganaki.* Lamb slowly roasts by the front window. The plush atmosphere sets Parthenon apart from other Greektown eateries. 🚹 🎵 📧

| ● | | | |

---

**NEAR WEST SIDE:** *Francesca's on Taylor.*                                          $$
1400 W Taylor St, Chicago, IL 60607. *829-2828.*
This Little Italy restaurant offers the same rustic Italian menu as the popular Mia Francesca *(see p151).* This location is open for both lunch and dinner and accepts reservations. One of several locations. 🚹 📧

| ● | | | |

---

**NEAR WEST SIDE:** *The Rosebud.*                                          $$
1500 W Taylor St, Chicago, IL 60607. *942-1117.*
Associated with Rosebud on Rush *(see p149),* this Little Italy establishment is said to be the home of chicken Vesuvio, a dish that is practically mandatory on Italian menus in Chicago. Music is Frank Sinatra or Italian opera. 🎵 📧

| ● | ■ | ● | |

---

**OAK PARK:** *Café Winberie.*                                          $
151 N Oak Park Ave, Oak Park, IL 60301. *(708) 386-2600.*
This bright spot serves reliable Euro-American fare with small continental flourishes. Fondues are also on the menu. 🚹 🎵 📧

| ● | | | |

## BEYOND CHICAGO

**EVANSTON:** *Lucky Platter.* $
514 Main St, Evanston, IL 60202. ☎ (847) 869-4064.
A great value restaurant that has an unpretentious, relaxed atmosphere and
excellent food. A good place to take the family. ⚄ ✇

**EVANSTON:** *Blind Faith Cafe.* $$
525 Dempster St, Evanston, IL 60201. ☎ (847) 328-6875.
A very popular restaurant that serves internationally-inspired vegetarian and
vegan food. There is a bakery, cafeteria, and take-out section as well as the
main dining room. ⚄ ✇

**EVANSTON:** *Davis Street Fishmarket.* $$
501 Davis St, Evanston, IL 60201. ☎ (847) 869-3474.
Clams and oysters can be enjoyed at the raw bar, while 20 varieties of fresh fish
are available in the dining room, many prepared with a Cajun accent. ⚄ ✇

**EVANSTON:** *Roxy Café.* $$
626 Church St, Evanston, IL 60201. ☎ (847) 864-6540.
A sleek dining room and diverse European menu draws a varied clientele.
Pastas cover all bases, and entrées run from chicken scallopini to *filet mignon.* ✇

**EVANSTON:** *Va Pensiero Ristorante.* $$$
1566 Oak Ave, Evanston, IL 60201. ☎ (847) 475-7779.
The quaint dining room of this intimate, upscale Italian restaurant is on the
lower level of the Margarita European Inn *(see p140).* Beef, lamb, and seafood
are highlights of the menu, though the pastas are also always good. ⚄ ✇

**EVANSTON:** *Trio.* $$$$$
1625 Hinman Ave, Evanston, IL 60201. ☎ (847) 733-8746.
A flawless blend of Asian and Mediterranean flavors is uniquely presented at
Trio. A nine-course chef's degustation is offered in addition to the menu.
Located in the vintage Homestead Hotel *(see p140);* the wearing of a jacket is
preferred. ● *Mon.* ❱ ✇

**GALENA:** *Bubba's Seafood, Pasta and Smokehouse.* $$
300 N Main St, Galena, IL 61036. ☎ (815) 777-8030 or (815) 777-8024.
Bubba's contains two dining rooms: the French Quarter is on the upper floor,
the Bourbon Street Cafe on the lower floor. Both feature slow-cooked,
hickory-smoked meats and Cajun flavors. Huge portions. ⚄ ✇

**GALENA:** *Vinny Vanucchi's Little Italy.* $$
201 S Main St, Galena, IL 61036. ☎ (815) 777-8100 or (815) 777-8140.
The menu at Vinny's, a three-story Italian restaurant with adjoining old-style
delicatessen, is extensive. Checkered tablecloths lend a homey atmosphere to
this family-owned spot. Cappuccino is served in the garden. ⚄ ✇

**GALENA:** *Fried Green Tomatoes.* $$$
1301 Irish Hollow Rd, Galena, IL 60136. ☎ (815) 777-3938.
The menu of this rustic Italian-style restaurant, in an 1850s building, features
traditional favorites such as lasagna, as well as unusual Italian fare, such as
*bistecca al espresso* and pork medallions rolled in pine nuts. The appetizer of
fried green tomatoes is a signature dish. Not wheelchair accessible. ✇

**LAKE GENEVA:** *Cactus Club.* $$
430 Broad St, Lake Geneva, WI 53147. ☎ (262) 248-1999.
The kitchen melds regional styles of Native American, Spanish, Mexican, and
American cuisine to produce flavorful southwestern dishes. Excellent
margaritas provide refreshment after a day of shopping. ⚄ ✇

**LAKE GENEVA:** *Kirsch's at the French Country Inn.* $$$
Highway 50, Lake Geneva, WI 53147. ☎ (262) 245-5756.
Elegant cuisine with a Hawaiian influence is standard in this charming
restaurant overlooking Lake Como. Its signature dishes – hibachi-grilled
Chilean sea bass and Kona coffee-crusted *chateaubriand* – are highly
recommended. Authentic New Orleans-style brunch on Sunday. ⚄ ✇

**LAKE GENEVA:** *Grandview Restaurant and Lounge.* $$$$
N2009 State Rd 120, Lake Geneva, WI 53147. ☎ (262) 248-5680 or (800) 441-5881.
Superb American and continental cuisine features fresh seafood, delicious
daily specials, and decadent desserts. Excellent service and a perfect location
highlighted by panoramic windows. A champagne brunch is available on
Saturdays and Sundays. ⚄ ✇

For key to symbols see back flap

# SHOPS AND MARKETS

SHOPPING, rather than sports, may well be the major pastime of Chicagoans. The sheer number of shops in the small area around Michigan Avenue alone makes Chicago a world-class shopping destination. Everything from basic necessities to outrageous luxuries can be found at

Clock at Marshall Field's, a favorite meeting spot

Chicago's boutiques, specialty shops, and legendary department stores. No matter what your passion, you will find a merchant in Chicago who shares it. Many of the shops listed on pages 156–9 will take you off the beaten track into the city's many distinct and charming neighborhoods.

**Ghirardelli Chocolate Shop and Soda Fountain**

## WHEN TO SHOP

MOST CHAIN STORES are open seven days a week, from 10am to 6pm. Some shops open an hour later and close an hour earlier on Sundays. Malls and shopping centers usually stay open evenings as well as on Sundays.

Neighborhood shops, antique dealers, vintage-clothing stores, and galleries keep more relaxed hours. Many are closed on Mondays and Tuesdays and may not open until noon on other days.

Shops are blissfully empty on weekday mornings, gradually becoming crowded as the evening approaches. On the weekends, downtown shops and malls are packed.

## SALES

PRE-SEASON SALES, end-of-season sales, 13-hour sales, Mother's Day sales – it is easy to find some kind of sale each day of the year.

Many sales, especially when shops want to clear their racks to make way for the next season's merchandise, offer great bargains.

Be wary of "going out of business" sales – some have been going on for years. However, some are legitimate sales; ask at nearby stores.

## TAXES

SALES TAX in Chicago is 8.75 percent and is added to everything except magazines and groceries. Sales tax is not refundable to visitors from overseas. However, if the shop ships your purchase to an address outside Chicago or Illinois, you can avoid city

and/or state sales tax. Foreign visitors may be required to pay duty on the purchase once they arrive home.

## PAYMENT

MAJOR CREDIT CARDS are accepted in most Chicago stores, as are bank debit cards, though small businesses may have a minimum-price policy (usually a $10 minimum) for purchases paid for this way. Traveler's checks must be accompanied by identification. Personal checks are discouraged; foreign currency is never accepted. A few smaller shops are still run on a cash-only basis.

## RETURNS

BE SURE YOU understand the shop's return policy before you make an important purchase. Keep your receipt as a proof of purchase.

Each store sets its own return-and-exchange policies; they are generally posted at the cash register. Some shops will give a full refund with no

**Vibrant window signs brightening a storefront in Chinatown**

**Sunday morning in the busy Maxwell Street Market (see p157)**

**Water Tower Place, with seven floors of boutiques and stores**

questions asked, whereas other shops maintain an all-sales-are-final policy. Some places offer an in-shop credit rather than a refund. Sale items are often not returnable.

## MALLS AND SHOPPING CENTERS

CHICAGO'S MALLS come in two varieties. Suburban malls resemble small cities surrounded by vast parking lots. City malls tend to rise upward from the ground. The most notable of these vertical malls are on the Magnificent Mile (see pp60–61).

**Water Tower Place** contains major department stores and seven floors with more than 100 boutiques and specialty shops, and, for those in need of a break from shopping, a movie theater.

Across the street is **900 North Michigan Avenue Shops**, with upscale shops and boutiques. A block south of these two powerhouse malls is **Chicago Place**, home to the flagship Midwest location of Saks Fifth Avenue, among other stylish shops.

## DEPARTMENT STORES

MANY DEPARTMENT stores have a prominent street location. **Marshall Field's** (see pp50–51) is the benchmark for luxurious department stores across the country. Don't leave Chicago without a box of its Frango mints.

In years past, critics said that Chicago's other major department store, **Carson Pirie Scott** (see p50), did not carry the high-end merchandise that Marshall Field's did, but this criticism has faded away in recent years.

Seattle-based **Nordstrom**, known for its quality clothing and shoes for men, women, and children, recently opened its flagship Midwest location.

Posh **Neiman Marcus** bills itself as a world-famous specialty store and prides itself on its personal service and exclusivity. The store specializes in clothing and accessories by many top fashion designers. Its epicurean shop offers delectable items, including caviar and wine.

**Saks Fifth Avenue** attracts a ritzy clientele with its fine selection of designer and private-label clothing.

**Bloomingdale's** is also stylish but less pricey. It has a great selection of fashionable clothing and shoes, and a floor devoted to housewares. Watch for its legendary sales.

The most traditional of the department stores is **Lord and Taylor**, which carries conservative clothing at very reasonable prices.

## PARKING

DOWNTOWN PARKING lots are expensive, street parking almost nonexistent (see p181). Many department stores offer discounted parking in their lots, but the few dollars saved are rarely worth the time spent in the parking maze. The CTA offers convenient public transit (see p181).

**An interior-furnishings shop on the street level of the historic Santa Fe Building (see p43)**

---

# Where to Shop

CHICAGO IS a shopper's paradise. The city's many neighborhoods attract locals and tourists alike with ethnic and one-of-a-kind shops. Visitors looking for fine and unusual artwork are sure to find a treasure in the River North Gallery District. Furnishing shops are clustered at Clybourn Corridor, while Oak Street is home to top fashion boutiques. Myriad shops, including chain and department stores, line the Magnificent Mile.

## ART

RIVER NORTH GALLERY District has Chicago's highest concentration of art galleries, though there are several good galleries outside its traditional boundaries. **Stephen Daiter Gallery** offers vintage 20th-century and experimental photography. **Carl Hammer Gallery** is known for its collection of "outsider art." Art with an emphasis on realism by emerging local artists is at **Lyonswier Packer Gallery**. **Zolla/Lieberman Gallery** specializes in contemporary painting, sculpture, drawings, and photographs; **Robert Henry Adams Fine Art** sells American and European paintings and prints from the 1930s and 1940s. **Mongerson Gallery** showcases Western art: paintings, sculpture, and photographs from the 18th to 20th centuries.

The collection of original European advertising posters dating from the late 1800s at **Spencer Weisz Galleries** is marvelous. **Vintage Posters** specializes in aviation, circus, food, and wine posters.

## ANTIQUES

MOST OF the antique shops in the former antique district at West Belmont and North Lincoln Avenues have dispersed. Although some of the shops remaining are worth visiting, many resemble thrift shops more than antique dealers. To find genuine antiques, go to **Jay Robert's Antique Warehouse**.

Visit **Salvage One** if you're looking for an antique door-knob, mantelpiece, or leaded stained glass. **Architectural Artifacts** has a great selection of salvaged pieces, everything from desks to church pews.

## ART AND CRAFT SUPPLIES

HUNDREDS OF Japanese papers are to be found at **Aiko's Art Materials**. **Pearl Art & Craft Supplies** stocks drafting, etching, and silk-screening supplies, in addition to paints, papers, and brushes. **Paper Source** sells specialized papers and the city's largest assortment of rubber stamps. **International Importing Bead & Novelty Co.** is known for handmade beads, pearls, crystals, and trim. **Tom Thumb Hobby & Crafts** offers a great selection of beads and craft materials.

## BOOKS

LOCAL BOOKSHOPS abound in Chicago. **Barbara's Book-store** specializes in small- and alternative-press titles. The **Chicago Architecture Foundation Shop** has an excellent selection of books on the city's architecture.

**Afrocentric Bookstore** stocks books by African Americans, from mysteries to histories; **Europa Books** stocks foreign-language publications. **Transitions Bookplace** is Chicago's – some say the country's – best new-age and self-help book-shop. The top bookshop for gay and lesbian literature in Chicago is **Unabridged Books**. **57th Street Books** has a great general selection but specializes in cookbooks, mysteries, and film, computer, and children's books. **Tower Records** carries books and magazines unavailable else-where in the city, on subjects ranging from cooking to the occult. **Powell's Bookstore** buys and sells used books, specializing in rare, out-of-print, and scholarly titles.

## BUTTONS AND FABRICS

BUTTONS FOR SEWERS and collectors alike are to be found at **Mayet Beads & Buttons**, and in the huge selection at **Tender Buttons**.

From decorator fabrics to bridal finery, the selection at **Vogue Fabrics** is dizzying. As well as silks, woolens, and cottons, **Fishman's Fabrics** carries theatrical fabrics, laces, and decorative trims.

## CAMERAS AND ELECTRONICS

CAMERA BUFFS will want to visit **Central Camera**, an old-world shop crammed with cameras of every make and model. **Helix Camera & Video** carries underwater equipment and used cameras.

Visit **Bang & Olufsen** for high-quality Danish entertain-ment centers. **Sony Gallery** is a wonderland of high-tech gadgets and electronics, while **United Audio** has superb home and car stereo systems and knowledgeable staff.

## COINS

THE FULL-SERVICE coin dealer **Harlan J. Berk** buys and sells all currencies of coins. It also deals in paper money and rare and ancient coins. Another respected dealer is **Chicago Coin Company**, located near Midway Airport.

## DISCOUNT CLOTHING

DISCOUNT CLOTHING stores are plentiful in Chicago. **Marshall's**, **TJ Maxx**, and **Filene's Basement** all have great selections.

Many department stores (*see p155*) also have discount outlets scattered throughout the suburbs.

## DESIGNER CLOTHING

FOR HIP men's and women's fashions by designers such as Gucci and Fendi, **Ultimo** is a must-visit. **Giorgio Armani** stocks the designer's entire collection, including eyewear and fragrances. Italian design house **Prada** sells its fashions from a sleek and ultra-hip

Oak Street shop. **Barneys New York** has an excellent selection of designer clothing.

For the more adventurous, there's New Yorker **Betsey Johnson**'s shop, and **Sugar Magnolia**, for fashions from European and US designers.

## SHOES

STOCKING STYLISH women's shoes, purses, and accessories, **Lori's Discount Designer Shoes** is a treasure. The somewhat hectic store is self-serve. **Altman's Shoes**, a Chicago mainstay since 1932, offers current men's styles and specialty sizes.

## FURS AND LEATHERS

THE MIDWEST's largest fur importer and wholesaler is **Chicago Fur Mart**. Chic furs and leathers by top designers are sold at **Elán Furs**. **Glove Me Tender** has a vast array of gloves for men, women, and children. **Alfred Dunhill** has a large selection of luggage, cases, and accessories.

## JEWELRY

THE GEMS of the jewelry district are clustered along Wabash Avenue between Madison and Washington Streets. Some are open only to the trade, but several open to the public. **Harold Burland & Son** sells diamonds and other precious stones. **Tiffany & Co.** sells designer jewelry, crystal, and clocks.

## FOOD AND WINE SHOPS

VISITING THE **Spice House** is an aromatic adventure. Its proprietors will gladly discuss the differences between the several varieties of cinnamon or basil they sell. **Treasure Island** carries hard-to-find imports and the city's best selection of gourmet foodstuffs. The organic food at **Whole Foods** is delicious.

For a rare Bordeaux or obscure Puerto Rican rum, visit **Sam's Wines & Spirits**. **House of Glunz** carries wines in vintages as early as 1804. It also has a tasting room and wine museum.

## MARKETS

FROM JUNE to October, Midwest farmers come to sell their produce at Chicago's 30 or so markets. Some markets are on weekdays, but Saturday is the main market day. Hours are usually from 7am to 1pm. **Near North Market** is held Saturdays, as is **Lincoln Park Market**. **Evanston Farmers' Market**, on Saturday mornings, has wonderful organic produce. The fabulous **Daley Plaza Market** is alternate Thursdays.

Chicago's famous **Maxwell Street Market** has been around since 1871. Up to 400 vendors sell new and used items, from power tools to fresh delicacies. The market runs Sundays, April to October.

Be prepared to pay with cash at the markets. Prices are generally not negotiable. Call the **Farmers' Market Information Line** for details and to confirm locations.

## GIFTS AND SOUVENIRS

FOR A PIECE – literally – of Chicago, visit the **City of Chicago Store**. It sells fragments of Chicago landmarks, such as bricks from the old Comiskey Park, as well as other, more commonplace, souvenirs. The **Chicago Architecture Foundation Shop** has a good selection of souvenir books, posters, and Chicago memorabilia.

Take home original arts and crafts from **Illinois Marketplace**. The **Illinois Artisans Shop** is an excellent source of affordable crafts by local artisans, while the **Gallery 37 Store** sells a wide range of artwork by teenagers enrolled in its nonprofit art program.

## HOME AND GARDEN FURNISHINGS

UPSCALE reproductions of vintage furniture and fixtures are the specialties of **Restoration Hardware**. **Jayson Home & Garden** carries unusual furnishings and garden pots. **Urban Gardener** sells interesting garden decorations, pots, and garden tools.

**Smith & Hawken** offers pricey but alluring garden supplies and accessories. Its discount outlet is next door.

## MEMORABILIA

YOU WILL FIND a fascinating and broad, collection of political, sports, and movie memorabilia at **Yesterday**. **Metro Golden Memories** has posters, movie stills, and vintage radio-show tapes from the 1920s onward.

## MUSIC

A VAST classical-music collection, as well as folk, jazz, rock, pop, and show tunes, is to be found at **Tower Records**. Its only competition is **Virgin Megastore**.

What is arguably the world's best collection of jazz recordings is found at **Jazz Record Mart**. Staff here are extremely knowledgeable. **Dr. Wax Records** is a fun place to browse through secondhand CDs.

## SPORTING GOODS

EVERYTHING the company manufactures can be found at **Nike Town**, while **Vertel's Authentic Running & Fitness** is serious about athletic shoes. If outdoor equipment is an interest, an expedition to **The North Face** is worthwhile.

## TOYS, GADGETS, AND SPECIALTY SHOPS

USEFUL GADGETS are stocked at **Hammacher Schlemmer** and **Sharper Image**, while **Kite Harbor** entices with an astonishing selection of kites and radio-controlled toys. Extraordinary miniature dollhouse furniture and figures are offered at **Think Small By Rosebud**. Everything from chemistry kits to telescopes is sold at **American Science and Surplus**. For children, **F.A.O. Schwarz** is a must-see for its huge stuffed animals and electronic toys. The popular **American Girl Place** sells historic and contemporary dolls and doll accessories.

## DIRECTORY

### ART

**Carl Hammer Gallery**
740 N Wells St.
**Map** 1 C4.
266-8512.

**Lyons Wier Gallery**
300 W Superior St.
**Map** 1 B4.
654-0600.

**Mongerson Gallery**
704 N Wells St.
**Map** 1 C4.
943-2354.

**Robert Henry Adams Fine Art**
715 N Franklin St.
**Map** 1 B4.
642-8700.

**Spencer Weisz Galleries**
214 W Ohio St.
**Map** 1 C5.
527-9420.

**Stephen Daiter Gallery**
311 W Superior St.
**Map** 1 B4.
787-3350.

**Vintage Posters**
1551 N Wells St.
**Map** 1 C1.
951-6681.

**Zolla/Lieberman Gallery**
325 W Huron St.
**Map** 1 B4.
944-1990.

### ANTIQUES

**Architectural Artifacts**
4325 N Ravenswood Ave,
**North Center**.
(773) 348-0622.

**Jay Robert's Antique Warehouse**
149 W Kinzie St.
**Map** 1 C5.
222-0167.

**Salvage One**
1840 W Hubbard St.
**Wicker Park**.
733-0098.

### ART AND CRAFT SUPPLIES

**Aiko's Art Materials**
3347 N Clark St,
**Lakeview**.
(773) 404-5600.

**International Importing Bead & Novelty Co.**
111 N Wabash Ave.
**Map** 4 D1.
332-0061.

**Paper Source**
232 W Chicago Ave.
**Map** 1 C4.
337-0798.

**Pearl Art & Craft Supplies**
225 W Chicago Ave.
**Map** 1 C4.
915-0200.

**Tom Thumb Hobby & Crafts**
1026 Davis St, **Evanston**.
(847) 869-9575.

### BOOKS

**Afrocentric Bookstore**
333 S State St.
**Map** 3 C2.
939-1956.

**Barbara's Bookstore**
233 S Wacker Dr,
Sears Tower. **Map** 3 B2.
466-0223.
*One of several locations.*

**Chicago Architecture Foundation Shop**
224 S Michigan Ave.
**Map** 4 D2.
922-3432.
*One of two locations.*

**Europa Books**
832 N State St.
**Map** 1 C3.
335-9677.

**57th Street Books**
1301 E 57th St.
**Map** 8 D4.
(773) 684-1300.

**Powell's Bookstore**
1501 E 57th St.
**Map** 8 D4.
(773) 955-7780.
*One of two locations.*

**Tower Records**
*See Music, p159.*

**Transitions Bookplace**
1000 W North Ave,
**Lincoln Park**.
951-7323.

**Unabridged Books**
3251 N Broadway,
**Lakeview**.
(773) 883-9119.

### BUTTONS AND FABRICS

**Fishman's Fabrics**
1101 S Des Plaines St.
**Map** 3 A4.
922-7250.

**Mayet Beads & Buttons**
826 W Armitage Ave,
**Lincoln Park**.
(773) 883-9508.

**Tender Buttons**
946 N Rush St. **Map** 2 D3.
337-7033.

**Vogue Fabrics**
718 Main St, **Evanston**.
1-847 864-9600.
*One of two locations.*

### CAMERAS AND ELECTRONICS

**Bang & Olufsen**
15 E Oak St. **Map** 2 D3.
787-6006.
*One of two locations.*

**Central Camera**
230 S Wabash Ave.
**Map** 4 D3.
427-5580.

**Helix Camera & Video**
233 N Michigan Ave.
**Map** 4 D1.
565-5901 or (800) 334-3549.
*One of several locations.*

**Sony Gallery**
663 N Michigan Ave.
**Map** 2 D4.
943-3334.

**Tweeter**
900 N Michigan Ave.
**Map** 2 D3.
664-3100.

### COINS

**Chicago Coin Company**
6455 W Archer Ave,
**Garfield Ridge**.
(773) 586-7666.

**Harlan J. Berk**
31 N Clark St.
**Map** 3 C1.
609-0016.
*One of three locations.*

### DISCOUNT CLOTHING

**Filene's Basement**
830 N Michigan Ave.
**Map** 2 D4.
482-8918.
*One of two locations.*

**Marshall's**
600 N Michigan Ave.
**Map** 2 D4.
280-7506.
*One of three locations.*

**TJ Maxx**
11 N State St. **Map** 3 C1.
553-0515.
*One of three locations.*

### DESIGNER CLOTHING

**Barneys New York**
25 E Oak St. **Map** 2 D3.
587-1700.

**Betsey Johnson**
72 E Oak St. **Map** 2 D3.
664-5901.

**Giorgio Armani**
800 N Michigan Ave.
**Map** 2 D4.
751-2244.

**Prada**
30 E Oak St. **Map** 2 D3.
951-1113.

**Sugar Magnolia**
34 E Oak St. **Map** 2 D3.
944-0885.

**Ultimo**
114 E Oak St.
**Map** 2 D3.
( 787-1171.

### SHOES

**Altman's Shoes**
120 W Monroe St.
**Map** 3 C2.
( 332-0667.

**Lori's Discount Designer Shoes**
824 W Armitage Ave,
**Lincoln Park**.
( (773) 281-5655.

### FURS AND LEATHERS

**Alfred Dunhill**
835 N Michigan Ave.
**Map** 2 D4.
( 467-4455.

**Chicago Fur Mart**
166 E Superior St.
**Map** 2 D4.
( 951-5000.

**Elán Furs**
675 N Michigan Ave.
**Map** 2 D4.
( 640-0707.

**Glove Me Tender**
900 N Michigan Ave.
**Map** 2 D3.
( 664-4022.

### JEWELRY

**Harold Burland & Son**
5 S Wabash Ave,
suite 712. **Map** 4 D2.
( 332-5176.

**Tiffany & Co.**
730 N Michigan Ave.
**Map** 2 D4.
( 944-7500.

### FOOD AND WINE SHOPS

**House of Glunz**
1206 N Wells St.
**Map** 1 C2.
( 642-3000.

**Sam's Wines & Spirits**
1720 N Marcey St,
**Depaul**.
( 664-4394.

**Spice House**
1941 Central St,
**Evanston**.
( 1-847 328-3711.

**Treasure Island**
75 W Elm St.
**Map** 1 C3.
( 440-1144.
*One of several locations.*

**Whole Foods**
1000 W North Ave,
**Lincoln Park**.
( 587-0648.
*One of several locations.*

### MARKETS

**Daley Plaza Market**
Richard J. Daley Center
Plaza, Washington &
Dearborn sts.
**Map** 3 C1.

**Evanston Farmers' Market**
( 1-847 866-2936 for
market times, location,
and further details.

**Farmers' Market Information Line**
( 744-9187 for market
times, locations, and
further details.

**Lincoln Park Market**
Armitage Ave & Orchard
St, **Lincoln Park**.

**Maxwell Street Market**
Canal St between W
Taylor St & 15th Pl.
**Map** 3 B4–B5.
( 922-3100.

**Near North Market**
Division & Dearborn sts.
**Map** 1 C3.

### GIFTS AND SOUVENIRS

**Chicago Architecture Foundation Shop**
*See Books, p158.*

**City of Chicago Store**
163 E Pearson St,
Chicago Water Works
**Map** 2 D4.
( 742-8811.

**Gallery 37 Store**
66 E Randolph St.
**Map** 4 D2.
( 744-7274.

**Illinois Artisans Shop**
100 W Randolph St.
**Map** 3 C2.
( 814-5321.

**Illinois Marketplace**
700 E Grand Ave, Navy
Pier. **Map** 2 F5.
( 595-5400.

### HOME AND GARDEN FURNISHINGS

**Jayson Home & Garden**
1915 N Clybourn Ave,
**Depaul**.
( (773) 525-3100.

**Restoration Hardware**
938 W North Ave,
**Lincoln Park**.
( 475-9116.

**Smith & Hawken**
1780 N Marcey St,
**Depaul**.
( 266-1988.

**Urban Gardener**
1006 W Armitage Ave,
**Lincoln Park**.
( (773) 477-2070.

### MEMORABILIA

**Yesterday**
1143 W Addison St,
**Lakeview**.
( (773) 248-8087.

**Metro Golden Memories**
5425 W Addison St,
**Portage Park**.
( (773) 736-4133.

### MUSIC

**Dr. Wax Records**
1203 N State St.
**Map** 1 C2.
( 255-0123.
*One of several locations.*

**Jazz Record Mart**
444 N Wabash Ave.
**Map** 2 D5.
( 222-1467.

**Tower Records**
214 S Wabash Ave.
**Map** 4 D2.
( 987-9044.
*One of two locations.*

**Virgin Megastore**
540 N Michigan Ave.
**Map** 2 D5.
( 645-9300.

### SPORTING GOODS

**Nike Town**
669 N Michigan Ave.
**Map** 2 D4.
( 642-6363.

**The North Face**
875 N Michigan Ave.
**Map** 2 D3.
( 337-7200.

**Vertel's Authentic Running & Fitness**
24 S Michigan Ave.
**Map** 4 D2.
( 683-9600.

### TOYS, GADGETS, AND SPECIALTY SHOPS

**American Girl Place**
111 E Chicago Ave.
**Map** 2 D4.
( 640-5895.

**American Science and Surplus**
5316 N Milwaukee Ave,
**Norwood Park**.
( (773) 763-0313.

**F.A.O. Schwarz**
840 N Michigan Ave.
**Map** 2 D4.
( 587-5000.

**Hammacher Schlemmer**
445 N Michigan Ave.
**Map** 2 D5.
( 527-9100.

**Kite Harbor**
109 N Marion St,
**Oak Park**.
( (708) 848-4907.

**Sharper Image**
835 N Michigan Ave.
**Map** 2 D4.
( 335-1600.

**Think Small By Rosebud**
3209 N Clark St,
**Lakeview**.
( (773) 477-1920.

# ENTERTAINMENT IN CHICAGO

TENS OF MILLIONS OF DOLLARS have been spent in recent years by the City of Chicago to rejuvenate old theaters and build cultural attractions. Today, a portion of the money raised through the hotel tax *(see p132)* is channeled directly to the department of culture. And it shows. Chicago's world-class orchestras and opera, intimate jazz ensembles, high-profile musicals, and

**Silver-painted street performer**

alternative theater help to attract more than 5 million tourists to Chicago each year. Festivals of all kinds, from music to dance to ethnic, are held in the city's many parks and more than 75 diverse communities *(see pp30–33)*. There are also numerous sports events throughout the year for visitors to Chicago to watch or participate in *(see pp162–3)*.

**Chicago's listings magazine, *Reader*, published weekly**

## INFORMATION

THE CITY'S MOST complete entertainment listings are in the *Reader*, a free newspaper distributed Thursdays throughout Chicago. The *Reader* lists even the most obscure theatrical and musical events. *Chicago Magazine*, available at newsstands, is a glossy monthly with listings of the city's major venues. The two daily newspapers, the *Chicago Sun-Times* and the *Chicago Tribune*, publish an entertainment section in their Friday editions, with movie, music, dance, and theater reviews and listings.

Chicago's **Visitor Information Centers** sell tickets as well as providing entertainment information.

**Moviefone** provides recorded details of movie show times and theater locations, as well as brief descriptions of the movies.

**Hot Tix**, a ticket agency run by the League of Chicago Theatres, provides half-price tickets to more than 125 Chicago-area theaters on the day of performance.

Most hotels carry a wide selection of entertainment brochures, and hotel staff will help orient you and may

arrange for tickets. The **Mayor's Office of Special Events** also provides information on local events, including the numerous neighborhood festivals that take place during summer.

## BUYING TICKETS

TICKETS for most major entertainment events are sold through **Ticketmaster**. You can buy tickets by phone or at one of its locations. You may be able to buy tickets for sold-out events from a ticket broker (see listings in the yellow pages of the telephone directory), but the price may be astronomical. Be wary of buying tickets from "scalpers" (ticket hawkers) on the street. Some try to sell tickets that are expired or counterfeit.

Many of the major concerts, plays, and musicals in Chicago are reviewed in the national press, which can lead to these shows selling out weeks in advance. It is best to buy tickets for such shows through a ticket agency or the

**The Civic Opera House, home to the Lyric Opera of Chicago**

venue's box office before arriving in Chicago.

Most people buy movie tickets at the theater. Prices range from $1.50 per ticket for second-run movies to $8.50 for first-run movies. You can buy tickets using a major credit card through **Moviephone**. This saves standing in line at the theater, but the tickets are nonrefundable and a surcharge of $1 to $2 is added to the price of each.

## DISCOUNT TICKETS

HALF-PRICE TICKETS for shows on the day of performance are available from **Hot Tix**. These tickets must be purchased in person and paid for in cash or, at most locations, by credit card.

**CityPass Traveler** packages admissions to six of the top attractions in Chicago, saving you both time and money. The passes can be purchased through its website or at the participating venues.

## TRAVELERS WITH DISABILITIES

MANY THEATERS and concert halls in Chicago are fully wheelchair accessible. Some of the smaller theaters and clubs try hard but are less than adequate when it comes to serving patrons with special needs. Even though a venue has the required seating area for persons in wheelchairs, the building may still be difficult to get around in.

Major theaters and halls provide amplifying headphones for people with hearing impairments.

The **Mayor's Office for People with Disabilities** provides details on which venues are accessible for people with disabilities.

## FREE EVENTS

ACCOMPLISHED young musicians play every Wednesday as part of the Dame Myra Hess series of free noontime recitals at the **Chicago Cultural Center** *(see p52)*. Harold Washington Library Center *(see p82)* also hosts concerts, many free.

The best free seats in the city are in Grant Park and, beginning in spring 2002, in the new Millennium Park *(see p53)*. The first-rate Grant Park Symphony gives evening concerts, mid-June to mid-August, Wednesday to Sunday, in Grant Park. (See page 162 for details on other free music events.)

Grant Park is also home to many summertime festivals. The Gospel Festival kicks off the season early in June, followed by the renowned Blues Festival. A country-music festival is usually held in July. The season winds down with the Viva! Chicago Latin Music Festival at the end of August, followed by the Jazz and World Music festivals, held in September.

Throughout the summer, dozens of Chicago's neighborhoods block off streets to traffic and hold weekend festivals. Most are free or require a minimal entrance fee. Vendors sell refreshments, artists show arts and crafts, and local bands perform. You can hear great salsa, gritty rock and roll, country music, blues, or jazz

**Buddy Guy, one of the world's greatest blues guitar soloists**

**Concert in Preston Bradley Hall at the Chicago Cultural Center**

– sometimes all on the same day. These festivals allow visitors to experience Chicago's neighborhoods.

**Oprah Winfrey**, **Jenny Jones**, and **Jerry Springer** all tape their TV talk-shows in Chicago. Tickets to the shows are free, but you must reserve them at least one month in advance.

**Sidewalk signs in the Loop's theater district**

## FREE-ADMISSION DAYS

**Monday**
Adler Planetarium (Sep–Feb; *pp92–3*).
Chicago Historical Society (*p74*).
Field Museum (Jan–Feb, Sep–Dec; *pp86–9*).
Museum of Science and Industry (*see pp106–109*).
Shedd Aquarium (Sep–Feb; *pp96–7*).
**Tuesday**
Adler Planetarium (Sep–Feb; *pp92–3*).
Art Institute of Chicago (*pp46–9*).
Brookfield Zoo (*see p117*).
Museum of Contemporary Art (*p65*).
Museum of Science and Industry (*see pp106–109*).
Shedd Aquarium (Sep–Feb; *pp96–7*).
**Thursday**
Brookfield Zoo (*see p117*).
Chicago Children's Museum (5–8pm; *p65*).
**Sunday**
DuSable Museum of African-American History (*p104*).

## DIRECTORY

### USEFUL NUMBERS

**Chicago Cultural Center**
744-6630, 346-3278.
w *www.ci.chi.il.us/Tourism/CulturalCenter*

**City Helpline**
311 *(event information)*.

**Dance Hotline**
987-1123.

**Mayor's Office for People with Disabilities**
744-6673, 774-3315.
w *www.ci.chi.il.us/Disabilities*

**Mayor's Office of Special Events**
744-3370.
w *www.ci.chi.il.us/SpecialEvents*

**Visitor Information Centers**
744-2400.
163 E Pearson St. **Map** 2 D4.
77 E Randolph St. **Map** 4 D1.
700 E Grand Ave. **Map** 2 F5.
w *www.cityofchicago/Tourism/GeneralInfo/VisitorsInformationCenters.html*

### TICKET AGENCIES

**CityPass Traveler**
w *www.citypass.net*

**Hot Tix**
163 E Pearson St. **Map** 2 D4.
214 S Wabash Ave. **Map** 4 D2.
*Two of several locations.*
554-9800.
Mon.
w *www.hottix.org*

**Moviefone**
444-3456.
w *moviefone.com*

**Ticketmaster**
559-1212.
w *www.ticketmaster.com*

### TV TALK-SHOWS

**Jenny Jones Show**
836-9400. w *www.jennyjones.warnerbros.com*

**Jerry Springer Show**
321-5365.
w *www.jerryspringer.com*

**Oprah Winfrey Show**
591-9222.
w *www.oprah.com*

# Arts, Film, and Sports

WHEN IT COMES TO ENTERTAINMENT, Chicago is second to none. The Chicago Symphony and the Lyric Opera are both world-class, while Steppenwolf Theatre grew from its beginnings in a basement to become one of the leading theater troupes in the country. Chicago also has its share of art film houses. Many events take place at the city's 550 parks and playgrounds. Ravinia Festival, in Highland Park, showcases music and dance throughout the summer. Spectator sports, especially baseball, are also enormously popular in Chicago, the numerous teams providing year-round entertainment.

## MUSIC

THE GUIDING LIGHT of classical music in Chicago is the **Chicago Symphony Orchestra**. From September through June, it performs at **Symphony Center**. During the summer, it performs at the **Ravinia Festival**.

The highly acclaimed **Lyric Opera of Chicago** presents lavish productions and brings international stars to **Civic Opera House** during its September-to-March season.

**Music of the Baroque** is Chicago's leading early-music ensemble. A consortium of Chicago's finest musicians, **Chicago Chamber Musicians** presents a series of free concerts throughout the year at the **Chicago Cultural Center**, held on the first Monday of each month.

Chicago's two world-class string quartets are the venerable **Vermeer String Quartet** and the **Chicago String Quartet**. Both perform frequently at the **DePaul University Concert Hall**.

**Mandel Hall** at University of Chicago hosts folk, jazz, and classical groups. Northwestern University presents concerts by leading touring ensembles at **Pick-Staiger Concert Hall**.

## DANCE

THE UNIQUE BLEND of jazz, ballet, and modern dance that **Hubbard Street Dance Chicago** offers will transport you to new places in entertainment. Performances take place at **Shubert Theatre** from September to May.

Each season, **Joffrey Ballet of Chicago** presents four performances of classical ballet with a contemporary edge, reflecting the dance company's mandate to present the works of 20th-century American artists.

## THEATER

CHICAGO HAS A vibrant theater scene. **Goodman Theater**'s new home is located in the Loop's theater district. The troupe presents contemporary plays as well as the classics directed with a fresh approach. Productions often star well-known stage and screen actors.

Nearby is the restored **Ford Center for the Performing Arts Oriental Theater**, which, along with **Shubert Theatre**, brings Broadway productions to the city. The **Chicago Theatre** is a multi-purpose venue that presents concerts and theater. The **Auditorium Theatre** (*see p42*) hosts mainstream musicals such as *Les Miserables* and *Showboat*.

Since its inception in a church basement, **Steppenwolf Theatre Company** has gained a national reputation for staging avant-garde plays. Although many of the actors who started at Steppenwolf, such as John Malkovich and Laurie Metcalf, have left, they frequently return to perform with the company or direct.

**Shakespeare Repertory Company** stages three productions a year in **Chicago Shakespeare Theater**, its new courtyard-style theater at Navy Pier.

**Performing Arts Chicago** brings in cutting-edge theater, dance, music, and puppetry groups. Performances are held at various venues.

Many notable theaters are located near Lincoln Park and in Lakeview, among them the **Royal George** and the **Victory Gardens Theater**.

## SUMMER PERFORMANCES

CHICAGO'S SUMMER HOME for the performing arts is in idyllic Highland Park, 25 miles (40 km) north of the city, at the internationally celebrated **Ravinia Festival**. Chicago Symphony Orchestra performs here, as do leading jazz ensembles, pop and folk acts, children's performers, and dance troupes, including Hubbard Street Dance and the Joffrey Ballet of Chicago.

The park's sound system is excellent. Reserved seats in the pavilion cost from $15 to $60. General admission to the park costs about $10.

Although Highland Park has several good restaurants, most people buy general-admission tickets, bring a picnic dinner (some, lavish spreads with candles, crystal, and fine wine), and sit on the lawn to enjoy the performances.

## FILM

LIKE MOST CITIES, Chicago has a cinema multiplex in almost every neighborhood showing first-run movies. There are also several art film houses in the city.

The **Harold Washington Library Center** screens a diverse selection of films. **The Music Box** is a fully restored 1929 movie palace designed to look as though you are outdoors at night. It shows an eclectic mix of foreign, American independent, and classic films. An organist entertains with vintage popular music during intermission on weekend evenings.

The **Gene Siskel Film Center of the Art Institute of Chicago** presents a wide range of standard-setting international cinema. Panel discussion and lectures provide context for the films.

Facets Multimedia has a small screening room where current innovative films from around the world – from South America to Eastern Europe to Africa – are shown. The theater also hosts retrospectives of great directors such as Alfred Hitchcock and Jean-Luc Godard. Facets has the country's largest collection of videos for rent or sale.

## SPECTATOR SPORTS

CHICAGO BOASTS several professional sports teams, including two baseball teams. The **Chicago White Sox** play for the American League at the new **Comiskey Park** on the city's South Side. The much-loved-but-often-disappointing **Chicago Cubs** of the National League play in

Wrigley Field, a marvelous inner-city stadium in the north end of Chicago (see p114).

The formerly great **Chicago Bulls** (winners of five world championships in the 1990s) play basketball at the **United Center**, as does Chicago's hockey team, the **Chicago Blackhawks**. The inimitable **Chicago Bears** play football at **Soldier Field**.

---

## DIRECTORY

### MUSIC

**Chicago Chamber Musicians**
225-5226; 692-9000.

**Chicago Cultural Center**
78 E Washington St.
**Map** 4 D1. 744-6630.

**Chicago String Quartet**
225-5226.

**Chicago Symphony Orchestra**
See Symphony Center.

**Civic Opera House**
20 N Wacker Dr. **Map** 3 B1.
419-0033; 372-7800.

**DePaul University Concert Hall**
800 W Belden Ave,
**Lincoln Park**.
(773) 325-7260.
(773) 325-7664.

**Lyric Opera of Chicago**
See Civic Opera House.

**Mandel Hall**
University of Chicago,
1131 E 57th St. **Map** 7 C4.
(773) 702-8068.

**Music of the Baroque**
551-1415.

**Pick-Staiger Concert Hall**
Northwestern University,
1977 S Campus Dr,
**Evanston**.
(847) 467-7425.
(847) 491-5441.

**Symphony Center**
220 S Michigan Ave.
**Map** 4 D2.
294-3000; (800) 223-7114.

**Vermeer String Quartet**
(773) 722-5463.

### DANCE

**Hubbard Street Dance Chicago**
850-9744.

**Joffrey Ballet of Chicago**
70 E Lake St.
739-0120.

### THEATER

**Auditorium Theatre**
50 E Congress Pkwy.
**Map** 4 D3.
922-2110.

**Chicago Shakespeare Theater**
800 E Grand Ave.
**Map** 2 F5.
595-5600.

**Chicago Theatre**
175 N State St.
**Map** 3 C1.
443-1130.

**Ford Center for the Performing Arts Oriental Theater**
24 W Randolph St.
**Map** 3 C1.
902-1500.

**Goodman Theater**
170 N Dearborn St.
**Map** 3 C1.
443-3800.

**Performing Arts Chicago**
(773) 722-5463.

**Royal George**
1641 N Halsted St.
**Map** 1 A1.
988-9000.

**Shakespeare Repertory Company**
See Chicago Shakespeare Theater.

**Shubert Theatre**
22 W Monroe St.
**Map** 3 C2.
902-1400 (tickets).

**Steppenwolf Theatre Company**
1650 N Halsted St,
**Lincoln Park**.
335-1650.

**Victory Gardens**
2257 N Lincoln Ave,
**Lincoln Park**.
(773) 871-3000.

### SUMMER PERFORMANCES

**Ravinia Festival**
Green Bay & Lake Cook
Rds, **Highland Park**.
1-847 266-5100;
(800) 433-8819.

### FILM

**Facets Multimedia**
1517 W Fullerton Ave,
**DePaul**.
(773) 281-4114.

**Gene Siskel Film Center of the Art Institute of Chicago**
164 N State St. **Map** 3 C1.
846-2800.

**Harold Washington Library Center**
400 S State St. **Map** 3 C2.
747-4999.

**The Music Box**
3733 N Southport Ave,
**Lakeview**.
(773) 871-6604.

### SPECTATOR SPORTS

**Chicago Bears**
Halas Hall, 1000 Football
Dr., **Lake Forest**.
1-847 295-6600.

**Chicago Blackhawks**
United Center.
455-7000.

**Chicago Bulls**
United Center.
559-1212 (tickets).

**Chicago Cubs**
(773) 404-2827;
(800) 843-2827 (tickets).

**Chicago White Sox**
674-1000.

**Comiskey Park**
333 W 35th St.
**Map** 5 B5–C5.
674-1000.

**Soldier Field**
425 E McFetridge Dr.
**Map** 4 E5. 747-1285.

**United Center**
1901 W Madison St,
**Near West Side**.
455-4500.

**Wrigley Field**
1060 W Addison Ave,
**Lakeview**.
(773) 404-2827.

# Taverns, Nightclubs, and Live Music

CHICAGOANS HAVE A REPUTATION for working hard and playing hard. Nowhere is the latter more evident than in the city's night life. The blues are a Chicago institution, but jazz, country, folk, and rock music thrive here as well. Acts both big and small play almost nightly, and many music venues are open into the early hours of the morning. Chicago night-life establishments tend to be clustered together. Singles' bars are gathered at the corner of Division and State streets, bars frequented by the college crowd abound on Lincoln Avenue. Clark Street near Wrigley Field, in Chicago's north end, has numerous sports bars. The gay scene is concentrated in the Lakeview neighborhood; Wicker Park offers a variety of alternative-music nightclubs.

## BARS AND TAVERNS

BARS AND TAVERNS are tucked into every neighborhood of Chicago. Some are rather basic drinking places, but others offer a glimpse into neighborhood life. Most bars in Chicago have limited food choices. Taverns, on the other hand, are serious about food. The American version of European pubs and bistros, taverns are relaxed places where locals go to eat, drink, and socialize.

The most venerable of the downtown taverns is **The Berghoff**. This establishment was the first in Chicago to be issued a liquor license once Prohibition ended. Some days it may seem that everyone in the Berghoff is from out of town, but locals also love this tavern. Two other notable downtown pubs are **Miller's Pub** and **Exchequer Restaurant & Pub**. Both succeed in maintaining a neighborhood atmosphere while catering to a good number of tourists.

Near the Magnificent Mile is **Boston Blackie's**, a dimly lit Art Deco-style sports bar. **Bar Louie**, a handsome bar with good drinks and large menu, is a great place to mingle with the upwardly mobile.

**Butch McGuire's** has a major presence on the bar-lined block of Division Street near the Gold Coast. Its atmosphere is pub-like, the food good (especially brunch). When the city celebrates a sports victory, fans celebrate in the many singles and sports bars near Division, Dearborn, and Rush streets.

Summer in Chicago is a great time to sit outside, enjoy a drink, and people-watch. There are several good beer gardens and patios in Lincoln Park. **John Barleycorn's** and **Charlie's Ale House** are two of the best. Nearby, **Ranalli's** serves good pizza and beer. **Goose Island Brewpub** sells brews made on the premises, some of the finest in town.

## NIGHTCLUBS

CHICAGO offers a variety of nightclubs: there is sure to be one to suit your taste. Expect to pay an admission charge, though some clubs may impose a drink-order minimum instead.

**Excalibur** is perhaps the most mainstream club in the city. Pool tables and video games fill the first floor; the dance floor is upstairs, where retrospective music is played.

If you are into tattoos and body-piercings, visit **CroBar the nightclub**. With the city's largest dance floor, complete with go-go dancers, it plays a mix of hip-hop, techno, and rock music.

One of Chicago's newest nightclubs, **Kustom** plays a mix of dance, hip-hop, and techno. There's ample dance space, as well as comfortable seating. But beware: this place gets loud once things warm up. Three VIP rooms, one complete with its own bar, offer some privacy.

## JAZZ

LIVE JAZZ, from salsa to swing, is played almost every night at the stylish **Green Dolphin Street**. The **Green Mill Cocktail Lounge** may not be impressive from the outside, and its Uptown neighborhood may be slightly run-down, but it is one of the city's coolest jazz clubs.

**Jazz Showcase** is the best place in Chicago to hear top jazz artists perform. **Andy's** is one of Chicago's most respected clubs and has been going for over 25 years.

## BLUES

MAJOR BLUES acts are presented at the **House of Blues**, a 1,500-seat venue with superb acoustics.

More intimate blues venues include **B.L.U.E.S.**, a small, busy bar with a friendly atmosphere that offers live music every night of the week. **Kingston Mines** also features nightly live blues on its two stages. Both stay open into the early morning hours.

**Buddy Guy's Legends** brings the big-name acts downtown. Guy himself plays here each January.

## FOLK AND COUNTRY MUSIC

THE CITY'S LEADING venue for folk music is the **Old Town School of Folk Music**. The **Abbey Pub** features local and touring groups, favoring Irish bands. It also offers barn dancing every Monday night.

**Heartland Cafe** is a throwback to the 1960s. It is a healthfood restaurant that also presents poetry readings, storytelling, and live music. **Schubas** is a neighborhood gem showcasing live folk and country music.

Although most of the line-dancing and two-stepping action is in the suburbs, it surprisingly can also be found in the city, at **Charlie's**. A gay bar serious about country music, Charlie's always welcomes straight folks.

## ROCK MUSIC

ROCK MUSIC is alive and well in Chicago. At **Brother Jimmy's**, bands play rock music from the 1970s onward while patrons experience authentic Southern cooking in the form of barbecued ribs.

**House of Blues** presents big-name rock stars. **Cubby Bear**, across from Wrigley Field *(see p114)*, is a huge sports bar that presents local bands and touring talents, whereas **Metro**, in Wrigleyville

*(see p114)*, is an independent-rock and dancing mecca. Wicker Park's *(see p114)* intimate **Double Door** is an excellent place to see live music. Many famous groups, such as the Smashing Pumpkins and the Rolling Stones, have played here under fictitious names, to the delight of unsuspecting patrons.

The **Wild Hare** is the city's best venue for live and reggae and African music. National or international acts are presented here nightly.

## COMEDY CLUBS

FOR WELL-KNOWN stand-up comedy acts, visit **Zanies**. Comedians Jerry Seinfeld and Jay Leno have entertained here.

**Second City**, the celebrated venue that produced many of the comedians who went on to *Saturday Night Live* fame, offers a mix of social-satire sketches and improvisation. Dinner-theater packages are available. Its offshoot, **Second City E.T.C.**, presents comedy revues next door.

## DIRECTORY

### BARS AND TAVERNS

**Bar Louie**
226 W Chicago Ave.
**Map** 1 C4.
337-3313.

**The Berghoff**
17 W Adams St.
**Map** 3 C2. 427-3170.

**Boston Blackie's**
164 E Grand Ave.
**Map** 2 D5.
938-8700.
*One of two locations.*

**Butch McGuire's**
20 W Division St.
**Map** 1 C3.
337-9080.

**Charlie's Ale House**
1224 W Webster Ave,
**Lincoln Park**.
(773) 871-1440.

**Exchequer Restaurant & Pub**
226 S Wabash Ave.
**Map** 4 D2.
939-5633.

**Goose Island Brewpub**
1800 N Clybourn Ave.
**Map** 1 A1.
915-0071.
*One of two locations.*

**John Barleycorn's**
658 W Belden Ave,
**Lincoln Park**.
(773) 348-8899.
*One of two locations.*

**Miller's Pub**
134 S Wabash Ave.
**Map** 4 D2.
263-4988 or 645-5377.

**Ranalli's**
1925 N Lincoln Ave,
**Lincoln Park**.
642-4700.
*One of several locations.*

### NIGHTCLUBS

**Crobar the nightclub**
1543 N Kingsbury St.
**Map** 1 A1. 413-7000.

**Excalibur**
632 N Dearborn St.
**Map** 1 C4. 266-1944.

**Kustom**
1997 N Clybourn Ave,
**Lincoln Park**.
(773) 528-3400.

### JAZZ

**Andy's**
11 E Hubbard St,
**Map** 2 D5. 642-6805.

**Green Dolphin Street**
2200 N Ashland Ave,
**Bucktown**.
(773) 395-0066.

**Green Mill Cocktail Lounge**
4802 N Broadway Ave,
**Uptown**.
(773) 878-5552.

**Jazz Showcase**
59 W Grand Ave.
**Map** 1 C5. 670-2473.

### BLUES

**B.L.U.E.S.**
2519 N Halsted St,
**Lincoln Park**.
409-7090.

**Buddy Guy's Legends**
754 S Wabash Ave.
**Map** 4 D3.
427-0333.

**House of Blues**
329 N Dearborn St.
**Map** 1 C5.
527-2583 or
923-2000 (tickets).

**Kingston Mines**
2548 N Halsted St,
**Lincoln Park**.
(773) 477-4646.

### FOLK AND COUNTRY MUSIC

**Abbey Pub**
3420 W Grace St,
**Northwest Side**.
(773) 478-4408.

**Charlie's**
3726 N Broadway Ave,
**Lakeview**.
(773) 871-8887.

**Heartland Cafe**
7000 N Glenwood Ave,
**Rogers Park**.
(773) 465-8005.

**Old Town School of Folk Music**
4544 N Lincoln Ave,
**Lincoln Square**.
(773) 728-6000
(tickets and classes).

**Schubas**
3159 N Southport Ave,
**Lakeview**.
(773) 525-2508.

### ROCK MUSIC

**Brother Jimmy's**
2909 N Sheffield Ave,
**Lakeview**.
(773) 528-0888.

**Cubby Bear**
1059 W Addison Ave,
**Wrigleyville**.
(773) 327-1662.

**Double Door**
1551 N Damen Ave,
**Wicker Park**.
(773) 489-3160.

**Metro**
3730 N Clark St,
**Wrigleyville**.
(773) 549-3604.

**Wild Hare**
3530 N Clark St,
**Lakeview**.
(773) 327-4273.

### COMEDY CLUBS

**Second City**
1616 N Wells St.
**Map** 1 C2.
337-3992 or (877)
778-4707.

**Second City E.T.C.**
1608 N Wells St.
**Map** 1 C2.
337-3992.

**Zanies**
1548 N Wells St.
**Map** 1 C1. 337-4027.

# SURVIVAL
# GUIDE

# PRACTICAL INFORMATION

CHICAGO LOVES VISITORS. Its Visitor Information Centers are an invaluable source of information, and a stop at one of them should be on every traveler's itinerary. The centers also have details of the many tours available, an excellent way to see the many different faces of Chicago. Getting around the city is both easy and

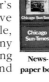

**News-paper box**

safe, if you follow a few guidelines *(see pp170–71)*. The practical information that follows offers a variety of tips, from locating banks *(see pp172–3)* to making a local phone call *(see pp174–5)*. There is also a section on transit in and around Chicago, as well as details on how to get downtown upon your arrival in Chicago *(see pp176–83)*.

## VISITOR INFORMATION

THE **Illinois Bureau of Tourism** will mail you information about Illinois hotels, restaurants, and attractions. The **Chicago Convention and Tourism Bureau**'s website will also help you plan your trip. Upon your arrival in Chicago, visit one of the three **Visitor Information Centers** for maps, entertainment and tour brochures, tickets, public transportation passes, and general information.

**Visitor Information Center**

**Sign for one of the city tourist offices**

## OPENING HOURS

MOST BUSINESSES are open from 9am to 5pm weekdays and do not close for lunch. Banks are generally open weekdays from 9am to 5pm. Some bank branches open from 9am to early afternoon on Saturdays.

Most major museums are open daily from 9am to 5pm, often with later hours on one weekday night. Smaller museums keep more limited hours; phone for details.

Banks and museums usually close on major holidays.

## ETIQUETTE

SMOKING IS PROHIBITED in public buildings and airports, except in designated areas. Restaurants provide separate seating areas for smokers. Smoking is usually permitted in the bar area. Some establishments have cigar rooms, but most do not permit cigar or pipe smoking.

Tipping is integral to Chicago's service industry. For

details on restaurant tipping, see page 143. Tip $1 per coat checked; taxi drivers, hairdressers, and bartenders, from 10 to 15 percent. Tip hotel or airport porters up to $1 per bag, valet-parking attendants $1 after they bring you your car. Tip tour drivers between $2 and $3 per group member. If a concierge was especially helpful, acknowledge it by tipping between $5 and $10.

## MUSEUMS

MUSEUMS either charge an admission fee or suggest a donation. Expect a separate charge to special exhibits. Smaller museums are often free. Entrance to large museums may be free either once a week or once a month *(see p161)*. Tours are often free.

Museum Campus, a park on the lakefront, is home to the Field Museum *(see pp86–9)*, Shedd Aquarium *(see pp96–7)*, and Adler Planetarium *(see pp92–3)*. Free trolleys run between these museums and public transportation stations. Call the **Museum Campus Information Line** for details.

## GUIDED TOURS

EXCELLENT WALKING, bicycle, bus, and boat tours are offered by the **Chicago Architecture Foundation** (CAF). A fabulous way to discover a few of Chicago's 77 neighborhoods is to take one of the Saturday tours offered by **Chicago Neighborhood Tours**. **American Sightseeing** offers two-hour narrated tours. **Chicago Trolley Company** sells an all-

day pass for tours aboard old-fashioned trolleys. **University of Chicago Walking Tours** *(see pp100–101)* are led by students on Saturdays.

Boat tour season is from April to October. **Wendella Sightseeing** offers evening and lakefront tours. **Mercury, Chicago's Skyline Cruiseline** has narrated 90-minute tours. **Shoreline Sightseeing** offers 30-minute narrated tours on Lake Michigan.

Many companies offer discounts when two or more tours per person are purchased; be sure to ask. **Antique Coach and Carriage** will pick you up at your hotel or a restaurant in a horse-drawn buggy.

New to the city are Italian-style gondola rides on the Chicago River, offering a unique view of downtown.

**A river cruise tour offered by the Chicago Architecture Foundation**

## NEWSPAPERS

CHICAGO HAS TWO major dailies: *Chicago Tribune* and *Chicago Sun-Times*. The *Chicago Defender* is published weekdays, primarily for

**Special-interest newspapers in Chicago**

the city's African-American readership. Business news is found in the weekly *Crain's*. For details on entertainment news, see page 160. Foreign newspapers are available at Europa Books *(see p156)*.

## CUSTOMS AND IMMIGRATION

HOLDERS of a valid EU passport and a return ticket do not need a visa if staying 90 days or less in the US. Canadians need only to show proof of their residence. New Zealanders and Australians need a current passport, tourist visa, and onward or return ticket. Foreign visitors may need to prove they carry sufficient funds for survival. Check current requirements and stipulations with your travel agent or the US embassy in your country.

## TRAVELERS WITH DISABILITIES

ALL FACILITIES operated by the city are wheelchair accessible. Most attractions, buildings (including restaurants), and public transportation are equipped for easy access. However, small entertainment venues may not be. Parking spaces reserved for vehicles with disabled permits are marked by the handicapped symbol either on a sign or painted on the concrete.
Phone the **Mayor's Office for People with Disabilities** for information.

## STUDENTS AND SENIORS

MANY businesses offer student and senior discounts. For seniors, all that is needed is picture identification with their birthdate on it.
Students will need current student photo ID. An international student ID card is widely accepted. Purchase one at your local youth travel association or

hostel organization. The card can also be purchased from **Council Travel** with proper credentials.

## CONVERSION CHART

**Imperial to Metric**:
1 inch = 2.5 centimeters
1 foot = 30 centimeters
1 mile = 1.6 kilometers
1 ounce = 28 grams
1 pound = 454 grams
1 US pint = 0.5 liter
1 US gallon = 3.8 liters

**Metric to Imperial**:
1 millimeter = 0.04 inch
1 centimeter = 0.4 inch
1 meter = 3 feet 3 inches
1 kilometer = 0.6 mile
1 gram = 0.04 ounce

Bear in mind that 1 US pint (0.5 liter) is a smaller measure than 1 UK pint (0.6 liter).

## ELECTRICITY

ALL US electric current flows at a standardized 110 to 120 volts AC (alternating current). You may need an adapter plug and voltage converter that fits standard US electrical outlets. US plugs have two flat prongs. Batteries are readily available.

**Standard US two-pin plug**

---

## DIRECTORY

### VISITOR INFORMATION

**Chicago Convention and Tourism Bureau**
📞 567-8500.
🌐 www.chicago.il.org

**Illinois Bureau of Tourism**
📞 (800) 226-66328.
🌐 www.enjoyillinois.com

**Visitor Information Centers**
📞 744-2400; 346-3278; (888) 244-2246.
**Chicago Cultural Center**
77 E Randolph St. **Map 4** D1. ⏰ 10am–6pm Mon–Fri; 10am–5pm Sat; 11am–5pm Sun. ● major public

hols. 🌐 www.ci.chi.il.us/tourism/culturalcenter

**Chicago Water Works**
163 E Pearson St. **Map 2** D4. ⏰ 7:30am–7pm daily. ● major public hols.

**Navy Pier**
700 E Grand Ave. **Map 2** F5. 📞 595-7437; (800) 595-7437.
⏰ 10am–8pm Sun–Thu; 10am–10pm Fri, Sat. 🌐 www.navypier.com

### GUIDED TOURS

**American Sightseeing**
📞 251-3100.

**Antique Coach and Carriage**
📞 787-1349; .

**Chicago Architecture Foundation**
📞 922-8687.
224 S Michigan Ave, Santa Fe Building.
**Map 4** D2. or 875 N Michigan Ave, John Hancock Center. **Map 2** D3.

**Chicago Neighborhood Tours**
📞 742-1190.

**Chicago Trolley Company**
📞 (773) 648-5000.

**Mercury, Chicago's Skyline Cruiseline**
📞 332-1368.

**Shoreline Sightseeing**
📞 222-0936.

**University of Chicago Walking Tours**
📞 (773) 702-8374.

**Wendella Sightseeing**
📞 337-1446.

### USEFUL NUMBERS

**Council Travel**
1160 N State St.
**Map 1** C3. 📞 951-0585.
🌐 www.counciltravel.com

**Mayor's Office for People with Disabilities**
📞 744-7050. 🌐 www.ci.chi.il.us/disabilities

**Museum Campus Information Line**
📞 409-9696.

# Personal Security and Health

CHICAGO IS A FRIENDLY CITY, and most visitors do not encounter any problems. However, it is always best to take common-sense precautions and be aware of your surroundings. If you don't feel safe, you probably aren't. Public transportation is generally safe during the day, but after dark, you may feel more comfortable taking a taxi to your destination. The best source of information is often your hotel concierge. Don't hesitate to ask if your destination or day's itinerary will take you into unsavory neighborhoods. Parks and the paths along the lakefront are populated during the day but are often fairly deserted at night.

Osco Drug, many locations with a 24-hour pharmacy

## LAW ENFORCEMENT

THE CHICAGO Police Department has bicycle, motorcycle, car, and foot patrols day and night. There is also a police presence at major community and cultural events. Police officers are usually very helpful if approached, but be mindful: they are not tour guides.

Parking-enforcement and traffic officers make their rounds on foot or in small vehicles. Airports, stores, and hotels have uniformed and plain-clothes staff who also provide security services.

## PERSONAL SAFETY

IN RECENT YEARS, violent crime has decreased in Chicago. However, petty crime is still a problem. Your best protection is common sense. Never walk in dark alleys or deserted streets. Don't leave purses or valuables unattended in public places, and don't carry a lot of cash or wear flashy jewelry. Keep one credit card in a concealed secondary

Chicago Fire Department on early-morning firefighting duty

wallet or in the hotel safe. Keep your wallet in an inconspicuous place, and have enough change handy for phone calls and bus fares. Defeat purse snatchers by carrying your bag with the clasp facing toward you and the shoulder strap across your body. Carry your passport separate from your money.

Do not allow anyone other than hotel and airport personnel to carry your belongings. Stow valuables in the room or hotel safe, keeping an inventory of items you deposit. Chicago's homeless sell the newspaper *Streetwise* for $1. Buying the paper is a help to the homeless. Otherwise, do not give money to, or make eye contact with, people asking for spare change.

Much of Chicago's West Side and South Side can be inhospitable. Notable exceptions are Little Italy, Chinatown, Hyde Park, and Pullman. Some safe North Side neighborhoods are next to troubled areas. And, like most US cities, the downtown is primarily a business district: bustling during the day and quieter at night. While the Loop is becoming busier during the evenings, in part because of its theater district, caution should still be exercised.

Chicago parks are safest when crowds are present. Avoid parks after dark, unless you're attending a special event held in one. If you want to go for a jog, ask the concierge at your hotel to map out a safe route.

Finally, be sure you fully understand your hotel's fire-escape procedures.

## MEDICAL MATTERS

MANY WALK-IN medical and dental clinics in Chicago are open 24-hours, and are often sufficient for minor injuries and ailments.

Without medical insurance, medical services can be expensive. Even with insurance, you may have to pay for the services yourself, then claim reimbursement from your insurance company.

Traveler's checks or cash are sometimes the only methods of payment accepted from visitors, though many practitioners take credit cards. Anyone taking a prescription drug should ask their doctor for an extra supply to take with them and a copy of the prescription in case more is needed. Both **Walgreen's** and **Osco Drug** have pharmacies open 24-hours. Call them to find the location nearest you.

## EMERGENCIES

CALL 911 for emergencies requiring medical, police, or fire services. For non-emergency police situations, such as theft, dial 311, to reach the **City HelpLine**.

Hospital emergency rooms and city hospitals are listed in the Yellow Pages of the telephone directory. Most Chicago hospitals have 24-hour emergency rooms. Your hotel concierge will know the one closest to the hotel. **Northwestern Memorial Hospital** has an emergency room convenient to both

Police car

Emergency ambulance

Fire boat

downtown and North Side visitors. It also provides a **Physician Referral Service**. The **Bernard A. Mitchell Hospital**, at the University of Chicago, serves the city's South Side.

Private hospitals are listed in the Yellow Pages of the telephone directory. Or, your hotel may be able to arrange for a doctor or dentist to visit you in your room.

For dental emergencies, call the **Chicago Dental Society**, which provides referrals 24 hours a day, every day.

## LOST PROPERTY

THE CHANCE of recovering stolen property is poor. Nevertheless, you should report all lost or stolen items to the police. Keep a copy of the police report if you plan to make an insurance claim.

The Chicago Police Department has a location at O'Hare Airport; call if you have misplaced something at the airport other than at a restaurant or on a plane.

Most credit card companies have toll-free numbers to call to report a loss, as do Thomas Cook and American Express *(see p173)* if you lose or have your traveler's checks stolen.

If you lose your passport, contact your embassy or consulate immediately.

## TRAVEL INSURANCE

TRAVEL INSURANCE coverage of a minimum of $1 million is strongly recommended, mainly because of the high cost of medical care in the US. Among the most important features the policy should cover are accidental death, dismemberment, emergency medical and dental care, trip cancellation, and lost or stolen baggage coverage. Your travel agent or insurance company should be able to recommend a suitable policy, but it is worth shopping around for the best deal.

Sign outside a Chicago medical center

---

# Banking and Local Currency

MOST NATIONAL AND INTERNATIONAL banks have branches in Chicago. The cheapest exchange, though, may be offered on your credit or debit card, which can be used at most ATMs (automated teller machines). It is a good idea to arrive in Chicago with about $100 cash in US currency, including a few dollars in coins, to cover incidental costs until you are able to exchange your money.

## BANKING

BANKS ARE GENERALLY open Monday to Friday from 9am to 5pm; 9am to early or mid-afternoon on Saturday.

Many banks charge fees to use a teller for routine matters

**Logos of two major Chicago banks**

such as withdrawing money. Always ask if any fees apply before making a transaction with a bank teller.

The major consumer banks in Chicago include **Bank One, LaSalle Bank**, and **Harris Trust and Savings**. Credit unions will usually serve only their members.

## AUTOMATED TELLER MACHINES

THERE IS NO NEED to carry large amounts of cash in Chicago. Hundreds of automated teller machines (ATMs) can be found throughout the city. They are almost always in bank lobbies or on an outside wall near the bank's entrance, as well as in many convenience and grocery stores. Some bars and fast-food outlets also have ATMs on their premises.

US currency, usually in $20 bills, can be electronically withdrawn from your bank or credit-card account through an ATM. Ask your bank at home which American ATM network your card can access in Chicago, and what transaction fees will apply.

**Cirrus** and **Plus** are common networks in Chicago. You can also do transactions with some credit cards at ATMs.

Use ATMs only in secure conditions, daylight hours, or when there are plenty of people nearby in order to deter robbers.

## CREDIT CARDS

CREDIT CARDS allow you to carry minimal cash and may offer merchandise guarantees or other benefits. American Express, Diners Club, MasterCard, and VISA are widely accepted.

Most hotels ask for a credit-card number to guarantee a reservation, taking an imprint of the card when you check in. Car rental agencies insist on a credit-card guarantee even if you are paying for the rental in cash (see p183).

Credit cards are very helpful in emergencies, should you have to fly home on short notice or need medical treatment during your stay. Many hospitals will accept a major credit card as a method of payment.

## EXCHANGING MONEY

EXCHANGE RATES are printed in the daily newspapers and posted in banks where exchange services are offered, usually at the main branches of large banks. Some banks have designated tellers for foreign exchange.

Foreign exchange brokers in Chicago are few. Among the solidly established is **Thomas Cook**. **World's Money Exchange** also deals in foreign currency. Two

exchanges are located at O'Hare Airport, in terminals 3 and 5 (open daily); there are no currency exchanges at Midway Airport. Keep in mind, however, that an ATM may provide a better exchange rate and charge a lower transaction fee than a bank or exchange bureau.

Chicago has hundreds of state-regulated "currency exchanges." Most do not exchange foreign currency but instead cash checks, sell money orders, and offer notary services.

## CASHING TRAVELER'S CHECKS

TRAVELER'S CHECKS issued by **American Express** and **Travelex/Thomas Cook** in US dollars are widely accepted without a fee by most shops, hotels, and restaurants, if accompanied by a recognized form of photographic identification, such as a passport, driver's license, or international student card (see p169).

US-dollar traveler's checks can be cashed at most banks. Checks in foreign currency can be cashed at a bank branch offering foreign-currency exchange, usually the banks' main locations.

American Express and Thomas Cook will cash their own checks at no fee.

**Automated teller machine (ATM)**

## Coins

*American coins (actual size shown) come in 1-, 5-, 10-, and 25-cent, as well as $1, denominations; 50-cent pieces are minted but rarely used. Each value of coin has a popular name: 1-cent coins are known as pennies, 5-cent coins as nickels, 10-cent coins as dimes, 25-cent coins as quarters, and 1-dollar coins (and bills) as bucks.*

**25-cent coin**
**(a quarter)**

**10-cent coin**
**(a dime)**

**5-cent coin**
**(a nickel)**

**1-cent coin**
**(a penny)**

## Bank Notes

*Units of currency in the US are dollars and cents, with 100 cents to a dollar. Notes, or "bills," come in $1, $2, $5, $10, $20, $50, and $100 denominations. The $2 bills are rarely seen. The US mint plans to gradually replace the $1 bill with the new "golden dollar" coin. New versions of the $20, $50, and $100 bills are the same color as the old versions, but the presidential portraits are larger and positioned off center.*

**1-dollar coin**
**(a buck)**

**1-dollar bill ($1)**

**5-dollar bill ($5)**

**10-dollar bill ($10)**

**20-dollar bill ($20)**

**50-dollar bill ($50)**

**100-dollar bill ($100)**

# Communications

CHICAGO'S COMMUNICATION systems are, for the most part, both efficient and reasonably priced. Public pay phones are located throughout the city, and at gas stations and tourist centers along the interstates. Ameritech is the major player in the Chicago telecommunications field. Regular letter service offered by the US postal system is reliable, if slow; two express services and independent courier services are also available. Visitors will find that Internet, e-mail, and fax services are readily available in Chicago.

**Express Mail box**

> ### CHICAGO TIME
>
> Chicago is on Central Standard Time (CST). It is one hour behind Eastern Standard Time (EST) and six hours behind Greenwich Mean Time (GMT). Daylight saving time begins on the first Sunday in April, when clocks are set ahead one hour. It ends on the last Sunday in October, when clocks are set back one hour.

## PHONE NUMBERS AND PREFIXES

MOST US phone numbers have seven digits. Some emergency and public-service numbers have only three. US prefixes (area codes) are always three digits.

Chicago and its environs use six prefixes: 312 (Downtown Core), 773 (surrounding downtown), 847 and 224 (north and northwestern suburbs; note that even local calls made in this area require dialling 1 and the area code, such 11-digit dialling for local calls will eventually apply to all areas), 708 (near western and southern suburbs), and 630 (far western suburbs).

## PUBLIC PAY PHONES

CHICAGO'S PAY PHONES are found throughout the city, particularly in restaurants, gas stations, and department stores. All are coin operated, though you can use a calling-card number to charge calls to your account. Some also accept credit cards.

Most pay phones are operated by Ameritech. Some may belong to a company other than Ameritech, though the phones often look similar. Phone companies set their own rates, so prices vary. Use only public phones that have details of the charges posted.

## PAY PHONE CHARGES

CALLING A NUMBER with the same prefix as the one from which you are calling is considered a local call. The minimum charge for a local call made from a pay phone is 35 cents and will buy from three to five minutes. When it is time to insert more money, a recording will interrupt to tell you how much to deposit.

When calling within the same area code, simply dial the phone number. When calling another area code, first dial 1 and the prefix.

Phone books are now rare at pay phones. Dial 411 to connect to national directory assistance. The minimum charge is 35 cents.

Rates for long-distance calls vary, depending on the time of day, the distance called, and the long-distance carrier. Be sure to have plenty of coins or a calling card before placing the call from a pay phone. If billing the call to a calling-card number, follow the instructions on the card or those on the phone. Dialing instructions are in the white pages of the phone directory.

Long-distance calls are less expensive when dialed without the help of an operator. Savings on calls within the US are available during the night and weekends. Discounts for calls to locations outside the US vary; ask the international operator for details. A list of country codes is in the Yellow Pages of the phone directory.

## USING A COIN-OPERATED PHONE

**1** Lift the receiver and listen for the tone.

**3** Press the number.

**Coins**
*Make sure you have the correct coins available before you dial and a sufficient quantity of them.*

**25 cents**

**5 cents**    **10 cents**

**2** Insert the required coin or coins. The coin drops as soon as you insert it.

**4** If you do not want to complete your call or the call does not connect, press the coin-release lever and take the coins from the coin return located at the bottom left-hand corner of the phone.

**5** If the call is answered and you talk longer than the allotted time, a recorded message will interrupt and tell you how much more money to deposit. Pay phones do not give change but will return unused coins to the coin return.

## CELL PHONES

IT IS POSSIBLE to rent a cell phone in Chicago. **International Sound** offers free downtown delivery. AT&T, Nextel, and Sprint are the largest mobile service providers. Chicago's cell phone network is not GSM-compatible. Check with your carrier whether you will be able to tune your own phone to local Chicago networks.

## TV AND RADIO

FIVE MAJOR TV networks are broadcast in Chicago: CBS on channel 2, NBC on channel 5, ABC on channel 7, WGN on channel 9, and FOX on channel 32.

AM radio stations include WBBM news (780Hz) and WGN talk/sports (720Hz). FM radio stations include WBEZ news and jazz (91.5M).

See pages 168–9 for details on Chicago newspapers.

## USEFUL DIALING CODES

• Long-distance direct-dial call outside your local area code, but within the US and Canada: dial **1**.
• International direct-dial call: dial **011**, followed by country code (Australia: 61; New Zealand: 64; UK: 44; Ireland: 353), then the city or area code, then the local telephone number.
• International call via the operator: dial **01**, followed by the country code, then the city code (minus the first 0), then the local telephone number.
• International directory inquiries: dial **00**.
• International operator assistance: dial **01**.
• An **800**, **866**, **877**, or **888** prefix indicates that the call is toll-free. Dial **1** before the prefix.
• Directory assistance for toll-free numbers: dial **1-800-555-1212**.
• Directory assistance for outside local area: dial **1-AREACODE-555-1212**.
• Local operator assistance: dial **0**.
• Local directory inquiries: dial **411**.

**Entrance to Oak Park's post office**

## POSTAL SERVICES

APART FROM post offices, letters can be mailed at most hotel concierge desks (which usually also sell stamps); at letter slots in the lobbies of office buildings; at air, rail, and bus terminals; and at a street mailbox, though these can be few and far between. Collection times are printed on the inside of the pull-down door of each mailbox, which are always painted blue, or red, white, and blue. Stamps can be bought at the **Chicago Main Post Office** or branch offices located throughout the city.

All letters are delivered on first-class service. The delivery time can sometimes be as long as five business days.

The US Postal Service offers two special delivery services. **Priority Mail** guarantees the delivery in two to three business days; **Express Mail** guarantees delivery on the next business day. If using either Express Mail or Priority Mail, first weigh your letters at a post office to determine the postage required.

Two other companies offer mail services. **FedEx** offers a variety of overnight mail services. **UPS** delivers parcels and packages. FedEx and UPS services are usually available through mailing businesses such as **Mail Boxes Etc**.

Letters and parcels will be held for 30 days for collection at the Main Post Office. Address mail with: Name, General Delivery, Chicago Main Post Office, 433 West Harrison Street, Chicago, IL 60607. You will need to show photo ID to collect mail.

## E-MAIL AND FAXES

VISITORS TO CHICAGO can use e-mail and the Internet, as well as fax machines, in the larger hotels and those with business facilities, or at one of the Internet cafés now beginning to dot the Loop and North Side. However, these businesses tend to close down as quickly as they open, so it is best to ask your hotel concierge or at a visitor center about current businesses. One popular Internet café in Chicago is **Screenz**, part of a national chain.

Online time at cafés may be charged by the minute (from 8 cents to 20 cents) or by the hour (from $4 to $10).

**Mail Boxes Etc., a national mailbox-service business**

# GETTING TO CHICAGO

CHICAGO IS ONE of the US's most important transportation hubs. All major airlines fly into one of its two airports: O'Hare or Midway. The major carriers often have similar fares, though you can sometimes find savings by flying into Midway. Discount ticket services, travel companies on the Internet, and charter airlines may also offer very substantial savings. Amtrak trains from across the US and from Canada arrive in Chicago daily, and several interstate highways run through Chicago (see pp182–3), making the city easily accessible by train, car, or bus. Long-distance bus travel is generally both comfortable and convenient.

**Star Alliance passenger jet**

## ARRIVING BY AIR

ASIDE FROM DRIVING into the city, the easiest way to get to Chicago is by air. Flights from the East Coast of the US take about two hours; from the West Coast about four hours.

All major airlines fly into Chicago, among them Air Canada, Continental, British Airways, Lufthansa, American Airlines, and United Airlines.

Chicago is served by two airports. The largest and busiest is O'Hare, located 17 miles (27 km) northwest of the city. Midway Airport is much smaller and located about 8 miles (13 km) southwest of downtown.

## AIR FARES

IT PAYS TO SHOP around for fares, especially if you are booking a departure flight less than 14 days in advance. Many major airlines offer discounts for tickets purchased at least 14 days before departure. These tickets usually carry restrictions and penalties for changes to your itinerary; ask before paying.

Investigate smaller carriers, especially if you are making last-minute plans; their fares are often less than half those of the major airlines. You may also find flights into Midway Airport to be less expensive than those into O'Hare.

For inexpensive consolidated tickets (those bought from a travel agent), contact **Travel City** or **Priceline.com** online. An extensive list of consolidators can be ordered from **Intrepid Traveler**.

When booking a flight, bear in mind that "direct" means that the plane may make one or two stops along the way, but you won't need to change planes. "Nonstop" means you fly directly to your destination.

## O'HARE AIRPORT (ORD)

CHICAGO'S O'HARE Airport is one of the world's busiest airports, servicing up to 70 million passengers each year. Three terminals are used for domestic flights, one for international flights.

O'Hare has been extensively remodeled in recent years. Today it is clean and spacious. The food at most of its restaurants is good, prices aren't grossly inflated, and the atmosphere is pleasing. There are also many upscale stores and kiosks throughout the airport. A branch of the Chicago Children's Museum (see p65) is in Terminal 2.

Rental carts are available for use within the airport. Skycaps (porters) will also transport your luggage to a taxi or shuttle; they should be tipped from 50 cents to $1 per bag.

Terminal 1 is dominated by United Express, United Airlines, and Lufthansa. Terminal 2 serves Continental, Air Canada, American Trans Air, Northwest Airlines, TWA, and US Airways. Terminal 3 serves American, American Eagle, Delta, Reno Air, and Singapore Air. Terminal 5 is for international flights. There is no Terminal 4.

To get between domestic terminals, the international terminal, and the long-term parking lot, take the free Automated Train System (ATS). There is also free shuttle service between parking lot F and the ATS terminal at parking lot E.

O'Hare has several Airport Information counters on the lower level of each domestic terminal, and on the lower and upper levels of the international terminal. The counters are open daily from 8:15am to 8pm. Multilingual specialists are on hand to provide directions and translation assistance.

Teletext phones for the hearing impaired are located next to the airport information booths as well as at phone banks located throughout the airport.

Automatic bank teller machines are located on the upper levels of all terminals. See page 173 for locations of foreign currency exchanges.

| AIRPORT | ( INFORMATION | DISTANCE TO CHICAGO | TAXI FARE (OFF-PEAK HOURS) | CONTINENTAL EXPRESS TO DOWNTOWN | OMEGA SHUTTLE TO SOUTH SIDE |
|---------|---------------|---------------------|----------------------------|---------------------------------|-----------------------------|
| O'Hare | (773) 686-2200 | 17 miles (27 km) | $30–$35 | $20 | $20 |
| Midway | (773) 838-0600 | 8 miles (13 km) | $20–$25 | $15 | $15 |

## MIDWAY AIRPORT (MDW)

**M**IDWAY IS everything O'Hare isn't. It is small, laid out on one level only, and relatively uncongested. It services about 13 million passengers each year. Although it is a bit worn around the edges, this is a small price to pay for the airport's advantages.

Terminals A, B, and C are within the airport's one building. The Airport Information counter is in the lobby by the main entrance.

A $761-million development project, to be completed in 2004, will triple the size of the existing building, expanding the concourse from 28 to 41 gates, and improve road links to and from the airport. New parking facilities and concessions are also planned.

Midway currently has no foreign currency exchange.

## GETTING INTO THE CITY

**A**CONVENIENT, inexpensive way to get into the city from either airport is via CTA train *(see p180)*.

Blue-line trains run directly to and from O'Hare Airport,

24 hours a day. The ride to the downtown Dearborn Street station takes about 45 minutes. Orange-line trains run between Midway Airport and downtown, stopping at all orange-line Loop stations, from early morning to late evening. Allow 35 minutes for the ride. Trains on both lines depart frequently. One-way train fare is about $1.50.

**Continental Airport Express** operates a shuttle service between each airport and downtown Chicago. Shuttles operate daily, beginning at 6am. Continental also provides service between both airports and McCormick Place Convention Center.

**Omega Airport Shuttle** operates shuttle service between O'Hare and Midway airports between 7am and 10pm daily. Omega also offers shuttle service to Hyde Park on Chicago's South Side.

It is possible to share a taxi ride from either airport to downtown. Airport curbside dispatchers will help get you a taxi or put you with other

**Blue line trains**
54/Cermak-Forest Park-O'Hare
**Sign for CTA blue-line trains**

**Concourse of the international terminal at O'Hare Airport**

persons going to the same area; it will cost you about $15 for the shared taxi ride.

Information counters of limousine and rental car agencies *(see p183)* are in the baggage claim areas of both Midway and O'Hare airports.

Driving time from O'Hare to downtown Chicago is about 45 minutes, and 30 minutes from Midway, but allow up to twice this during rush hour (from 6am to 9am; 3pm to 7pm). Taxis are not immune to traffic jams. During rush hour, it is much faster to use public transportation to and from either of the airports.

---

### DIRECTORY

**AIRPORTS**

**Midway Airport**
☎ (773) 838-0600.
🅆 www.ohare.com/midway/home.cfm

**O'Hare International Airport**
☎ (773) 686-2200 or (800) 832-6352.
🅆 www.ohare.com

**AIRLINE NUMBERS**

**Air Canada**
☎ (888) 247-2262.

**American Airlines**
☎ (800) 443-7300.

**British Airways**
☎ (800) 247-9297.

**British Midland**
☎ (800) 788-0555.

**Continental Airlines**
☎ (800) 525-0280.

**Lufthansa**
☎ (800) 645-3880.

**United Airlines**
☎ (800) 241-6522.

**AIR FARES**

**Intrepid Traveler**
☎ (203) 488-5341.
🅆 www.intrepidtraveler.com

**Priceline.com**
🅆 www.priceline.com

**Travel City**
☎ (858) 581-5656.
🅆 www.travelcity.com

**AIRPORT SHUTTLES**

**Continental Airport Express**
☎ 454-7800, (800) 654-7871, or (888) 284-3826.

**Omega Airport Shuttle**
☎ (773) 483-6634.

**AIRPORT HOTELS**

**At O'Hare Airport**
Holiday Inn O'Hare
5440 N River Rd,
Rosemont, IL.
☎ (847) 671-6350 or (888) 642-7344.

Hyatt Regency O'Hare,
9300 W Bryn Mawr Ave,
Rosemont, IL.
☎ (847) 696-1234 or (800) 233-1234.

Embassy Suites Hotel O'Hare
5500 N River Rd,
Rosemont, IL.
☎ (847) 678-4000 or (800) 362-2779.

Westin O'Hare
6100 N River Rd,
Rosemont, IL.
☎ (847) 698-6000 or (800) 228-3000.

**At Midway Airport**
Holiday Inn Express Hotel & Suites
6500 S Cicero Ave,
Chicago, IL.
☎ (708) 458-0202 or (888) 643-4667.

Courtyard Chicago
Midway Airport
6610 S Cicero Ave,
Bedford Park, IL.
☎ (708) 563-0200 or (888) 236-2427.

## ARRIVING BY CAR

IF YOU ARRIVE in Chicago from the south, on I-55 (Stevenson Expressway), follow the freeway to its end, to Lake Shore Drive, then follow Lake Shore Drive north. Shortly you will pass the city center, and have one of the best views of Chicago's skyline. Several exits lead off Lake Shore Drive into downtown or the North Side, including the Wacker Drive exit. Taking Lake Shore Drive is a good way to traverse the city.

Historic Route 66 running from Los Angeles joins I-55 on the outskirts of Chicago.

I-90 East (Northwest Tollway to Kennedy Expressway) running from the north, from O'Hare Airport, will bring you into the city. Take the Ohio Street exit for downtown.

Arriving by car from the west, I-290 East (Eisenhower Expressway) will become Congress Parkway at the southwest edge of Chicago's downtown Loop. From the parkway, drive north for destinations downtown or beyond.

I-90 and I-94 converge in the city. For destinations in the Loop, there are a number of options. The Washington Street or Monroe Street exits will put you on one-way streets that run into the Loop. For destinations just north of the Loop, such as the Magnificent Mile, take the Ohio Street exit east.

The **Illinois Department of Transportation** has a useful website, which details driving directions to Chicago and throughout Illinois, providing information on interstate rest areas, welcome centers, road and weather conditions, as well as how to obtain state highway maps. See pages 182–3 for more details on driving in Illinois.

## ARRIVING BY LONG-DISTANCE BUS

THE MAIN TERMINAL in Chicago for **Greyhound Bus Line**, the bus line that services almost all parts of the US, is in the Downtown Core. However, it is not within easy walking distance to hotels in the Loop, so plan on taking a taxi or public transportation to your final destination.

Greyhound also stops near O'Hare Airport at the CTA Cumberland station and on the city's South Side at 95th and Dan Ryan Expressway.

Greyhound buses are clean and modern. Ask when purchasing tickets about any discounts. They are usually offered to children, seniors, students, members of the military, and US veterans. Ask also about any promotional packages that may be available.

Greyhound's Ameripass allows up to 60 consecutive days of unlimited travel anywhere in the continental US. Tickets may be less expensive if you buy them in advance, though walk-up, or unrestricted, fares are also readily available.

Greyhound provides assistance to travelers with disabilities with 48 hours' notice, including priority seating. In some cases, a personal care assistant may travel for free. Call the Greyhound **ADA Assist Line** for details.

**Sign for historic Route 66**

**Amtrak train in train yard near Union Station**

## ARRIVING BY TRAIN

CHICAGO IS the national rail hub of **Amtrak**, the US's passenger rail line. Fifty trains linking to hundreds of US destinations, as well as those from Canada, arrive at or depart from Chicago's **Union Station** daily. Amtrak also services 35 destinations in Illinois, either through trains or connecting buses.

Its commuter trains have refreshment cars. Long-distance routes have both dining cars and sleeping cars.

Amtrak offers discounts to travelers with disabilities, students, seniors, and children. There are also group and convention rates. Ask too about any promotional discounts or package deals.

Reservations are necessary on many Amtrak routes and advised for all travel during peak periods: the summer months and major holidays.

The 1925 building housing Union Station was renovated in the early 1990s. Ticket agents, a food court, lounge, 10-story waiting area, storage lockers, and Metra commuter train station *(see pp182–3)* are all to be found within the building, which is wheelchair accessible. "Red cap" Amtrak porters are available to help you with your luggage.

Although Union Station is just west of the Loop and close to downtown Chicago, it is not an easy walk to hotels or CTA trains when you are carrying luggage. If arriving in Chicago by train, it is best to plan on taking a taxi to your hotel.

**Long-distance Greyhound bus**

**A typical Chicago taxi cab**

## GETTING TO McCORMICK PLACE

L OCATED ONE MILE (1.5 km) south of downtown Chicago, McCormick Place Convention Center is the largest exhibition and meeting facility in North America. Even though it is close to the Loop, the walk is not a practical one. A taxi ride from the Loop to McCormick Place will cost about $6. Large conventions often provide shuttle bus services from major downtown hotels, and sometimes, from the airports. The McCormick Place Busway has improved travelling times from downtown to the Center.

The Metra Electric line *(see pp182–3)* services the 23rd Street/McCormick Place station. Trains depart from the Randolph Street and Van Buren Street stations.

If you are arriving in Chicago at Union Station, take the No. 1, 7, or 126 eastbound CTA bus to Michigan Avenue. Transfer to either southbound bus No. 3 or 4; both will take you to the 23rd Street bus stop outside the convention center.

If driving to McCormick Place from O'Hare Airport, take I-90 (Northwest Tollway) east to I-94 (Kennedy/Dan Ryan Expressway), exiting to

I-55 north (Stevenson Expressway). Follow the signs to Lake Shore Drive South (31st Street exit) and to McCormick Place.

From Midway Airport, take Cicero Avenue north to the I-55 (Stevenson Expressway), then continue north to Lake Shore Drive South, following the signs to McCormick Place.

The convention center can be reached via public transportation from O'Hare and Midway airports. However, you may find it more convenient to take a taxi or, if available, a shuttle bus, as there is no direct transit route: you will need to transfer to a CTA bus once downtown.

If using public transportation from O'Hare Airport, take the blue-line CTA train *(see p177)* downtown, transferring to the brown, green, orange, or purple line to reach Adams station. Then take the southbound CTA bus No. 3 or 4 from Michigan Avenue to 23rd Street.

From Midway Airport, take the orange-line CTA train *(see p177)* to Roosevelt Street station, then southbound CTA bus No. 3 or 4 to 23rd Street.

The **Chicago Convention and Tourism Bureau** provides information on meeting services, convention planning, and accommodations.

**LONG-DISTANCE BUS SERVICES**

**Greyhound Bus Line**
630 W Harrison St. **Map** 3 A3.
( 408-5800 or
*(800) 231-2222.*
or
14 W 95th St.
( 408-5999.
w *www.greyhound.com*

**Greyhound ADA Assist Line**
( *(800) 752-4841.*

**TRAIN INFORMATION**

**Amtrak at Union Station**
( *(800) 872-7245.*
w *www.amtrak.com*

**Union Station**
210 S Canal St.
**Map** 3 B2.
( 322-4269.

**PUBLIC TRANSIT**

**Chicago Transit Authority (CTA)**
( 836-7000 or (888) 968-7282.
w *www.yourcta.com*

**Metra Passenger Information**
( 322-6777 8am–5pm Mon–Fri.
( 836-7000 evenings and
weekends. w *www.metrarail.com*

**USEFUL NUMBERS AND ADDRESSES**

**Chicago Convention and Tourism Bureau**
2301 S Lake Shore Dr,
Chicago, IL 60616.
( 201-8847 or (877) 244-2246.
w *www.chicago.il.org*
w *www.choosechicago.com*

**Illinois Department of Transportation**
Map Sales
Room 121, 2300 S Dirksen Pkwy,
Springfield, IL 62764.
( *(217) 782-0834.*
w *www.dot.state.il.us/idot.html*

**McCormick Place**
2301 S Lake Shore Dr,
Chicago, IL 60616.
( 791-7000.
w *www.mccormickplace.com*

**Trade show in Hall B, North Building, McCormick Place**

# Getting Around Chicago

No parking from 11pm to 6am

ALTHOUGH CHICAGO is a sprawling Midwestern metropolis, many of the city's sights and main cultural centers are located downtown, making the city a walker's dream. The city's public transportation is inexpensive and efficient. The train system, known as the "L" for "elevated," is the easiest way to get around. Buses crisscross the city, but the system is complicated and best left to regular commuters. Taxis are affordable, convenient, and readily available.

Cyclist taking advantage of a quiet spell on Chicago's lakefront path

## PLANNING YOUR JOURNEY

PUBLIC TRANSIT in Chicago is extremely busy during the rush hours, which are weekdays from 6am to 9am and 3pm to 7pm. You may wish to avoid it at these peak times. Ask your hotel concierge and check a calendar of events to avoid getting caught in the middle of a particular celebration, of which there are many (see pp30–33).

## STREET LAYOUT AND NUMBERING

CHICAGO STREETS are laid out on a grid system. Most streets run north and south or east and west, though some run on the diagonal.

The zero point in the city is at Madison and State Streets, in the Loop. Street numbers ascend by 50 or 100 numbers in each block as they radiate out from Madison and State. Most streets in the Loop are one-way streets.

**Typical pedestrian and vehicular traffic on busy State Street**

## TRAFFIC SIGNS

ALL TRAFFIC SIGNS, including those denoting speed limits, are black and white. Informational signs, such as those indicating highway exits, are green and white. Most intersections are also marked with green-and-white signs bearing the name of the streets. These signs are posted high on utility poles.

"Caution" and "Yield" signs are yellow and black. White-and-brown signs indicate the major city sights and landmarks.

## WALKING

**Walkway sign**

THE BEST WAY to explore downtown Chicago is on foot. Many of the major sights and shopping areas are only a short walk from each other. Streets are relatively flat, so you will not have to tackle hills during your outings.

Traffic lights signal drivers to stop (red), go (green), and proceed with caution (yellow). For pedestrians, electronic "Walk" signs show an illuminated human figure. A red hand indicates that pedestrians should not cross the street. Never rely solely on the traffic lights; look both ways before crossing the street, and watch for cars making right turns or racing through yellow lights.

In the Loop, an extensive system of pubic underground pedestrian walkways, or pedways, links train stations with major buildings.

## BICYCLING

CHICAGO IS NOT a bike-friendly city: traffic can be heavy and snarled. Very few dedicated bike paths exist, so cyclists are forced to share the streets with drivers. It is advisable to wear a safety helmet when cycling.

The lakefront, however, offers miles of scenic path for recreational riding. **Bike Chicago** rents bicycles and in-line skates; the **Bike Stop** also rents bicycles.

Informal rules-of-the-road exist on the path, but it is still often difficult for walkers, cyclists, and in-line skaters to coexist on it. The best time to take advantage of the lakefront path is during business hours, when traffic on it is quieter.

## TAXIS

MOST CHICAGO taxi drivers are good drivers. But, as in any city, there are exceptions. For a serious complaint, note the name of the taxi company and the car number (on the side of the taxi) and call **Consumer Services**.

You likely will be able to flag a vacant taxi on a busy street, or find one waiting outside a hotel. If the taxi's roof light is lit, it is available. To be picked up at a specific time, phone to reserve at least one hour in advance.

Taxis charge a base fare of about $1.90, plus 50 cents for each additional passenger. A $1 surcharge is added to all airport trips. Fare information is posted inside each taxi.

## DRIVING

VEHICLES ARE DRIVEN on the right-hand side of the road in the US, except on one-way streets. The Illinois speed limit is 35 mph (56 km/h) on city and residential roads, 55 mph (88 km/h) on metro highways. You must wear a seatbelt.

A right turn on a red light is permitted unless a sign prohibits it. Left turns are not allowed at some intersections during peak times, or are allowed only when the green arrow signal is illuminated.

See pages 182–3 for details on interstates and renting a car.

## PARKING

STREET PARKING in Chicago falls into three categories: free, metered, and restricted. Free street parking is scarce. Metered street parking is most readily available. The parking meters usually take quarters only. Depending on the area, 25 cents will buy from five minutes to one hour of parking time. The vehicle may be ticketed once the time runs out. Parking is free in some metered areas after 9pm and on Sundays.

Residential areas often have permit-only parking at night; restrictions are noted on signs. Parking tickets are expensive and tickets for a rental car will follow you home. Never park in front of a fire hydrant or driveway; your car will likely be towed.

The city operates a few parking lots that have low rates. Commercial lots abound; the closer the lot is to downtown, the more expensive. Some businesses offer customers validated parking (discounted or free parking if you have your ticket stamped in the store).

**Parking meter for street parking**

## PENALTIES

IF YOUR CAR is towed off a downtown city street, call **City Services** to locate it. If it is towed from a privately managed parking lot, call the telephone number on the sign posted nearby.

Expect to pay at least $100 to retrieve your car. If it is a rental car, be prepared to show your rental contract.

Parking tickets and minor traffic violations may be paid by money order or credit card. For moving violations, your ticket will have information about where and how to pay or contest the ticket.

## TRAVELING BY PUBLIC TRAINS AND BUSES

THE **Chicago Transit Authority** (CTA) operates an extensive system of trains and buses. The train system is called the "L," for "elevated" – even when the lines run underground. There are seven train lines: blue, brown, red, green, yellow, orange, and purple.

Free CTA system maps *(see inside back cover)* are available at the stations. Many CTA train stations are wheelchair accessible.

Buses stop about every two blocks at posted CTA signs that indicate the number and name of the route, but not the direction. Some buses do not travel the entire route; check the destination sign on the bus. To board a bus, hail the driver and remain on the curb until the bus has come to a stop.

Adult fare is about $1.50; child fare about 75 cents. Transferring between routes costs 30 cents. Change is not provided on CTA buses.

Machines in the stations will dispense cards that can be used on both CTA trains and buses. Passes for unlimited travel are available at the CTA website, Visitor Information Centers, and other locations.

Trolleys and shuttle buses provide free service to several

**CTA transit card**

**A Chicago Transit Authority elevated train in the Loop**

city sights. Visit the **Department of Transportation** website or a Visitor Center *(see pp168–9)* for details.

---

### DIRECTORY

#### BICYCLE RENTALS

**Bike Chicago**
at Navy Pier. **Map** 2 F5.
📞 755-0488 or (800) 915-2453.
or North Ave Beach. **Map** 2 D1.
📞 (773) 327-2706. ⬤ winter.

**Bike Stop**
1034 Belmont Ave, **Lincoln Park**.
📞 (773) 868-6800.

#### TAXI NUMBERS

**American-United Cab**
📞 (773) 248-7600.

**Checker Taxi**
📞 243-2537.

**Flash Cab**
📞 (773) 561-1444.

**Yellow Cab**
📞 829-4222.

#### USEFUL NUMBERS

**Chicago Transit Authority (CTA)**
📞 836-7000 or (888) 968-7282.
Ⓦ www.transitchicago.com

**City Services**
📞 744-7550 or 744-7275 to pay tickets by credit card.

**Consumer Services**
📞 744-9401.

**Department of Transportation**
Ⓦ www.ci.chi.il.us/Transportation

# Traveling Outside Chicago

Traveling outside chicago is most convenient by car, though there is also an inexpensive and extensive public transportation system to the many suburbs and beyond. Rush hours are the only real obstacle to smooth traveling. The so-called reverse commute has vanished. At peak times during the day, city dwellers are going to work at industry headquarters located in the suburbs; at the same time, suburbanites are heading into the city to office jobs. Rush hour can start as early as 5:30am and last until 9am. The afternoon rush begins as early as 3pm and often lasts until past 7pm.

## METRA

A NETWORK of 12 commuter train lines that begin in the city center and stretch out like tentacles to the suburbs is operated by **Metra**. The 495-mile (795-km) system has 230 stations in the Illinois counties of Cook, Du Page, Lake, Will, McHenry, and Kane. It also services some cities in Indiana and Wisconsin. Trains run on a published schedule, frequently during rush hour and every one to three hours at other times. The trains are more comfortable than CTA trains *(see p181)*. They do not have baggage check.

On weekends and holidays, youngsters ages 12 to 17 ride for half fare. Kids under 12 may ride free when accompanied by a fare-paying adult. Weekend passes are also available for unlimited travel on all Metra lines.

Metra trains depart from five stations surrounding the Loop: Union Station, Ogilvie Transportation Center, Randolph Street Station, Van Buren Street Station, and LaSalle Street Station.

Union Station, at Adams and Canal streets, is the main Metra station. The Electric Main Line, which runs to McCormick Place, stops at three stations along Michigan Avenue: at Randolph and Van Buren Streets and at Roosevelt Road. The Union Pacific North Line runs to Highland Park, stopping just outside the Ravinia Festival gate.

Metra has wheelchair-accessible cars; phone for details or visit the **Metra Passenger Services** center.

## PACE

The suburban bus system, **Pace**, is a division of the Regional Transportation Authority (RTA), which also oversees Metra and the CTA. Pace provides fixed bus routes, Dial-a-Ride services for travelers with disabilities, vanpools, and special-event buses throughout Chicago's six-county suburban region. Pace buses also provide good connections between Metra stations and shopping malls.

Much of the Pace system is wheelchair accessible; phone for details, or visit the **RTA Customer Service Center** for information, along with free maps and timetables.

## INTERSTATES

The several highways running through and around Chicago are of two types: freeways and tollways. Freeways are tollfree public highways. The charge for driving on a state tollway ranges from 15 cents to $2, which will be collected at a tollbooth.

**CTA bus No. 56, which terminates at Jefferson Park**

Generally, lanes at the tollbooths are designated as exact change (automatic), needing change (manual), and I-Pass (an electronic system that allows specially equipped cars to drive through, automatically deducting the toll from the vehicle's account). Getting on or off a tollway usually also involves a fee, and because those booths are unattended, exact change is necessary.

Interstates are divided multilane highways and are the main routes between cities. Most swell to six or more lanes as they near large cities. Interstate numbers are posted on red, white, and blue shield-shaped signs.

Main interstate routes have two-digit numbers, with those with even numbers generally running east-west and those with odd numbers generally running north-south. There are exceptions, however. While I-94 runs east-west across the US, it runs north-south in Illinois.

Interstates with three digits are loops (if the first digit is 2, 4, 6, or 8) or spurs (first digit

**Stairs to main concourse at Chicago's historic Union Station**

View from scenic US Route 20, running northwest through Illinois

of 1, 3, 5, 7, or 9) of the main interstate route.

I-55 (Stevenson Expressway) runs from US-41 (Lake Shore Drive) in Chicago to St. Louis, then to New Orleans via Memphis.

I-90 runs from Boston to Seattle, and in Illinois from the Indiana line on the Chicago Skyway through Chicago on the Dan Ryan and Kennedy Expressways, and to Rockford and the WI line on the Northwest Tollway. The Chicago Skyway, however is no longer designated as I-90, but rather, as TO I-90.

I-190 is the spur from I-90 to O'Hare Airport.

I-94 runs from Montana to Michigan. In Illinois, it is called Edens Expressway and merges with I-90, the main highway through Chicago.

## NAMED HIGHWAYS

Many illinois highways are commonly referred to by name rather than by number. The stretch of I-90/94 that runs from the city center south to 95th Street is called the Dan Ryan Expressway.

The stretch that runs from the city center northwest to O'Hare Airport is known as the Kennedy Expressway.

I-290 is also known as the Eisenhower Expressway, and as Congress Parkway within the city center. I-55 is called the Stevenson Expressway.

## SPEED LIMITS AND FINES

The speed limit for cars on Illinois' open highways is 65 mph (105 km/h) and 55 mph (88 km/h) on metro highways. Speeding tickets

carry heavy fines. A minimum speed regulation in Illinois means you also could be ticketed for driving so slowly that you impede traffic.

**Speed limit (in mph)**

**Rest area, indicated off an interstate**

Roadside tests and fines for drinking and driving are increasingly common.

## RENTAL CARS

To rent a car, you must be at least 25 years old, with a valid driver's license (for foreign visitors, an international driver's license) and a major credit card in your name.

Before leaving home, check your insurance policy to see if you are covered in a rental car. If not, you should buy damage and liability insurance when renting the car.

Most agencies offer a range of vehicles, from "economy" models to convertibles. All rental cars are automatic and have power steering.

Refill the car with gasoline before returning it or you will pay a service charge.

Two car rental agencies in Chicago

# STREET FINDER

**M**AP REFERENCES given in this guide for sights, hotels, restaurants, shops, and entertainment venues refer to the Street Finder maps on the following pages (*see* How the Map References Work *below*). A complete index of the street names and places of interest marked on the maps can also be found on the pages that follow. The map opposite shows the area of Chicago the eight *Street Finder* maps cover. This includes the sightseeing areas (which are color-coded) as well as the whole of central Chicago. The symbols used to represent sights and useful information on the *Street Finder* maps are listed below in the key.

## HOW THE MAP REFERENCES WORK

**The first figure** tells you which *Street Finder* map to turn to.

## Sears Tower ❶

233 S Wacker Dr. **Map** 3 B2
875-9696. **M** *Quincy.*
○ *Mar–Sep: 9am–11pm daily;*
*Oct–Feb: 9am–10pm daily; last*
*adm 30 min before closing.*

**The letter and number** are a grid reference. You will find the letters at the top and bottom of the map and the numbers at the sides.

**The map** continues on map 5 of the *Street Finder.*

### KEY TO STREET FINDER

| | |
|---|---|
| | Major sight |
| | Minor sight |
| | Station building |
| **M** | CTA train station |
| | Metra train station |
| **P** | Parking |
| | Tourist information |
| | Hospital with emergency room |
| | Police station |
| | Church |
| | Synagogue |
| | Buddhist temple |
| ⊠ | Post office |
| | Railroad line |
| | One-way street |

### SCALE OF MAPS 1–6

| 0 meters | 500 |
|---|---|
| 0 yards | 500 |

### SCALE OF MAPS 7 & 8

| 0 meters | 500 |
|---|---|
| 0 yards | 500 |

| 0 kilometers | 2 |
|---|---|
| 0 miles | 1 |

NORTH SIDE

DOWNTOWN CORE

Lake Michigan

SOUTH SIDE

Visitors enjoying a Chicago Architecture Foundation walking tour

# Street Finder Index

Pedestrian Tunnel

*North Avenue Beach*

**P**

**1**

BLVD

■ *Archbishop's Residence*

N ASTOR ST

Pedestrian Tunnel

*International Museum of Surgical Science*

■ *1500 North Astor Street*

E BURTON PL

E   *Edward P. Russell House*

E SCHILLER ST

N ASTOR

*Charnley-Persky House*

NORTH

EAST BANKS STREET

RITCHIE CT

*Lake Michigan*

**2**

EAST GOETHE STREET

*GOUDY SQUARE*

N STONE STREET

ASTOR

EAST SCOTT STREET

N LAKE SHORE DRIVE

**DIVISION ST**

Pedestrian Tunnel

**GOLD COAST**

EAST ELM STREET

★

*Oak Street Beach*

EAST CEDAR STREET

**3**

EAST BELLEVUE PLACE

Pedestrian Tunnel

N MICHIGAN AVE

EAST OAK STREET

**EAST LAKE SHORE DRIVE**

■ *Drake Hotel*

EAST WALTON PLACE

CONNORS PARK

*John Hancock Center*

MIES VAN DER ROHE WAY

N DE WITT PL

EAST DELAWARE PLACE

*Fourth Presbyterian Church* ✝

EAST CHESTNUT STREET

*Quigley Seminary and Chapel of St James*

*Water Tower Place*

50>>

*Water Tower and Pumping Station* **i**

*SENECA PARK*

EAST PEARSON STREET

*LAKE SHORE PARK*

Pedestrian Tunnel

N WABASH AVE

E **CHICAGO**

*Museum of Contemporary Art* ✚

**AVE**

250>>

**4**

EAST SUPERIOR STREET

N ST CLAIR ST

**STREETERVILLE**

*St James Episcopal Cathedral* ✝

E HURON ST

*MILTON LEE OLIVER PARK*

ickerson House

*Terra Museum of American Art*

EAST ERIE STREET

**P**

NORTH MCCLURG COURT

**P**

ble House

**EAST ONTARIO STREET**

**NORTH**

**EAST OHIO STREET**

**P**

*NAVY PIER PARK*

**P**

**EAST GRAND AVENUE**

N RUSH ST

**FAIRBANKS**

N PESHTIGO CT

**P**

**EAST**

**P**

*Hotel Inter-Continental Chicago*

**COURT**

N STREETER DRIVE

*Navy Pier* **i**

EAST ILLINOIS STREET

*Chicago Children's Museum*

E HUBBARD ST

*GATEWAY PARK*

**5**

*Tribune Tower*

*Wrigley Building*

KINZIE ST

*Chicago*

N LAKE SHORE DRIVE

*IBM Building*

**EAST WACKER DRIVE**

*River*

*Michigan Avenue Bridge*

# General Index

Page numbers in **bold** type refer to main entries.

# Acknowledgments

Dorling Kindersley and International Book Productions would like to thank the following people whose contributions and assistance have made the book possible:

**AT DORLING KINDERSLEY:**
Managing Art Editor: Jane Ewart
Managing Editor: Helen Townsend
Senior Publishing Manager: Louise Lang
Production Controllers: Marie Ingledew, Michelle Thomas
Cartographers: Casper Morris, Dave Pugh

**MAIN CONTRIBUTORS**
LORRAINE JOHNSON is a freelance writer living in Toronto who has a lifelong fascination with Chicago. She is the author of six books and contributes articles and book reviews regularly to magazines and newspapers.

JOHN RYAN lives in Chicago. A professional musician and former chef, he manages the Elgin Symphony Orchestra in addition to writing regular food columns for America Online.

**ADDITIONAL CONTRIBUTOR**
Penney Kome

**SPECIAL RESEARCH**
Dana Joy Altman
Deanna Cates

**PROOFREADER**
Maraya Raduha

**INDEXER**
Barbara Sale Schon

**CARTOGRAPHY**
Visutronx, Ajax, Ontario, Canada

**SPECIAL ASSISTANCE**
Particular thanks go to Vanetta Anderson, Chicago Office of Tourism
Norah Zboril, City of Chicago, Mayor's Office, Special Events
Daniel J. Curtin, City of Chicago, Department of Aviation
Jeff Stern, Chicago Transit Authority
Diana Holic and Dawn Kappel, Adler Planetarium and Astronomy Museum
Brigid Murphy, Newberry Library
Mily Anzo, Museum of Science and Industry
Patricia Kremer, Field Museum
Corey Tovian and Gwen Biassi, John G. Shedd Aquarium
Rosemary Haack, City of Lake Forest
Janice Klein, Mitchell Museum of the American Indian
Ms. Chase Ruppert, McCormick Place Convention Center
Stephen Majsak, Chicago Architectural Foundation
Lois Berger, Chicago Public Library, Harold Washington Library Center
Jennifer Swanson, Lincoln Park Zoo
Adam Davies, Chicago Place
Angela Sweeney, Water Tower Place
Kelly Boggs and Michael Rilley, Chicago Theatre
Sarah Hamilton Hadley, Terra Museum of American Art
Karen Irvine, Museum of Contemporary Photography
Zarine Weil, Robie House
Ken Price, Palmer House Hilton Hotel
Michilla Johnson, Buddy Guy's Legends
Jennifer Kocolowski, Goose Island Beer Co.
Jan Berghoff, Berghoff Restaurant
Janet Femarek and David Caruso, Ed Debevic's Restaurant

**PHOTOGRAPHY PERMISSION**
Dorling Kindersley and International Book Productions would like to thank everyone for their assistance and kind permission to photograph at their establishments.

**PICTURE CREDITS**
KEY: t=top; tl=top left; tlc=top left center; tc=top center; trc=top right center; tr=top right; cla=center left above; ca=center above; cra=center right above; cl=center left; c=center; cr=center right; clb=center left below; cb=center below; crb=center right below; bl=bottom left; b=bottom; br=bottom right; bcl=bottom center left; bc=bottom center; bcr=bottom center right.

Every effort has been made to trace the copyright holders. Dorling Kindersley apologizes for any unintentional omissions and would be pleased, in such cases, to add an acknowledgment in future editions.

The Publishers are grateful to the following museums, companies, and picture libraries for permission to reproduce their photographs:

© ADLER PLANETARIUM AND ASTRONOMY MUSEUM: 19bl, 92tr, 93tc.

THE ART INSTITUTE OF CHICAGO: All rights reserved – Mary Cassatt, American, 1844–1926, *The Child's Bath*, oil on canvas, 1893, 39 1/2 x 26 inches, Robert A. Waller Fund, 1910.2 – 47tl; Marc Chagall, French, born Russia, 1887–1985, *American Windows*, glass, 1977, Gift of the City of Chicago and the Auxiliary Board of The Art Institute of Chicago commemorating the American Bicentennial in memory of Mayor Richard J. Daley, 1977.938, © 2000 – 46c; Rembrandt Harmenszoon van Rijn, Dutch, 1606–1669, *Old Man with a Gold Chain*, oil on panel, c.1631, 83.1 x 75.7 cm, Mr. and Mrs. W.W. Kimball Collection, 1922.4467 – 47bc.

BUDDY GUY'S LEGENDS: 161bl.

THE CANADIAN PRESS/ASSOCIATED PRESS AP: 29ca; AP/Wide World Photos Inc. Charles Bennett 170bl.

CHICAGO ARCHITECTURE FOUNDATION: Bill Richert 168br, 185bl.

CHICAGO HISTORICAL SOCIETY: 74bl; ICHi-2212 – 8–9; ICHi-08732 – 13bl; ICHi-30084 – 15cb; ICHi-31412 – 17tl; ICHi-31413 – 29tr; ICHi-31411 – 71br; ICHi-09440 – 72cla; ICHi-31414 – 72c; ICHi-14063 Currier & Ives 14crb; ICHi-05630 Inger & Bodtker 167 (inset); ICHi-10889 Edward Kemeys 13c; ICHi-05769 Louis Kurz 9 (inset), 35 (inset); ICHi-05836 Leslie's Weekly 15bc; ICHi-06291 Scribner's Magazine 131 (inset); ICHi-13946 US Treasury Department 121 (inset); ICHi-27363 Paris Raoul Varin 13bc.

CHICAGO PUBLIC LIBRARY, HAROLD WASHINGTON LIBRARY CENTER: 82tl; *Events in the Life of Harold Washington* ceramic tile mosaic by Jacob Lawrence 22br; *Sleeping Beauty* sculpture by Alison Saar 80tr.

CHICAGO TRANSIT AUTHORITY: 182c.

CITY OF CHICAGO, DEPARTMENT OF AVIATION: 16cb, 177tr.

CITY OF CHICAGO, OFFICE OF TOURISM: © Willy Schmidt 33bl, 60bc; © Peter J. Schultz 19tr, 31br, 180bl; Chicago Air and Water Show 31cr.

COLUMBUS ASSOCIATION FOR THE PERFORMING ARTS: 54b.

CORBIS: © Corbis 16cra, 109cra; © Sandy Felsenthal 26cl, 30cl; © Mitchell Gerber 28br; © Robert Holmes 48br; © Layne Kennedy 46tr, 48cl; © Francis G. Mayer, *The Basket of Apples* by Paul Cézanne 49tr, *The Gourmet* by Pablo Picasso 49cl, *On the Seine at Bennecourt* by Claude Monet 49br; © Archie A. Thomas, Dat's Jazz 28tr; © AFP/Corbis 17crb, 29clb; © Bettmann/Corbis 15tl, 27cla, 28cl, 29bc, *A Sunday on La Grande Jatte* by Georges Seurat 47cr, *American Gothic* by Grant Wood 47br, 77crb, 77br; © Hulton-Deutsch Collection/Corbis 16tl; © UPI/Corbis-Bettmann 16bc.

THE DAVID AND ALFRED SMART MUSEUM OF ART, THE UNIVERSITY OF CHICAGO: reproduced with permission 101tc; University Transfer – Dining Table and Six Side Chairs, Frank Lloyd Wright 102cr.

FIELD MUSEUM: Courtesy of the Field Museum, 86cl, 89bl; John Weinstein © 1998 – 21ca, © 1994 – 87ca; George Papadakis © 1998 – 86tr; Ron Testa 87crb.

GOOSE ISLAND BEER COMPANY: © Daniel J. Wigg 143br.

THE GRANGER COLLECTION, NEW YORK: 12.

HENRY MOORE FOUNDATION: *Sundial* 1965–66 (LH 528) on the title page and *Nuclear Energy* sculpture illustrated on pages 4tr and 103tc are reproduced by permission of the Henry Moore Foundation.

INTERNATIONAL MUSEUM OF SURGICAL SCIENCE, CHICAGO: 20clb; *Hope and Help* sculpture by Edouard Chaissing reproduced with permission 75c.

JANE ADDAMS' HULL-HOUSE: Jane Addams' Hull-House Museum, University of Illinois at Chicago 116tl.

JOHN G. SHEDD AQUARIUM: © Edward G. Lines 96tr, 96cl, 96bc, 97tl, 97ca, 97c, 97cb.

KIMPTON GROUP: 132cl, 133tl, 133bc.

LINCOLN PARK ZOO, CHICAGO: © Grant Kessler 19crb; © Todd Rosenberg 113tc.

MCCORMICK PLACE CONVENTION CENTER: 179bl.

MILLENNIUM PARK PROJECT: Skidmore, Owings & Merrill LLP 53b.

MITCHELL MUSEUM OF THE AMERICAN INDIAN: 125tl.

MUSEUM OF CONTEMPORARY PHOTOGRAPHY, COLUMBIA COLLEGE CHICAGO: Tom Nowak 81tl, 84tr.
MUSEUM OF SCIENCE AND INDUSTRY: 106tr; © 2000 Dirk

Fletcher 21br, 107tl, 108bl, 109tl.

THE NEWBERRY LIBRARY: 67br.

PALMER HOUSE HILTON HOTEL: 5tr, 132br.

SOCIETY FOR REPRODUCTION RIGHTS OF AUTHORS, COMPOSERS AND PUBLISHERS IN CANADA (SODRAC) INC: SODRAC (Montreal) © Estate of Pablo Picasso (Paris)/SODRAC (Montreal) 2000 – 37 (inset); SODRAC (Montreal) © Estate of Joan Miró/ADAGP (Paris)/SODRAC (Montreal) 2000 – 44tr; SODRAC (Montreal) © Estate of Marc Chagall/ADAGP (Paris)/SODRAC (Montreal) 2000 – 44bl.

SPERTUS MUSEUM: *Flame of Hope* by Leonardo Nierman, 1995. Collection of Spertus Museum 81tc.

WATER TOWER PLACE: 155tl.

FRANK LLOYD WRIGHT HOME AND STUDIO FOUNDATION: Courtesy of Henrich Blessing and the Frank Lloyd Wright Home and Studio Foundation, 23br.

WRIGLEY BUILDING: The Wrigley Building and design are registered trademarks of the Wm. Wrigley Jr. Company, used by permission 60br, 62tl.

JACKET
Front - DK PICTURE LIBRARY: Andrew Leyerle br, bc; GETTY IMAGES/ALLSPORT: Matthew Stockman bl; Vito Palmisano main image. Back - DK PICTURE LIBRARY: Andrew Leyerle t; JOHN G. SHEDD AQUARIUM: Edward G. Lines b. Spine - GETTY IMAGES: Vito Palmisano.

All other images © Dorling Kindersley. For more information see www.DKimages.com

## DORLING KINDERSLEY SPECIAL EDITIONS

Dorling Kindersley books can be purchased in bulk quantities at discounted prices for use in promotions or as premiums. We are also able to offer special editions and personalized jackets, corporate imprints, and excerpts from all of our books, tailored specifically to meet your own needs.

To find out more, please contact:
(in the United Kingdom) –
SPECIAL SALES, DORLING KINDERSLEY LIMITED, 80 STRAND, LONDON WC2R 0RL;
(in the United States) –
SPECIAL MARKETS, DK PUBLISHING, INC., 375 HUDSON STREET, NEW YORK, NY 10014.